Birmingham University Field Archaeolo
Monograph Series 3

The Excavation of a Romano-British Shrine at Orton's Pasture, Rocester, Staffordshire

I.M. Ferris, L. Bevan and R. Cuttler

with contributions by

A.S. Esmonde Cleary, A. Hammon, K. Hartley, C. Hewitson,
T. Joyce, D.F. Mackreth, A. Monckton, R.S.O. Tomlin,
D. Williams, S. Willis

and illustrations by

M. Breedon and N. Dodds

BAR British Series 314
2000

Published in 2016 by
BAR Publishing, Oxford

BAR British Series 314

Birmingham University Field Archaeology Unit Monograph Series 3
The Excavation of a Romano-British Shrine at Orton's Pasture, Rocester, Staffordshire

ISBN 978 1 84171 205 5

© BUFAU and the Publisher 2000

BAR Publishing is the trading name of British Archaeological Reports (Oxford) Ltd.
British Archaeological Reports was first incorporated in 1974 to publish the BAR
Series, International and British. In 1992 Hadrian Books Ltd became part of the BAR
group. This volume was originally published by Archaeopress in conjunction with
British Archaeological Reports (Oxford) Ltd / Hadrian Books Ltd, the Series principal
publisher, in 2000. This present volume is published by BAR Publishing, 2016.

Printed in England

PUBLISHING

BAR titles are available from:

        BAR Publishing
        122 Banbury Rd, Oxford, OX2 7BP, UK
EMAIL   info@barpublishing.com
PHONE   +44 (0)1865 310431
  FAX   +44 (0)1865 316916
        www.barpublishing.com

The Excavation of a Romano-British Shrine at Orton's Pasture, Rocester, Staffordshire

by I.M. Ferris, L. Bevan and R.Cuttler

with contributions by A.S. Esmonde Cleary, A. Hammon, K. Hartley, C. Hewitson, T. Joyce, D.F. Mackreth, A. Monckton, R.S.O. Tomlin, D. Williams, and S. Willis, and illustrations by M. Breedon and N. Dodds.

For my mother,
Rosemary Ferris
I.F.

The Excavation of a Romano-British Shrine at Orton's Pasture, Rocester, Staffordshire

Contents

List of Figures

List of Tables

List of Plates

Frontispiece   Copper alloy patera handle   (G. Norrie)

The plates follow the bibliography

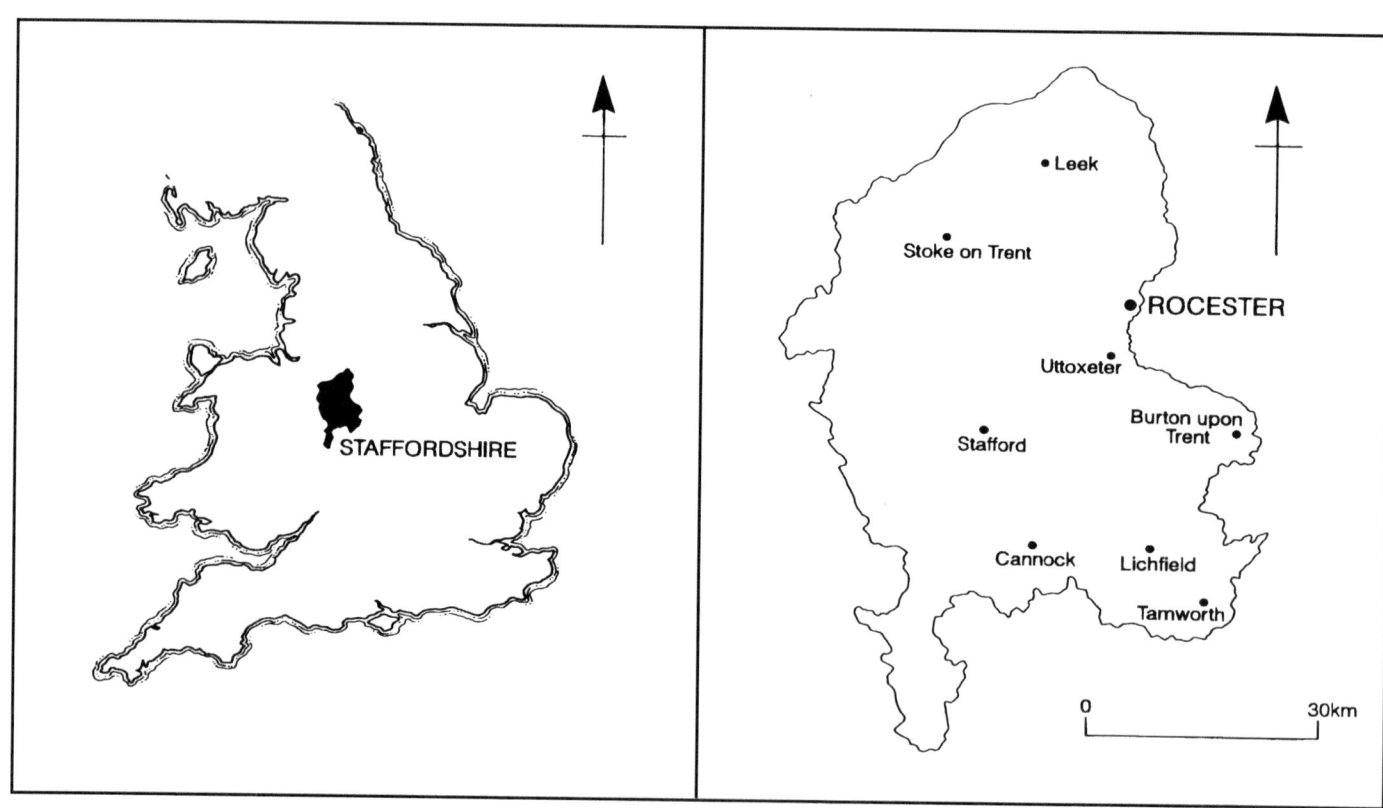

Fig. 1   Rocester : location map

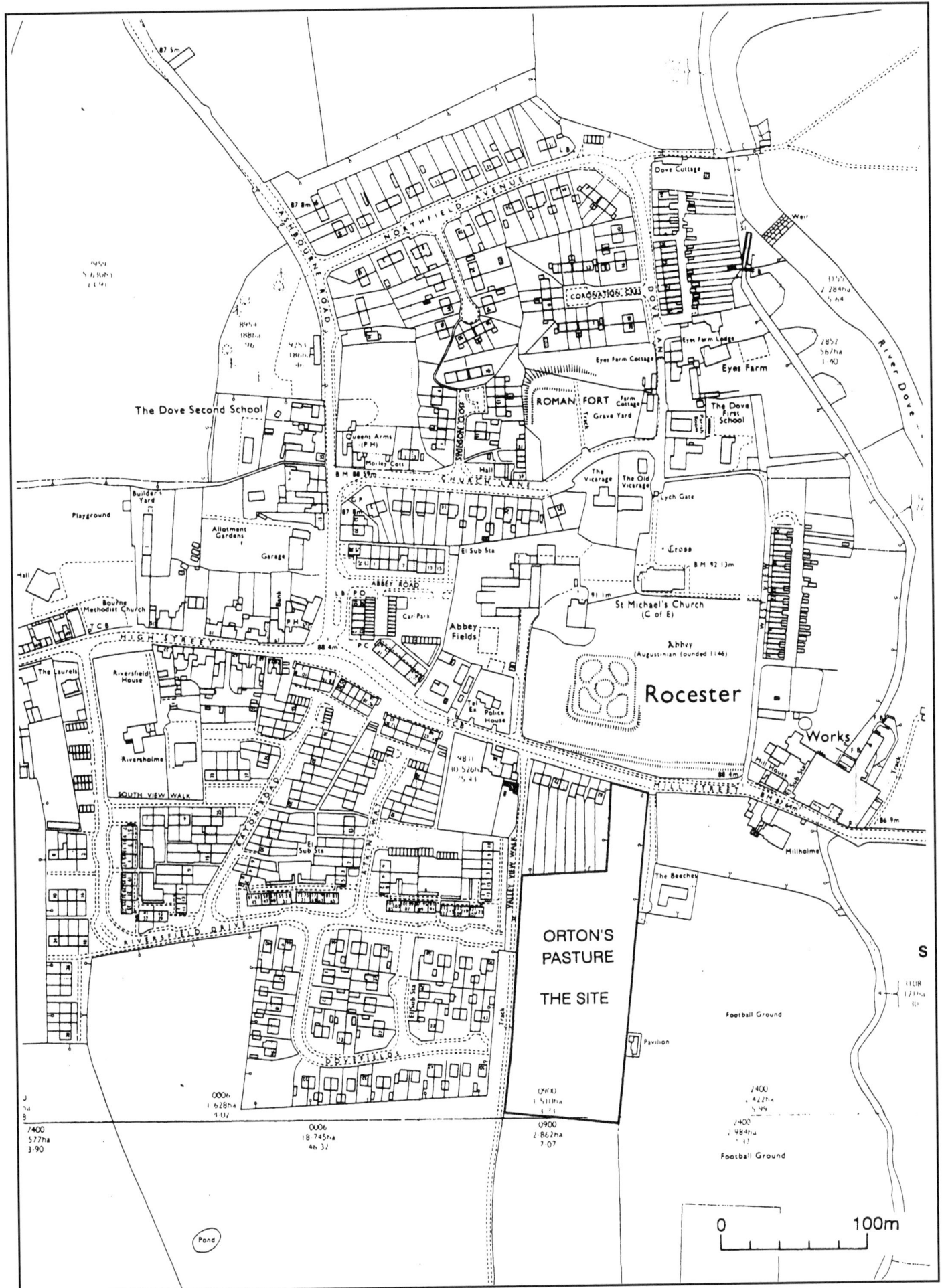

Fig. 2   Rocester : map of the village

vii

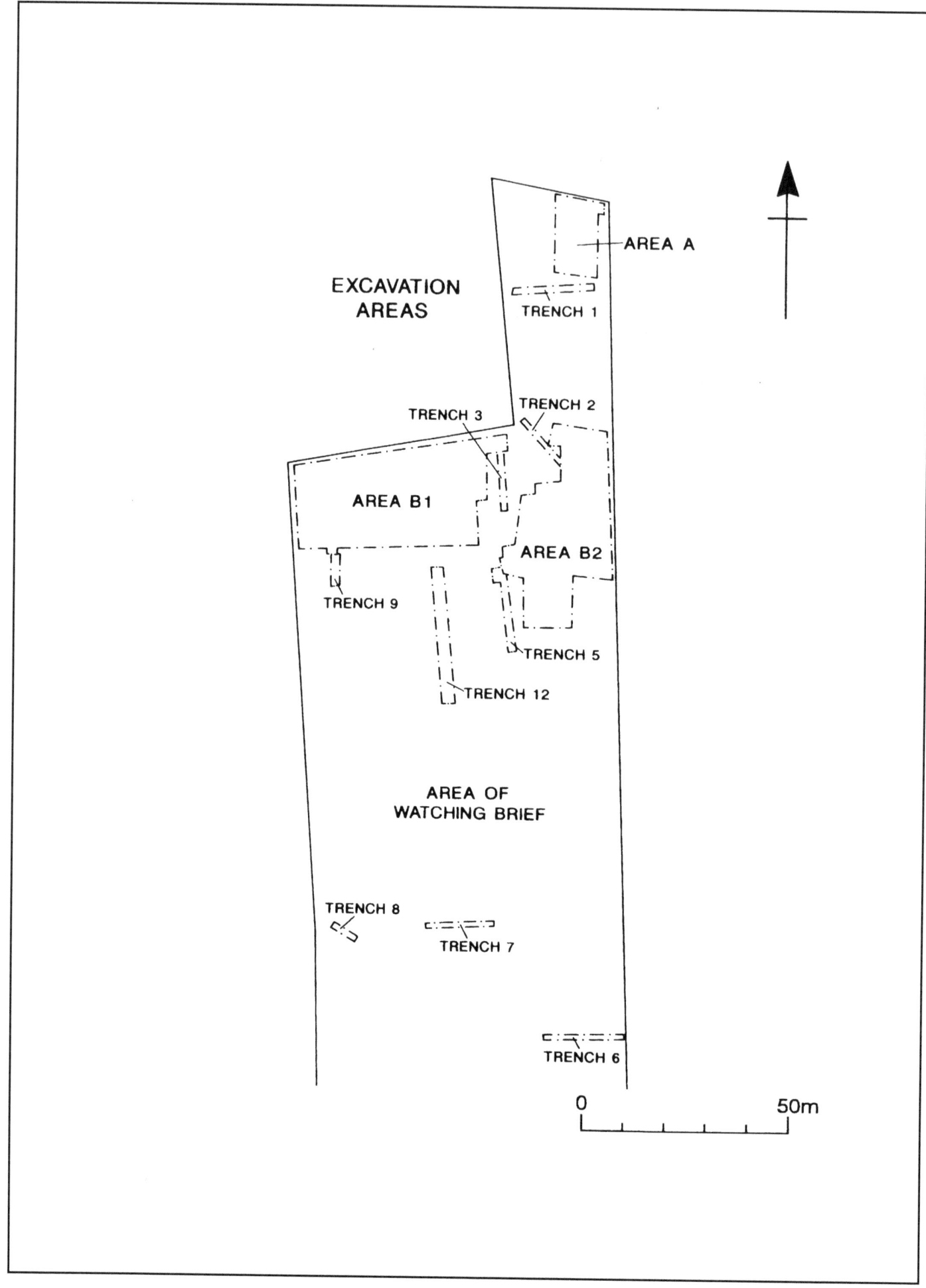

Fig. 3 Orton's Pasture : location of evaluation and excavation

The Excavation of a Romano-British Shrine at Orton's Pasture, Rocester, Staffordshire

by I.M. Ferris, L. Bevan and R.Cuttler

with contributions by A.S. Esmonde Cleary, A. Hammon, K. Hartley, C. Hewitson,
T. Joyce, D.F. Mackreth, A. Monckton, R.S.O. Tomlin, D. Williams, and S. Willis,
and illustrations by M. Breedon and N. Dodds.

Summary. *Rescue excavations ahead of a housing development at the site of Orton's Pasture, Rocester recorded a sequence of Romano-British activity principally of the late first to mid-second century AD, though some less intensive later Roman activity was also recorded in one area of the site. Parts of two adjacent, contemporary enclosures, also contemporaneous with, and probably associated with, the Roman fort complex which lay to the north of the site, were excavated. Pits inside, and outside, the enclosures produced significant quantities of both general domestic rubbish, in the form of pottery, animal bone and other finds, and more unusual finds, including a fragment of an altar, which suggest that the site may have been the focus of occasional ritual or religious acts. A small stone building in the southern enclosure has been identified as a shrine.*

INTRODUCTION

The field named Orton's Pasture (Figs. 1–3) lies on the south side of Mill Street, on the eastern fringes of the village of Rocester, Staffordshire (centred on National Grid Reference SK 11053937). The boundary of Abbey Field, on the north side of Mill Street, forms the southern boundary of the Scheduled Ancient Monument of Rocester Abbey and Roman Settlement (County Monument Number, Staffordshire No. 66). The main, central part of the village of Rocester lies on a gravel knoll between the rivers Churnet and Dove, with land on the lower slopes and around the fringes of the knoll, including parts of Orton's Pasture, having been prone to flooding, from the River Dove in particular, up to recent times.

In late-September/early-October 1990 the Birmingham University Field Archaeology Unit was commissioned by Philip Atkins of Abbey Farm, Rocester to undertake an initial archaeological evaluation of Orton's Pasture (hereafter called the site), in advance of the proposed sale of the land for a housing development. The evaluation consisted of a desktop study, site inspection, geophysical survey and trial trenching. Without specific details of the proposed development being available, this evaluation provided at this stage only a broad overview of the archaeological potential of the site, with first indications being that archaeological activity here was extensive across the area, but was confined to the Romano-British period. A further, targeted evaluation, comprising geophysical survey and trial trenching, was commissioned by Mrs M.Atkins in September 1995, to assess the archaeological potential of areas now directly threatened by more specific development proposals.

Following the second stage evaluation in 1995, three discrete but extensive areas of archaeological potential were identified (Fig. 3). Area A, closest to Mill Street, contained a complex, well-preserved stratigraphic sequence of archaeological deposits, where the build-up of ploughsoil at a plough headland had acted to protect buried archaeological features and deposits here. In contrast, in Area B only features cut into the natural subsoil had survived what appeared to be severe truncation by the plough, with no stratigraphic sequence surviving here above the natural gravels and alluvium. The northern part of Area C contained a few, widely spaced features, again quite obviously affected by the ploughing regime carried out here over the years, while little of archaeological potential was recorded in the southern part of Area C, where the evaluation demonstrated that this land had been regularly flooded, as reflected by a build-up of alluvial wash which was up to one metre thick in places.

Proposals for the development initially took on board the possibility of preserving the archaeology *in situ* across the whole site by levelling-up the area. This, however, proved impractical, particularly in view of the need for services to the site, and the provision of garden areas where continued protection into the future could not be monitored or guaranteed. Furthermore, the level of Orton's Pasture was significantly higher than that of Mill Street, and in order to provide a suitable access to the development the Mill Street frontage required levelling down below the level of any archaeological deposits at the street frontage.

A strategy of total stripping, planning, and sample excavation in the threatened parts of Areas A and B was therefore adopted, though in those parts of Area A where sympathetically planted open spaces could be provided by development preservation *in situ* was achieved. The excavation ran concurrently with, and was periodically followed by, a watching brief over the remaining areas of Orton's Pasture, to the south of the main excavated areas during topsoil stripping and groundworks (Fig. 3). The 1996 rescue excavations took place over an eight-week period between October and December. Weather conditions were generally appalling, and much of the site cleaning and recording was undertaken in conditions that would have ruled the site to be unworkable in a non-rescue situation. Such circumstances will undoubtedly have created a perhaps significant recovery bias in the artefactual record.

In order to facilitate understanding of the overall results, the evidence from the evaluations has been integrated into the main body of presentation and discussion of the 1996 excavation. Descriptions of those evaluation trenches that lay outside the main areas subsequently examined by the excavation and detailed watching brief can be found in the site archive which will be deposited at the City Museum and Art Gallery, Hanley, Stoke-on-Trent.

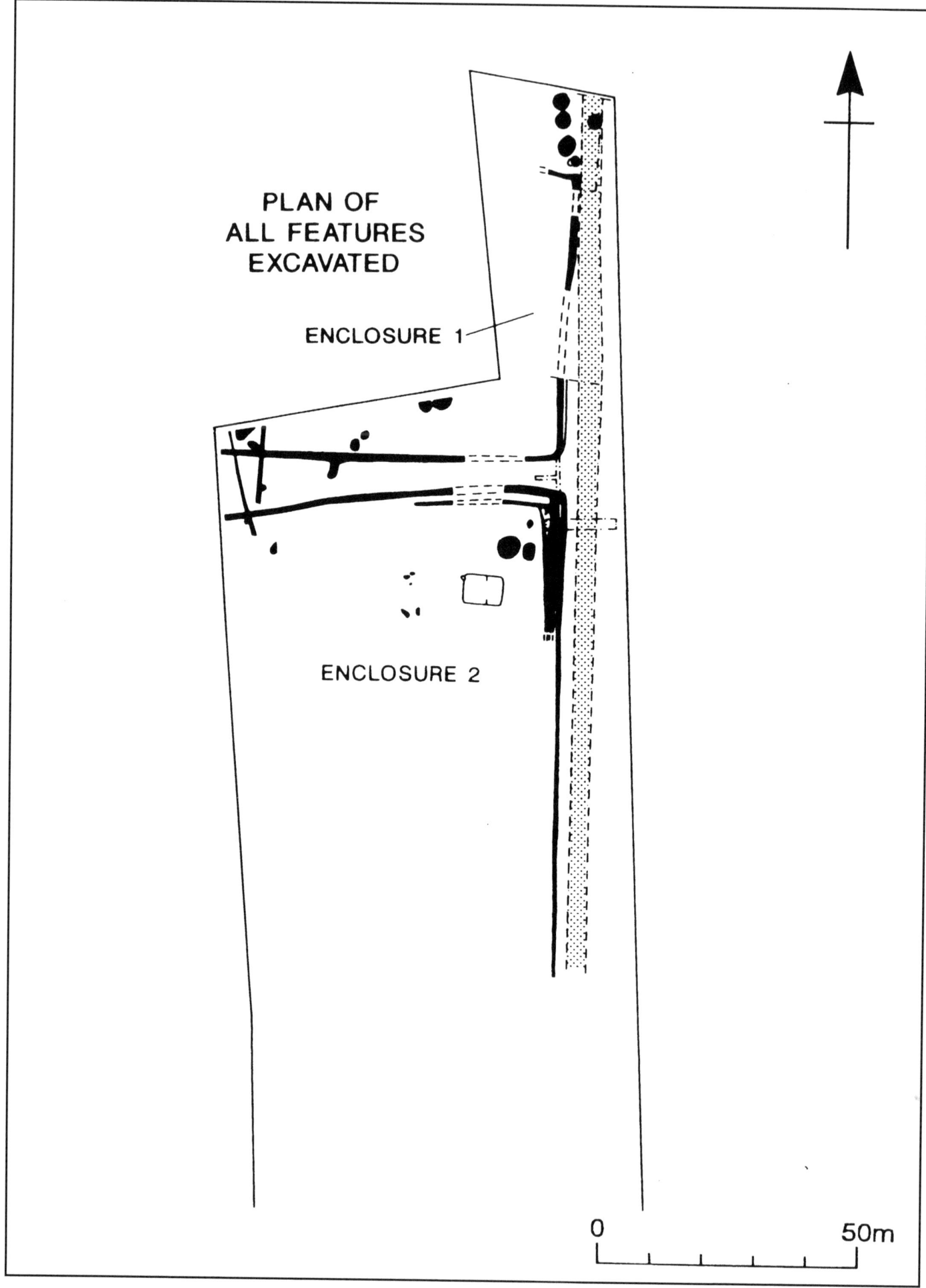

PLAN OF
ALL FEATURES
EXCAVATED

ENCLOSURE 1

ENCLOSURE 2

0   50m

Fig. 4   Orton's Pasture : plan of all excavated features

THE EXCAVATED SEQUENCE

by Richard Cuttler and Iain Ferris

Project Aims, Excavation and Recording Methodology

The aim of the excavation was to record in plan as extensive an area of the Roman features and structures as could be achieved within the constraints of development, and to sample-excavate a sufficient number of features and deposits to enable the construction of a coherent interpretation of the sequence of activities in the threatened areas. In this report, the results of excavations at Orton's Pasture will first be described in detail, and a presentation of both finds and environmental data will then be made. Finally, the overall results will be interpreted and discussed alongside those from other, previous excavations at Rocester.

On site, standard Birmingham University Field Archaeology Unit recording systems were employed. Feature numbers, with the prefix F, were allocated from number F1, F200, F300, F400, F500, F600 and F700 onwards in different areas, and context

or layer numbers began in individual areas at 1000, 2000, 3000, 4000, 5000, 6000, and 6500. Each deposit or feature was recorded on a separate pro-forma record sheet. A total of 89 features and 292 contexts was recorded, this total including those excavated during the evaluations of 1990 and 1995. Where appropriate, archaeological features and deposits were drawn at a scale of 1:50, utilising 'multi-context planning'. Single contexts requiring finer, more detailed recording were planned at a scale of 1:20. Section drawings were recorded at a scale of either 1:10 or 1:20, again depending on the detail required. A comprehensive photographic record of all features and deposits was kept, in monochrome and colour transparency. Sealed and stratified archaeological deposits were sampled for environmental analysis. The full site archive, comprising both the paper record and the artefacts, will be deposited with the City Museum and Art Gallery, Hanley, Stoke-on-Trent.

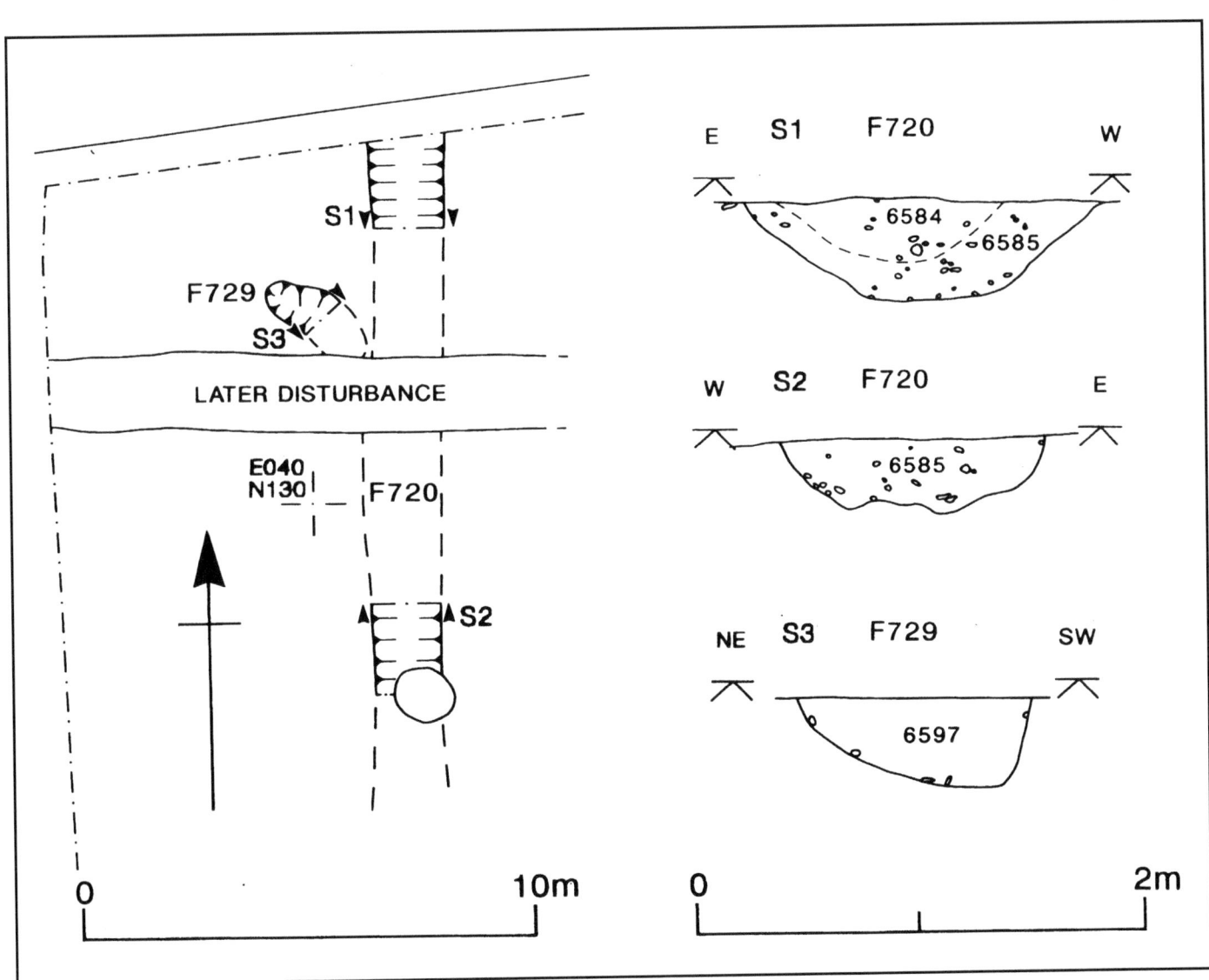

Fig. 5 Phase 0 : plan and sections

3

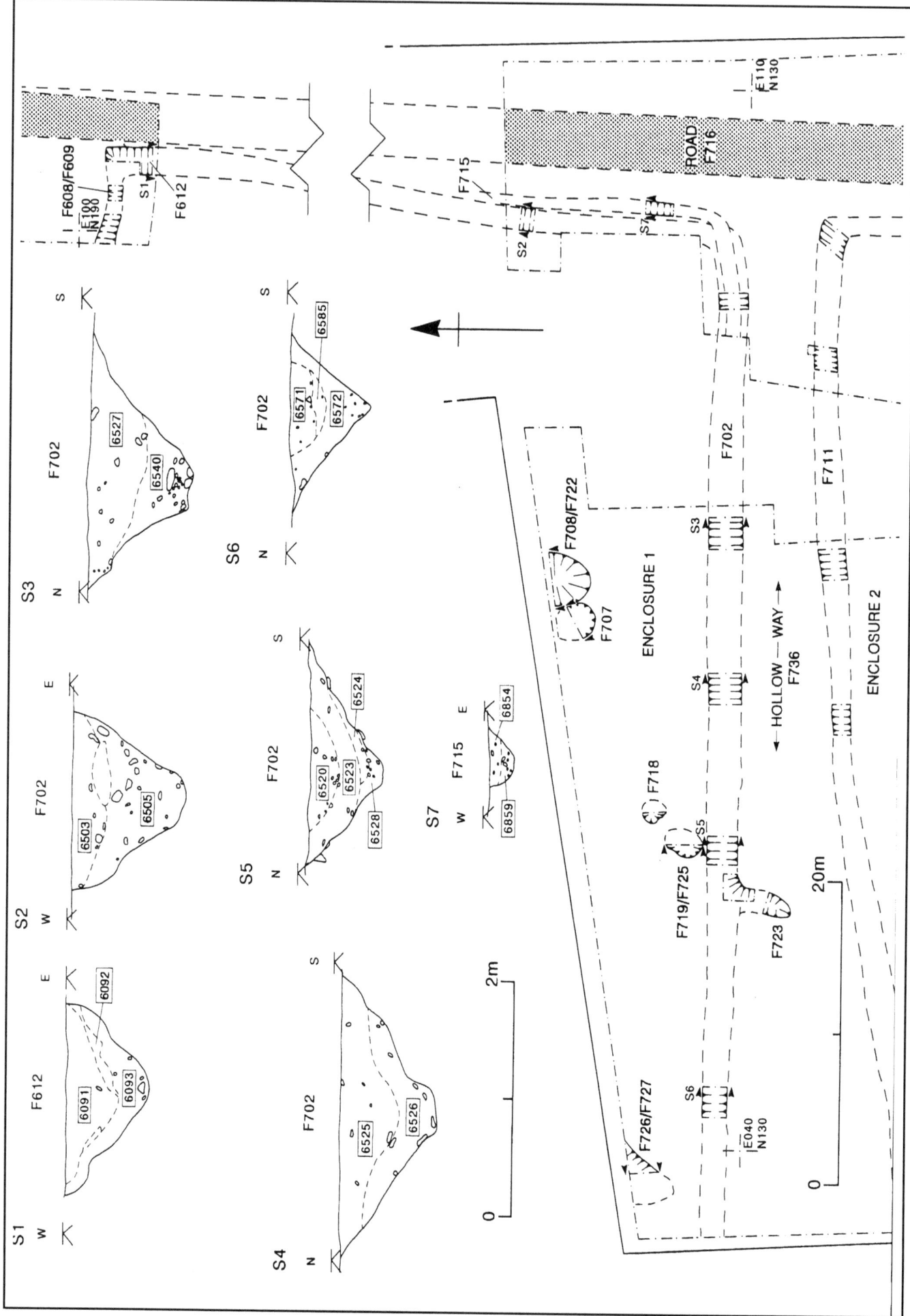

Fig. 6 Phase 1 : Enclosure 1 (Northern Enclosure), plan and ditch sections (F612, F702, F715)

Over the areas of excavation, the ploughsoil was removed by a JCB mechanical excavator fitted with a toothless ditching bucket, working under archaeological supervision. Machined surfaces were then hand-cleaned to define the nature of deposits present. The remainder of Orton's Pasture was subject to a watching brief during topsoil stripping by a 360 degree mechanical excavator. With the exception of a Roman road or trackway, a 20% sample of all linear deposits and a 50% sample of all other features was excavated. Pottery, bone and bulk finds were collected, numbered and recorded by context. Small finds (mostly metal objects) were additionally allocated an individual number — prefixed by the letters SF — and were recorded three dimensionally.

The Stratigraphic Sequence

Three main phases of Roman, or earlier, activity were defined during excavation and post-excavation analysis, and one post-Roman phase (Fig. 4). These comprise:

Phase 0   pre-enclosure activity. *?Prehistoric or late first century AD* .

Phase 1   creation and use of two ditched enclosures. *c. 95 AD – c. 130 AD* .

Phase 2   post-enclosure Roman activity. *Third to fourth century AD* .

Phase 3   post-Roman activity. *Post-medieval and modern.*

Phase 0
(Fig. 5)
Pre-enclosure activity, represented by a short length of boundary ditch and a related pit.

It seems likely that the earliest feature at Orton's Pasture was a north–south-aligned ditch (F720), located close to Valley View Walk, towards the western edge of the excavated area. The ditch, sampled in two 2m-long sections, measured approximately 1.5m in width and was cut with steep sides and a rounded base to a depth of 0.45m (Fig. 5). A *c.*12m length of this ditch was recorded in plan before the feature shallowed out to the south, perhaps as the result of plough truncation. Cut by two Phase 1 features, ditch F720 contained no finds. Its backfills (6584 and 6585) of dark brown sandy silt — there was some minor variation in consistency only between the two identified fills — were quite distinct in the overall context of the site, though adjacent pit F729 was also backfilled with a similar material.

Associated with this early ditch (F720), and lying to its west, was a small ovoid pit (F729), which likewise yielded no finds. Filled with a dark brown sandy silt (6597), similar in matrix to the backfill of ditch F720, the pit measured approximately 1.80m by 1.02m and was 0.40m in depth. It was also cut by a Phase 1 ditch.

Phase 0 – Dating and Interpretation
Given the density of Roman pottery recovered from other features, F720 and F729 would appear to pre-date any significant and extended Roman activity within the area of Orton's Pasture. Since no finds were recovered from the features, they could be later prehistoric in origin, or alternatively the ditch and pit could relate to the very earliest phases of Roman military presence in the area, though the forts associated with this early presence lie to the north of the site.

The ditch (F720) may be an early, possibly prehistoric, field boundary, or it may be early Roman in date and relate to the first phases of military activity recorded to the north of the Orton's Pasture site. There is the possibility that F720 may be a marching camp ditch (A.S. Esmonde Cleary pers. comm.), though once more this suggestion is very tentative. Pit F729 has a similar fill, and, since both are cut by the same later ditch, it seems probable that the two features are contemporary.

Phase 1
(Figs. 6–11 and Plates 1–11)
The creation and use of two adjacent enclosures, separated by a hollow-way. A metalled track ran to the east of the enclosures. There was evidence for the recutting and redefinition of lengths of the boundary ditches around both enclosures. The interior of the northern enclosure (Enclosure 1) contained a number of pits and/or wells, while the southern enclosure (Enclosure 2) likewise contained pits, but in this case associated with a small stone building. Either just outside the northern ditch of Enclosure 1, or in the area of an entrance into the enclosure, there was situated another group of pits. Each of these individual elements will be described separately before an integrated discussion of the dating and interpretation of the phase is offered.

The Northern Enclosure (Enclosure 1)
The enclosure ditches
(Fig. 6)
The northern enclosure, its long axis being aligned east–west, enclosed an area of at least 3944m², with parts of its northern (F608 and F609), eastern (F612 and F715) and southern (F702) defining ditches being within the area of excavation and watching brief (Plate 1). Its western limit was not established. The dimensions of the enclosure were 58m (north–south) by at least 68m (east–west). Both the northern and eastern ditch lines exhibited signs of recutting and redefinition (respectively F609 and F715). There was no evidence of an associated bank.

Internal features will be considered below, as will a group of pits lying outside the enclosure to the north, quite possibly in the area of an entry gap into the enclosure.

The original northern ditch cut F608 had been severely truncated by a later recut. Measuring 0.25m in depth and 0.79m in width, the remaining, undisturbed portion of the ditch was backfilled with a single deposit of mixed, dark brown sandy silt (6077). Its profile was unreconstructable. The original cut for the eastern ditch (F612), which had survived to a depth of 0.70m, had a V-shaped profile and measured 2.30m in width. In the excavated section, the ditch contained substantial amounts of pottery, charcoal flecking and large stone inclusions in a mixed silty matrix (6093) which was overlain by a very clean orange-brown sandy gravel (6092), containing no finds, and a mixed brown silt with stone and charcoal inclusions (6091).

It is possible that rather than being the northern boundary of the enclosure, ditch line F608/F609 could mark the southern side of an entrance into the enclosure through its east side. If this was in fact the case, then the entrance gap would have been at least 15m in width, with its northern side lying beyond the area of excavation, under Mill Street. However, there was no indication of the existence of a spur road leading off road F716 at this point, which may suggest that an entrance into the enclosure here is unlikely.

Five sections were excavated across the southern boundary ditch (F702), whose V-shaped profile varied considerably in depth from east to west, probably as a result of plough truncation (Plate 2). In places up to 2.60m wide and 0.75–0.85m deep, a considerable variation in the nature of its backfills was noted during excavation, these numerous individual deposits including: lower fills of a mixed grey silt (*e.g.* 6505) and in another stretch of a dark brown silty clay (*e.g.* 6540 and 1025); and upper fills again of mixed silt, but rich in charcoal and containing occasional inclusions of burnt red clay (*e.g.* 6503) and of dark grey-brown silt clay with charcoal and pebble inclusions (*e.g.* 1002 and 6525). A significant variation in the quantities of finds from each excavated section was noted. Approximately 47m eastwards along the line of ditch F702 was a ditch spur, leading off to the south (F723). This feature was approximately 0.50m in depth and 1.70m in width.

The recut (F609) of the northern boundary ditch almost totally truncated the original cut (F608). With a V-shaped profile, F609 measured 1.8m in width and 0.70m in depth. Its lower fills consisted of dark brown sandy silts (6078, 6098 and 6099), which were extremely prolific in finds, containing quantities of animal bone and, more unusually, lead-glazed Roman pottery.

Along the eastern boundary ditch, the recut (F715) became progressively shallower towards the south where its alignment lay slightly to the east of F612. With a U-shaped profile, F715 measured approximately 0.40m in depth and 1.00m in width. It was backfilled with mixed sandy silts and clays (6854 and 6859).

The northern enclosure interior (Enclosure 1)
(Figs. 6 and 7)

Only a very small portion of the enclosure interior lay within the area of excavation, the majority of the interior lying under the back gardens of those properties to the west and fronting onto Mill Street. Internal features consisted of four pits and two shallow scoops (Figs. 6 and 7).

In the extreme north-west corner of Area B, close to Valley View Walk, was a pit (F726), approximately 0.62m in depth and 2.10m in width. The full extent of the pit could not be determined since it extended beyond the northern baulk. Filled by three deposits of dark brown sandy silt (6595, 6613 and 6614), the feature yielded an unusual find, a partially preserved piece of leather strap with rivetted copper-alloy fittings attached, along with a quantity of Roman pottery sherds. Pit F726 was cut by a shallow scoop (F727), measuring approximately 0.24m in depth and 1.10m across and filled by a single deposit of charcoal-rich clay (6596).

Located approximately 20m to the east of F726, and close to the southern boundary ditch of the enclosure, were two further, intercutting, pits (F725 and F719). The earliest of the two pits (F725) was circular in plan and measured 2.9m across and 1.40m in depth. The mixed silt clay fills of pit F725 (6582, 6586 and 6592) were truncated to the north by the cut of a second pit (F719), which was sub-rounded in plan and 0.78m deep, with mixed silt clay fills (6577 and 6581). Both pits contained substantial amounts of Roman pottery and animal bone. A few

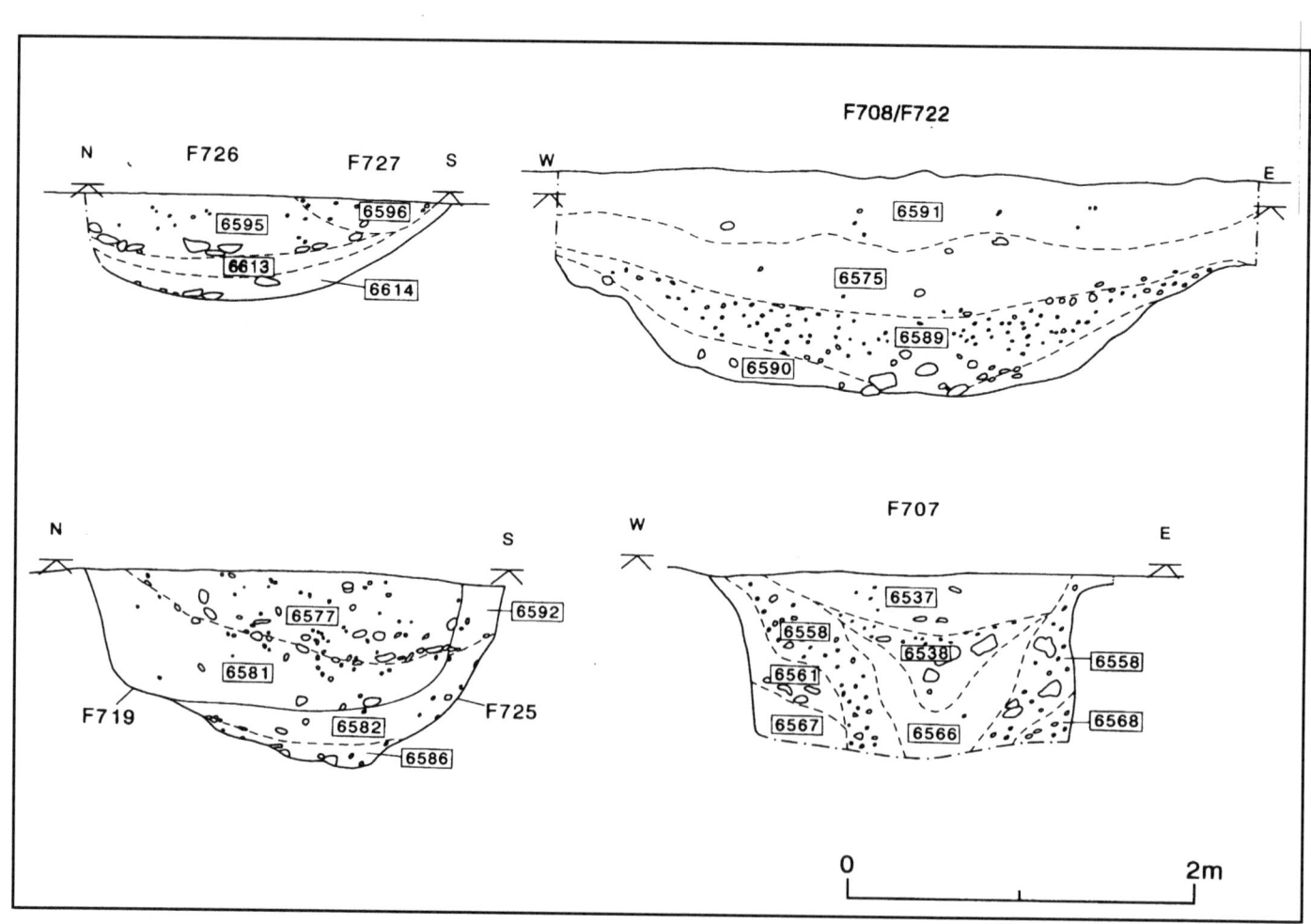

Fig. 7 Phase 1 : Enclosure 1 (Northern Enclosure), pit sections (F707, F708/F722, F719/F725, F726/F727)

metres to the north-east of pit F725 was cut a shallow scoop (F718), *c.* 0.16m in depth and 0.80m in width. The fill of the scoop, a dark grey-brown silt (6576), contained pottery and a copper-alloy spoon.

Two more pits were recorded within the northern enclosure. The deepest of these (F707) was circular in plan with vertical sides, measured 2.2m in diameter and was excavated to a depth of 1.2m, but not bottomed. It was backfilled with a number of gravel-rich sandy silt deposits (6558, 6561, 6567 and 6568) at the sides of the pit, which probably represent weathering of natural material and its collapse into the feature, and three central fills of mixed dark brown-grey silty clay (6566), overlain by a similar clay with charcoal inclusions and occasional sub-angular stones (6538). This, in turn, was overlain by a much siltier dark clay with charcoal, stones and burnt clay (6537). Immediately to the east was another shallower, but much wider, pit (F708/F722), measuring 3.80m in width and 0.45m in depth. It was backfilled with four, very different and distinct deposits, of yellow sand and stones (6590), a compact, stony mixed clay (6589), a dark brown silty sand with occasional stones (6575) and an upper fill of dark mixed silt (6591) which may have dished into the backfilled feature following compaction and subsidence of its fills.

The pits/wells lying to the north of Enclosure 1
(Fig. 8, Plates 3 and 4)
A few metres to the north of Enclosure 1 were dug several pits (F602, F603, and F604). These measured between 2.7 and 3m in diameter, and varied between 2.9 and 3m in depth. The stratigraphic relationship of these features to other deposits initially proved difficult to assess during excavation, due to the considerable extent of subsidence into the pits, whereby the fills had compacted and settled, causing the slumping of later deposits by up to a metre. Each pit was excavated by hand to a safe depth of *c.* 1.2m. Subsequent excavation was by machine, working under archaeological supervision, in order to allow a record of the full depth to be made, with the sorting of spoil for the recovery of artifactual and environmental material taking place at the side of the features.

The northernmost pit (F603) had a primary fill of dark brown sandy silts (6100 and 6097), overlain by successive layers of brown sandy silt, clay, and stone ((6027, 6033, 6041, 6042 and 6050). Approximately 1m to the south of pit F603 lay pit F602. Its primary fill of dark brown sandy silt (6096) was overlain by a mixed brown silt, clay and rubble deposit (6062), and two further layers of brown silt (6054 and 6032). A central, V-shaped fill of mixed silt clays (6031) was overlain by dished deposits of clay and cobble. The last of the large pits here (F604) was located approximately 2m to the south of F602 and was excavated by hand to a depth of 1.6m. The primary fills consisted of a light brown sandy silt (6094 and 6095), to a depth of approximately 3.5m. Visible at 1.6m was a light brown sandy silt with charcoal, clay, iron slag and deposits with the appearance of cess (6060 and 6064). Considerable dishing of Phase 2 deposits and surfaces had again taken place.

The three pits lay to the west of the metalled road surface F716.

The Southern Enclosure (Enclosure 2)
The enclosure ditches
(Figs. 9 and 10, Plates 1 and 5)

Only two sides of the southern enclosure were defined during the excavation, its northern ditched boundary, with one instance of boundary redefinition evident, and its eastern boundary, marked by a series of recut ditches. The enclosure may have been either square or rectangular in shape, and would have had an internal area of at least 9100m².

The eastern boundary was defined by four parallel, and in places intercutting, ditches (F704, F705, F706 and F714), all aligned north–south and cut into the natural gravels and, to the south, into alluvium. The ditch profiles were all similar, having steeply sloping sides and flat, or rounded, bases. The earliest ditch (F714), located furthest to the west, measured 0.58m in width and 0.37m in depth. No east–west return of Feature F714 was recorded. Any east–west alignment of this ditch may have been truncated by recutting. Again, there was no evidence for an associated bank, though any such bank would probably have been removed by deep ploughing of the field.

Feature F706 (also recorded in the evaluations as F4 and F301), aligned north–south, ran parallel with Feature F714 and appeared to have been cut originally with a northern return, which was later truncated by ditch F705. Feature F705 was cut between ditches F714 and F706, and truncated both. Full descriptions of the mixed silty clay fills of these three ditches, which varied only in the quantities and densities of charcoal and small cobble inclusions, can be found in the archive. The latest, and largest, of the four enclosure ditches was the easternmost ditch (F704, also recorded in the evaluations as F3 and F300). This measured 0.84m in width and 0.43m in depth, and was backfilled with a mixed grey-brown silt (6529, 6532, 6542,1011 and 3004), in places overlain by a linear deposit of river cobbles (1010) along its eastern edge. These were overlain by a 0.30m-deep deposit of very dark grey-brown silt clay with charcoal and cobbles (1005). This upper fill was undoubtedly a single, dumped deposit. The eastern boundary line was traced in plan and by geophysical survey for 70m southwards into Zone C and the area of the watching brief. However, it is not possible to say whether the boundary was recut along the whole of its length, as it had been in the north where excavation was able to establish this sequence.

Along the northern boundary, one stretch of recut ditch (F713), ending at a terminal, was identified. This is probably part of the same phase of recutting that created F705. The main boundary line though was formed by ditch F711, which continued up to, and beyond, the western extent of the excavated area, *c.* 65m to the west. Two sections were excavated across the line of F711, where it was demonstrated that the feature measured approximately 1.40m in width and 0.43m in depth, with a V-shaped profile and a flat base. The ditch became shallower towards the west, perhaps as the result of a differential ploughing regime. The lower fill comprised a compact dark, orange-brown gravel (6551), probably representing primary slumping off the ditch sides. This was overlain by a deposit of soft mid-brown silt (6549), and that in turn was overlain by a dark grey-brown sandy silt clay with small stones, charcoal inclusions and some flecking of burnt clay (6548). The uppermost fill of the ditch was a soft dark silt (6543) that possibly represents inwash into the dished and compacted upper surface of the backfilled ditch. Ditch F711 would appear to be part of the same operation that involved the cutting of the major eastern boundary ditch F704.

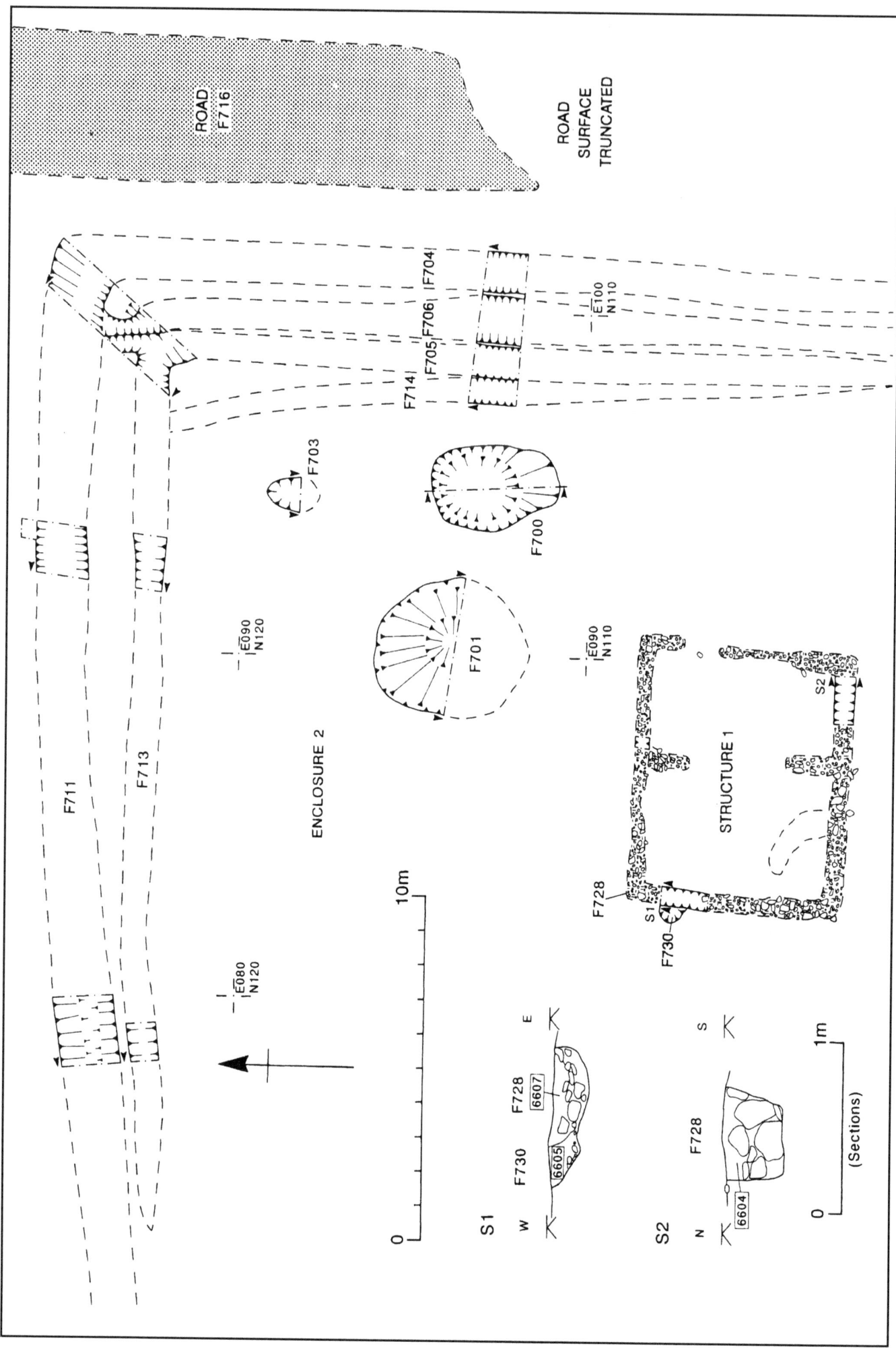

Fig. 8 Phase 1 : to north of Enclosure 1, plan and pit sections (F602, F603, F604)

The southern enclosure interior (Enclosure 2)
(Figs. 9–11, Plates 5–11)

Features inside the southern enclosure consisted of a small, stone-footed building, two large pits and a number of shallow pits or scoops.

The most significant internal feature of Enclosure 2 was a small building (F728, Structure 1) whose stone and cobble foundations (1007 and 6604) had escaped the denudation of the plough which had otherwise unfortunately removed any floor surfaces and internal features which may once have been present inside the structure (Fig.9, Plates 10 and 11).The evaluation in 1990 (Trench 5) had encountered this building, but its full significance had not been appreciated at the time. Rectangular in plan, the structure measured 8m by 4m, and was aligned east–west. A north–south central partition divided the structure into two more-or-less equally sized rooms, with an entrance to the east and another to the west. Four sections were excavated across the foundation trench which was revealed to be 0.70m wide and 0.35m deep, with almost vertical sides and a flat base, packed with clean yellow clay and river cobbles (1007 and 6604). No finds were recovered from the backfill of the foundation trench.

Two substantial pits (F701 [F302 in the evaluation] and F700 [F303 in the evaluation]) were also dug in the north-east corner of the enclosure, to the northeast of, and only a few metres away from, Structure 1, both cut into the yellow/orange sand which here formed the natural subsoil (Figs. 9 and 10). The larger of the pits (F701, Plates 6, 7 and 8) was circular in plan, measuring 3.70m in diameter and *c.* 2m in depth. The pit narrowed to a width of 1.70m at a depth of 1.10m. The lower fills consisted of a 0.75m-thick series of grey-brown silt sands with clay and varying quantities of charcoal inclusions (6521, 6522 and 6557), which contained very few sherds of pottery, or indeed other finds. Overlying these was a very light brown silty, sandy clay (6556), again more-or-less devoid of finds, though the presence in the matrix of a number of large stones was noted. Above this, a very dark grey-brown sandy silty clay with charcoal inclusions (6518), again recorded as containing fragments of stone, in this case pieces of sandstone, was overlain by a sterile, orange-brown, sandy clay (6517) and a mottled dark, grey-brown, sandy silty clay with frequent charcoal inclusions (6507). The uppermost, dished fills of mixed grey-brown silty clays (3017 and 6504) formed the matrix for about two dozen blocks of sandstone that on the surface of the feature at first were thought to be a stone lining for the pit around its northern edge, an appearance probably caused by compaction and subsidence post-dating the use of the pit. One of these blocks was a fragment from an altar, while one or two of the other blocks displayed evidence of dressing and facing, suggesting that they represented building stone. The other blocks were unworked.

To the east of pit F701 was another, slightly smaller, ovoid pit (F700). Feature F700 measured 2.6m in width (east–west) by 3.5m (north–south) and was 1.40m deep (Plates 6 and 9). The lower fills consisted of a charcoal-rich, brown sandy silt (3011, 6516, 6514 and 6511), which contained several lenses of alternating charcoal and clean orange sand (3010, very similar to the natural subsoil).The uppermost of the charcoally fills (6511) contained a greater concentration of burnt material than the lower deposits with which it has here been grouped. The layering of clean sand may have been the result of a collapse of

the sides, or may represent a deliberate attempt to seal off and cap each successive layer of charcoal. The upper fills (6510 and 3007) measured 0.28m in depth, and contained an extremely dense concentration of Roman pottery. At some period, the pit appears to have collapsed from the south, as represented by a layer of cleanish silty sand and gravel (6514, 6512), creating an oval appearance in plan.

In the north-eastern corner of the southern enclosure was a shallow ovoid pit (F703), measuring approximately 0.10m in width and 0.25m in depth. To the south-west of pit F703 was another small ovoid pit (F730), measuring 1.40m in length, 0.90m in width and 0.22m in depth. Feature F730 was cut to the north-east by the foundation trench for structure F728.

Also lying within the area of the enclosure, at the northern end of evaluation Trench 12 and in an area that was not re-examined during the main excavation other than during machine stripping, was a number of small, isolated features (Fig. 11). These included two possible post-holes (4006 and 4007), measuring 0.28m and 0.25m in diameter respectively. To the south, and to the west of these, were two shallow circular features (F401 and F403), both approximately 0.14m in depth. Feature F403 was filled with a light brown silt (4004), which contained patches of yellow-brown clay. Feature F401 was filled with a dark orange-brown sandy silt (4002). A few, small and abraded sherds of Roman pottery came from the fill of F401.

The road/trackway and hollow-way

The evaluation in 1990 identified a possible metalled surface which the main excavation subsequently confirmed to be a north–south-aligned road or track, traversing both Area A (F601), and Area B (F716), to the east of Enclosures 1 and 2, but not extending further south into Area C. The road surface (from now on simply called F716) appeared to have two phases of construction, and was repaired in several places. In Area A, foundation make-up layers of sandy silt and gravel (6104), varying between 0.15m and 0.40m in depth, were overlain by the earliest road surface (6034). This surface comprised a layer of large cobbles and smaller stones (6034), in turn overlain by a layer of clean orange gravel and cobbles, up to 0.20m in thickness.The eastern edge of the road lay beyond the eastern baulk in Area A, so its full width remains unknown, though within the area of excavation it was recorded as having a width of *c.* 4m.

In Area B, the alignment of the road gradually diverged from the eastern boundary of Orton's Pasture, and it was possible to record a full section across the road. The make-up below the road surface (6608 and 6609) was not as deep as in Area A, measuring approximately 0.05 to 0.15m in depth. As in Area A, the lower phase of the road consisted of large cobbles and gravel (6617), sealed by a clean, compact, orange-brown gravel (6573). No evidence of a ditch related to the road was recorded to the west, but to the east the road had been truncated by a later ditch which lay on a similar north–south alignment. Further to the south, the metalled surfaces (6617 and 6573) showed a gradual reduction in depth, and were not evident beyond the southern extent of the excavation in Area B. This may result from truncation by the plough.

A possible hollow-way (F736), aligned east–west, ran between the northern and southern enclosures. This was only evident in the eastern half of Area B, where it extended as far as the better-

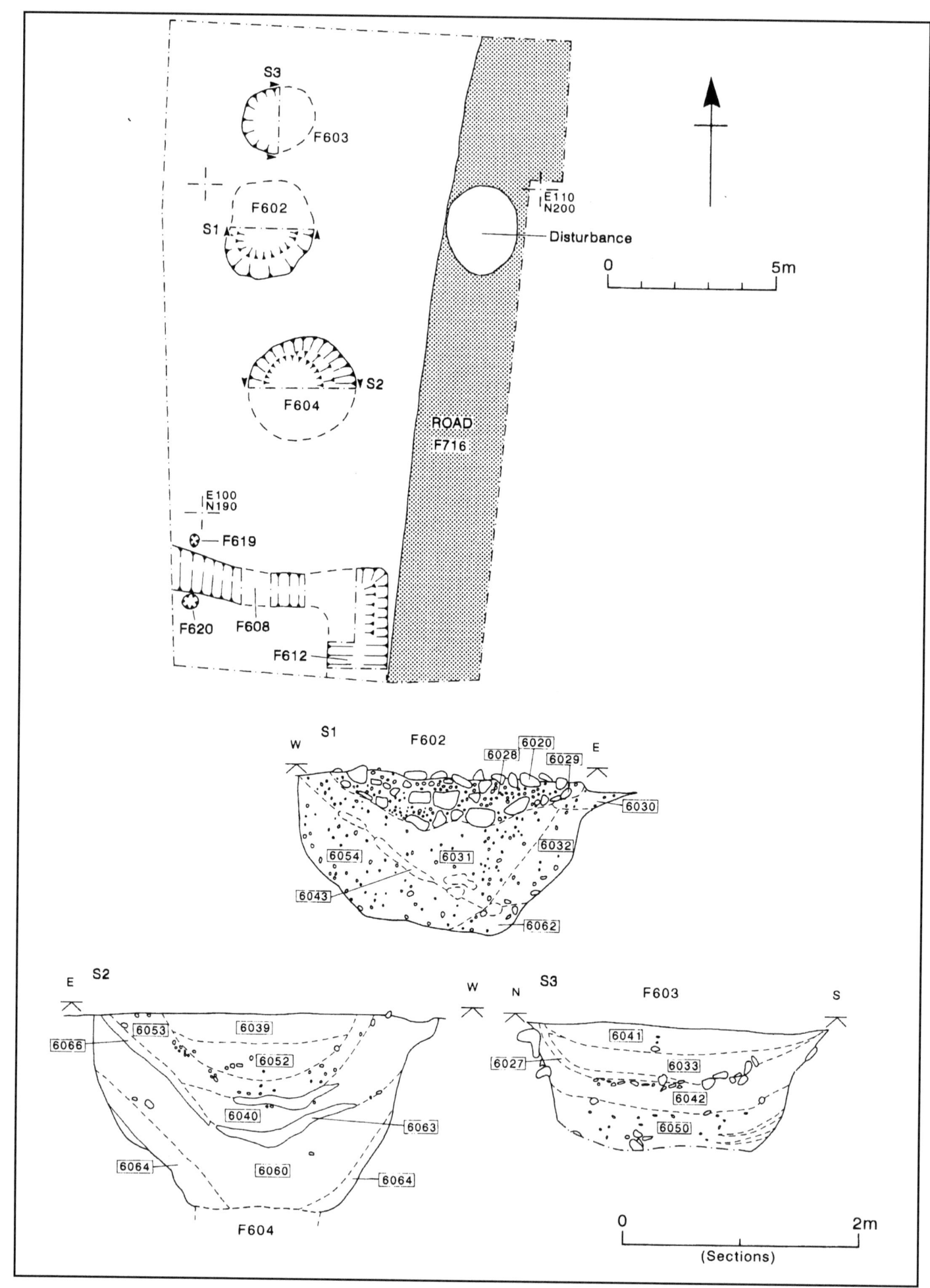

Fig. 9   Phase 1 : Enclosure 2 (Southern Enclosure), plan and sections (F728, F730)

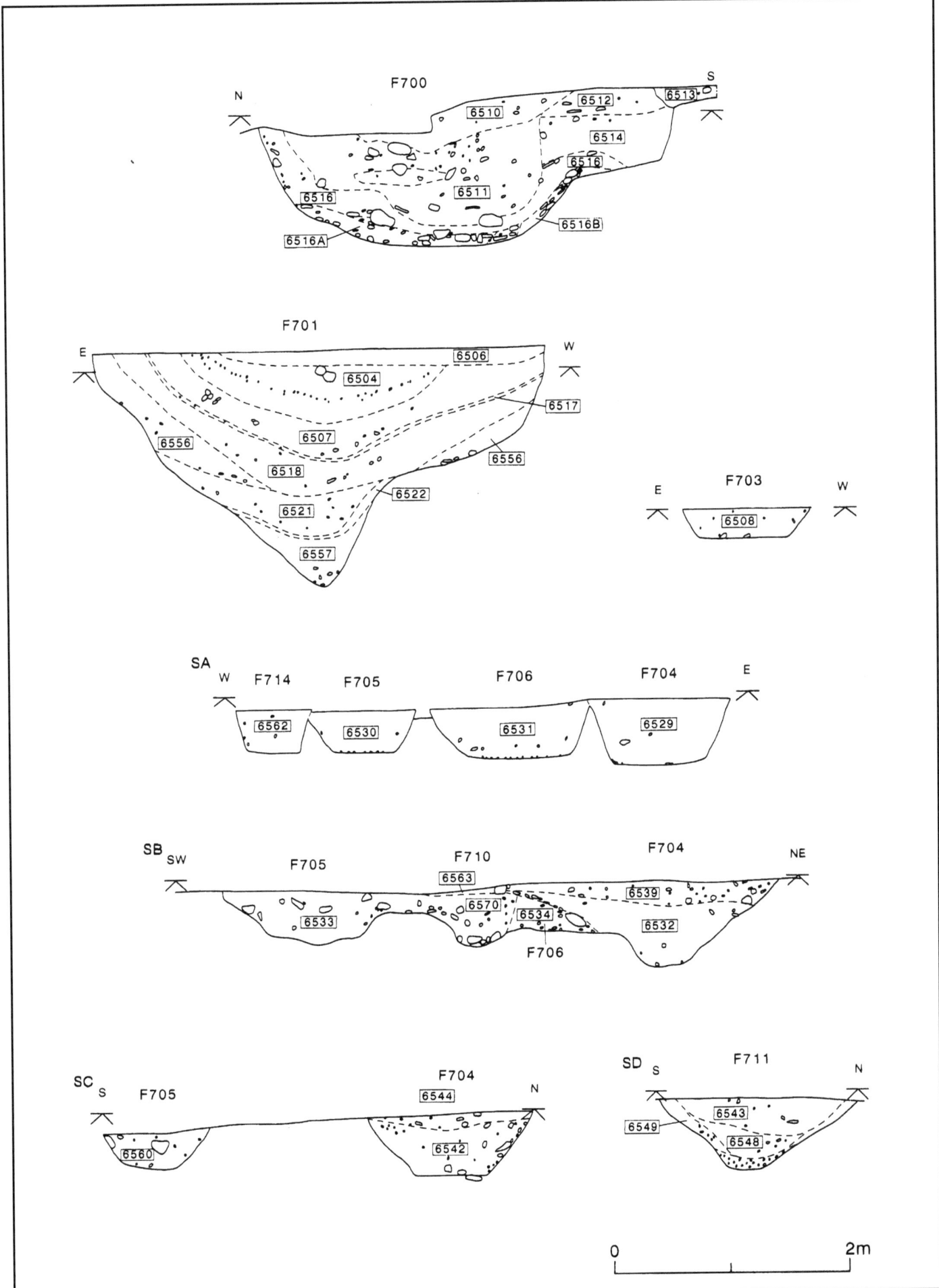

Fig. 10   Phase 1 : Enclosure 2 (Southern Enclosure), pit sections (F700, F701, F703) and ditch sections (F704, F705, F706, F710, F711)

constructed road F716. The hollow-way was *c.* 2m in width, 0.15m in depth and was infilled with a grey sandy silt (6607). A compacted layer of orange-brown gravel (6606), 0.08m in depth and in places overlying the silt, may have at some stage formed a metalled surface. This later metalled surface over the line of the hollow-way appears to be of a similar matrix to the later surface of the road to the east.

Phase 1 – Dating and Interpretation

An integrated discussion of the site follows the presentation of the finds and environmental data from the site. Here the opportunity will be taken briefly to interpret the excavated structures on their own. An examination of the layout of the enclosure complexes suggests that the two enclosures were laid out in relation to each other, there being no intercutting of enclosure ditches or overlapping of their plans. Either they were created at the same time, or one was created while the other

was still in use and clearly visible on the ground. It would also seem that the east–west-aligned hollow-way running between the two enclosures and the metalled road running alongside the eastern boundary of both enclosures also form part of an integrated plan, though it can be seen in plan that the line of the metalled road or track is almost impinged upon by Enclosure 1 in the north, perhaps suggesting that Enclosure 1 is the later of these features sequentially.

Excavation of the enclosure ditches demonstrated two main phases of ditch digging for Enclosure 1, and as many as three instances of boundary redefinition of Enclosure 2, principally along its eastern boundary. Although the cuts for the enclosure ditches were continuous, the fills in different areas were extremely varied. This almost certainly reflects the functional range of activities in the vicinity, in various parts of the enclosures.

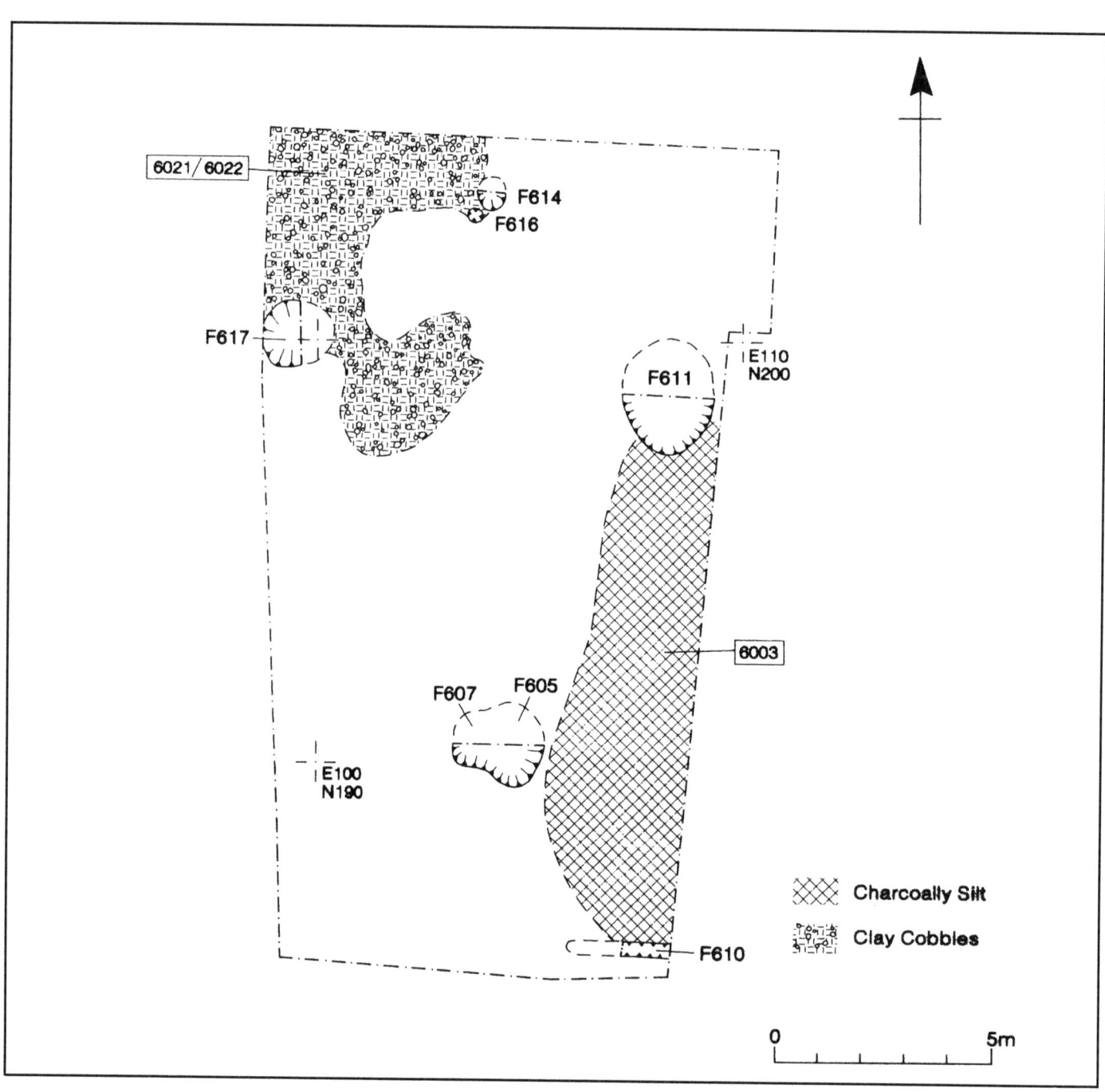

Fig. 11   Phase 2 : plan

The recovery of military fittings exclusively from the fills of features within the northern enclosure, Enclosure 1, must relate in some way to the initial occupation of the fort at Rocester, though the status and function of the Orton's Pasture site cannot be determined from examination of the plan of the site or from individual features or structures here. There was no evidence of buildings inside the enclosure.

The morphology of the pits within Enclosure 1 would tend to suggest that they were originally intended for different purposes. Features F719, F722, F725 and F726 seem likely to have been rubbish pits, since none of them is deeper than 1.4m. Feature F718 may be a shallow, partially truncated pit. Feature F707 may have been used as a well, since it has sharply defined vertical sides and was originally lined, although its original function is unclear since the feature was not excavated to its base.

Of the three large pits (F602, F603 and F604) lying outside Enclosure 1 to its north, it may be that they were originally intended as wells, which could be periodically backfilled with rubbish as a new well was dug. The absence of any well lining, however, tends to suggest that this was not the case. Although the pits widened considerably around the surface, giving them the appearance of having been robbed out, no trace of a well lining was encountered further down, where it may have been expected to survive. Due to the nature of the geology, a lining would have been essential for a well to function efficiently and to prevent the sides from collapsing within a few days. Since the deepest of the pits is only 3.5m deep (approximately the level of the water-table), assuming that the water-table remains the same as during the Roman period, the pits were not cut sufficiently deep enough to draw water effectively. Containing substantial amounts of pottery, glass, bone and cess, the pits would appear to have been utilised for the disposal of rubbish rather than simply being allowed to infill naturally.

The interior of the southern enclosure, Enclosure 2, contained a small, stone-footed building (Structure 1) whose function is not immediately clear from its plan and internal layout. Two large pits (F700 and F701), and a smaller feature (F703), lay to its north. These features and the building are grouped together in the very north-east corner of the enclosure. Other, isolated, small internal features were also recorded during both the evaluation and the excavation watching brief. The pits do not appear to be classic rubbish pits, though they contained quantities of finds and charcoal etc, and their stepped profiles suggest that they may have been dug in this way to allow access into the features. The presence of clean, sterile deposits in the backfill of pit F700 suggests a controlled backfilling process at some stages of the feature's use-span.

No help in dating the site is given by the single coin recovered from the northern enclosure; this was unfortunately illegible. This was the only coin found during the combined evaluation and excavation exercise. Dates provided by the samian indicate that if all features assigned here to Phase 1 are assessed together, then the phase would appear to extend from the later first century, *c.* AD 95, up to *c.* AD 130. There are quite significant clusterings of dates, and Willis (below) has pointed out that in the case of the ditches of Enclosure 1 the samian groups from different stretches of the ditches are not necessarily contemporary from stretch to stretch. This observation would seem to confirm the excavator's interpretation of the ditches being backfilled in a somewhat piecemeal fashion, with different types of spoil in different stretches, though this was a subjective rather than an objective observation, due to the sampling strategy necessarily employed during the excavation. Only total excavation would have allowed a quantification of this presumed phenomenon to be made.

Certainly the samian indicates that Phase 1 was mainly of an early second-century date, with little suggestion that activity here continued much beyond AD 120–130. There is a consistency in the dating of the samian from the three large pits (F602, F603 and F604) lying outside Enclosure 1, to its north, which may suggest that these features went out of use in the early Antonine period, perhaps a little later than the terminal dates for activity inside the enclosures.

With regard to the earliest dated samian on the site, its presence need not necessarily date the start of Phase 1. Indeed, the very early material generally appears in contexts with later first- and early second-century material, and in those cases is in the minority within the assemblages. In assessing samian use and discard dates, as opposed to manufacturing dates, it is a cautionary tale to consider that at the New Cemetery site at Rocester, inside the Roman fort, a cache of Flavian samian vessels was found in a context that placed their breaking and deposition at a time when the vessels would have been almost one hundred years old (Esmonde Cleary and Ferris 1996, 91 and 224).

The two copper-alloy brooches recovered from the backfill of pit F700, in the interior of Enclosure 1, are types to which Mackreth (below) has assigned dates of, in one case, *c.* AD 75 to *c.* AD 150/175. and, in the other, mid- to late first century. Again, though, a distinction needs to be made between use dates and loss dates.

As to the coarse pottery and the mortaria, the coarse pottery from this phase would appear to include much Flavian–Trajanic material, though the latest vessels are Hadrianic–Antonine types, with some distinct clustering of material of slightly different dates in different features, a pattern also evident amongst the samian. The majority of the stamped mortaria further confirms a bias in date for mortaria at Rocester that had already been noted by Mrs Hartley from her study of the mortaria from the New Cemetery and the as-yet-unpublished Dove First School sites. Though there is some first century material, the majority is of an early second-century date, with little material that suggests that this floruit extended beyond *c.* AD 130.

Phase 2
(Fig. 11)
Later Roman Activity
Following backfilling of the Phase 1 pits in the northernmost excavated area, and presumably after Enclosure 1 had gone out of use, a series of floors, yards or working surfaces was laid down here. Associated structures lay within the area of excavation and other such structures presumably lay further to the north and west. The north–south aligned road had now gone out of use. A number of pits and scoops was associated with this phase of activity.

Three successive floor surfaces were recorded in the north-western corner of Area A. The earliest of these was a layer of grey clay (6043 and 6050), approximately 0.08m in depth, which contained deposits of burnt red clay within its matrix. This surface survived in patches across the area and appeared to be limited by a band of red clay to the south. Remains of this clay layer had also survived where they had subsided into the upper fills of two earlier pits of Phase 1 (recorded in section as clay layers 6043, F602 and 6050, F603). The clay was overlain by a brown sandy silt (seen in pit sections as contexts 6031 and 6042), which was possibly used to backfill areas of slumping around pits F602 and F603. A metalled surface of small gravel and stones (6021) was then spread and laid over the silt make-up deposit, which was, in turn, sealed by another surface of red clay (6022). Both surfaces survived as disjointed, isolated deposits due to the subsidence into the earlier features.

An accumulation of layers of brown sandy silt with numerous inclusions of burnt red clay (6024 and 6035) sealed most of the features in the southern half of Area A. Evident within the upper surface of layer 6024 was a small hearth (F600). Partly obscured by the western baulk in Area A, the hearth measured 1.10m in width and 0.15m in depth, and was built of a solid, plastic red clay (6004).

To the east, and cutting through the former Phase 2 road surface, was a large pit (F611). The feature was hand-excavated to a depth of 1.4m, at which point excavation ceased. In this instance, it was not possible to machine-excavate the feature further, due to the instability of the feature's sides. Having subsided to a depth of 1.0m below the level of the ground surface, the dished, upper part of the feature was backfilled with small cobble, silts and clay (6046 and 6071), the true upper fill of F611 being identified as a brown sandy silt with large stones and cobbles (6083).

A second, smaller, two-phase pit was located approximately 6m to the south. The earliest pit (F607) was cut with steep sides to a depth of 0.80m. Filled by grey-brown sand (6072, 6074 and 6103) it was heavily truncated by another pit to the east (F605). Measuring approximately 1.65m in width and evident to a depth of 0.85m, pit F605 was cut with steep sides and a flat base. The lower, mixed silty clay fill of the pit (6084) contained a lens of charcoal, while the upper fills again were characterised by several lenses of charcoal (6065, 6073 and 6061), which may suggest that it was in some way related to industrial activity on the site. This is further hinted at by the presence of a spread of charcoally silt and burnt clay (6003) lying between pits F611 and F605/F607. Forming the southern limit of this spread of burnt material was a beam-slot or gulley (F610), aligned east–west and measuring approximately 0.3m in depth and 0.3m in width. The feature continued beyond the eastern baulk. The slot was filled with charcoal and mixed deposits with cobbles (6082).

A third pit or scoop (F617), towards the northern end of the western baulk, and only partially within the area of excavation, measured 0.55m in depth and 1.5m in width. With steep sides and a rounded base it was filled with a single deposit of brown sandy silt (6108).

In the northern part of Area A were two, adjacent, small post-holes or stake-holes (F614 and F616). Both were of a similar depth, of 0.16m, and backfilled with a similar deposit of dark brown silt (6105 and 6107 respectively). If structural, they were presumably associated with a building that lay largely to the north, beyond the limits of excavation.

Phase 2 – Dating and Interpretation

It is not altogether easy to understand the nature of the activity taking place in the northern part of the site in this phase. Beam slot or gulley F610, and post-holes/stake-holes F614 and F616, appear to be isolated and may not therefore be structural elements of anything other than ephemeral or flimsy timber buildings or workshops. The pits and scoops (F605/F607, F617 and F611) have fills which contain quantities of charcoal and burnt clay which may suggest a link to craft or industrial activity, perhaps metalworking. Spreads of burnt charcoal and clay (6003 and 6079), a hearth (F600) and the successive floor surfaces (6043/6050, 6031/6042, 6021 and 6022) in the north-east corner of Area A, along with albeit low densities of iron smithing slag in these deposits suggest the same. A crucible in layer 6089 and copper-alloy slag in the upper backfill of recut ditch F609 of Phase 1 could be derived from this phase, and would seem to point towards just such an interpretation of the function of this phase. The form of the largest pit F611, with its near-vertical sides, suggests that it represents a backfilled well, a type of feature which again might be expected in an area in close proximity to industrial activities probably requiring an easily available source of water.

Although the samian pottery from Phase 2 was not catalogued in detail, as it was considered that at this period the vast majority of this material was residual, a scan of the material suggested that there was indeed little difference between the Phase 1 and Phase 2 groups, with few pieces dating to after 150 AD. Exactly the same observation can be made about the coarse pottery assemblage, with obviously residual material being in the majority.

Although little of the material from this phase was selected for publication, when the archive catalogues are compared to Ruth Leary's characterisation of the third- and fourth-century assemblage at the New Cemetery site it can be seen that later BB1 rim forms and decorative trends are more-or-less absent at Orton's Pasture, while quantities of Derbyshire ware in Phase 2 are low enough to suggest that at Orton's Pasture this too is probably largely residual, pre-dating the expected increase in such material in the third and fourth centuries. Late Oxfordshire red colour-coats and Dales ware are also absent at Orton's Pasture in these later deposits. All of this suggests that the activity of Phase 2 was on the fringes of the third- and fourth-century settlement at Rocester, in an even more peripheral location than the New Cemetery site.

However, the mortaria provided the key dating for activity of this phase. From the make-up of the floor deposits dished into the three large pits F602, F603 and F604 came mortaria dating respectively: to the mid-second to third century and to the third century (F602); to the second half of the second century (F603); and to a post-AD 230 date (F604). Other mortaria of similar date came from the uppermost surfaces of pit F707 in the northern enclosure and of pit F701 inside the southern enclosure, where once more they probably represent dishing, in this case of ploughsoil deposits, and from ploughsoil itself.

Phase 3 (Not illustrated)
Post-Roman activity
To the east of, and partially cutting, the Phase 2 road (F716) was a ditch (F731), aligned north–south and measuring approximately 0.40m in depth and 1.10m in width. Although

truncating the road, this ditch contained no material within its fill (6610) to suggest its date, and it has therefore here been assigned to the post-Roman period. A shallower ditch (F732), on a similar alignment, truncated the upper fills of F731 to a depth of 0.15m.

Two features were cut into the upper surface of the road, a small pit (F724) and a possible post-hole (F733). No finds were recovered from either feature. A small pit was also recorded between the northern and the southern enclosures, truncating the north–south-aligned ditch F721. The fill of this feature contained fragments of clay pipe. Immediately to the west of

Feature F721, close to the western baulk in Area A, was a shallow ditch (F734), aligned north–south, which truncated both the northern and the southern enclosure ditches. It seems likely that this feature is relatively modern in origin.

Drawings, photographs, and descriptions of all these features can be found in the site archive.

Phase 3 – Dating and Interpretation
Given the lack of firm dating evidence for these features and the lack of any proven inter-relationship between them, no further discussion of this phase will be undertaken.

—✧—

Table 1. Fabrics present in assemblage by number, weight and relative percentages

Fabric Code	Quantity	Weight (grams)	% no / % weight
AMPH	829	89882	11.78/47.85
SAM	740	9800	10.52/5.21
MORT	124	11230	1.76/5.97
BB1	902	14660	12.82/7.69
BB1 (variant)	1	209	>1/>1
CC1	37	423	>1/>1
CC2	45	752	>1/>1
CTA	10	657	>1/>1
CTA2 DW	7	581	>1/>1
DBY	309	7437	4.40/3.95
FLA1	221	4602	3.14/2.45
FLA2	335	5960	4.76/3.17
FLA3	42	1016	>1/>1
FLA4	25	607	>1/>1
FLB1	51	989	>1/>1
FLB2	13	297	>1/>1
GLZ1	35	435	>1/>1
GLZ3	1	11	>1/>1
GRA1	943	3946	13.82/2.10
GRA2	665	7621	9.45/4.06
GRA3	93	1267	1.32>1
GRA4	23	326	>1/>1
GRB1	295	5681	4.20/3.02
GRB2	55	1079	>1/>1
GRB3	218	2844	3.10/1.51
GRC1	161	2383	2.29/1.27
GRC2	70	1166	>1/>1
GRC3	2	23	>1/>1
GTA	3	45	>1/>1
MG1	4	90	>1/>1
MG2	6	125	>1/>1
NG1	44	270	>1/>1
NV1	33	345	>1/>1
NV2	5	20	>1/>1
0AA1	150	1560	2.13/>1
0AA2	71	1104	1.01/>1
0AA3	20	351	>1/>1
0AB1	74	1242	1.05/>1
0AB2	57	921	>1/>1
0AB3	59	895	>1/>1
0BA1	43	599	>1/>1
0BA2	17	203	>1/>1
0BB1	110	2619	1.56/1.39
0BC1	61	791	>1/>1
0BC2	20	220	>1/>1
SMST	10	544	>1/>1
Totals	**7039**	**187828**	

THE FINDS

ROMAN COARSE POTTERY
by Lynne Bevan

Some 7,039 sherds of Romano-British pottery, weighing a total of 187,828 grams and representing the remains of at least 428 vessels, were recovered. Of these, 68% came from stratified Romano-British contexts. The pottery was catalogued by context, recording fabrics and forms present, and quantified by sherd count and vessel equivalent using rim percentage values respectively (Orton 1989, 94–6). Percentages by sherd count only are used in the text. The archive comprises a form type series with written descriptions and illustrations; pottery recording sheets which include factors such as burning, sooting, perforation, decoration, distortion and sherds with post-firing *graffiti*; and quantification of fabric and forms for all groups of contexts and phases, using sherd counts and rim percentage values/estimated vessel equivalents. The samian, mortaria and amphorae are reported on separately below.

Fabrics

Sherds were related to Ruth Leary's 1966 published Type Series from the New Cemetery site (reproduced as an appendix to this report) using a hand lens with x10 magnification. Indeterminate sherds were further examined under a x30 microscope. With the exception of an additional fabric (SMST) identified during the analysis of this assemblage, the fabric descriptions below are reproduced from Ruth Leary's original Rocester series from the New Cemetery site (Esmonde Cleary and Ferris 1996, 40–41). A selective approach was taken to illustration in view of the fact that the majority of identifiable rim forms could be related to material previously published by Leary (Esmonde Cleary and Ferris 1996).

Apart from some of the material from the ploughsoil, the general condition of the pottery was very good with little evidence for abrasion. The general sizes of sherds, with an average weight of 26.68 grams (15.77 excluding the amphorae), tended to be large, and there were several almost complete vessels in the assemblage, particularly from F609, a re-cut stretch of ditch defining the northern enclosure.

Catalogue of Illustrated Sherds

Unstratified

1. BB1 (variant) 'dog bowl' with segmented interior, irregular, diamond lattice decoration on the exterior and a crudely carved ?wheel motif and cross-hatching scratched on the underside of the base. The basic bowl form conforms to a type dated to *c.* AD 190–340 (Gillam 1970, 329), which was also present at Derby (Dool *et al.* 1985, fig.87: 383). See discussion (p.24) for possible parallels and alternative interpretation. Context 6000. Fig.12:1.

2. FLB1 ring-necked flagon, of Antonine type (Gillam 1970, No. 5 dated AD 110–50; Dool *et al.* 1985, fig.39:16, Table 8, early–mid-Antonine; Leary 1996,21:45,46). This example is a waster with a distorted rim. Context 6500. Fig.12:2.

3. FLB1 flagon base. Context 6500. Fig.12:3.

4. OAB2 dish, similar to an example from a well deposit in the Roman industrial settlement at Derby, of a Hadrianic to Antonine date (Dool *et al.* 1985, fig.81:182). Context 6500. Fig.12:4.

5. OBB1 flat lid. Possibly a Dressel 20 amphora stopper. Context 6500. Fig.12: 5.

Northern Enclosure (Enclosure 1) Ditch: F702

6. OAA2 Curved fragment from the base of a triple vase, showing the hollow base of one vase. Context 1025. Fig.12:6.

7. GRA1 everted-rim jar with a cordon at the shoulder and a distorted, ovoid rim. This type of jar was 'the most common jar form of the Flavian–Trajanic period', a form which became more globular in the later period, and has been found in quantity at Wall, where it is difficult to distinguish between earlier and later examples (Leary 1998, fig.13: 17,18). Context 6505. Fig.12:7.

8. GRB3 narrow-necked jar with out-curving rim and grooves at base of neck and upper body, 'a long-lived type' with many examples from Wall (Leary 1998, fig.13: 34, 30 and 32), and among a Hadrianic to Antonine assemblage from a well (F24C) at Derby (Dool *et al.* 1985, fig.79:117). Context 6525. Fig.12:8.

Northern Enclosure (Enclosure 1) Ditch: F715

9. FLA2 ring-necked flagon, of Antonine type (Gillam 1970, No. 5 dated AD 110–50, Dool *et al.* 1985, Fig.36:16, Table 8, early–mid-Antonine; Leary 1996, 21:45,46). Context 6564. Fig.12:9.

10. FLB2 flanged bowl with trailed, orange-brown slip decoration, a form with numerous parallels at Derby, particularly in Kiln Group 5, which was abandoned during the mid-second century (Brassington 1980, fig.15), and also in the industrial settlement where the closest parallel (in terms of fabric and decoration) has been assigned a Hadrianic to Antonine date range (Dool *et al.* 1985, fig.40: 36). Context 6565. Fig.12:10.

11. CC1 flanged bowl with omphalos base and striped white slip decoration on the flange (for similar forms see Brassington 1980). Context 6554. Figure 12:11.

12. OAA1 plain-rimmed dish. Context 7000. Fig.12:12.

Northern Enclosure (Enclosure 1) Ditch: F608

13. GRA1 rusticated jar with lid, apparently a pair since they are well-matched in size and fabric. Flavian–Trajanic. Context 6077. Fig.13:13.

14. GRA1 reeded-rim bowl. Flavian–Trajanic. Similar forms have been recovered from Derby (Kiln Group 5), with an abandonment date in the mid-second century (Brassington 1980, fig.14: 393, 394). Context 6077. Fig.13:14.

Northern Enclosure (Enclosure 1): F612

15. GRA1 lid, similar lids, many in grey fabrics, were recorded from Derby, especially from the well (F24B) dated to the Hadrianic/Antonine periods, terminating during the latter (Dool *et al.* 1985, fig.81:193–198). Context 6088. Fig.13:15.

16. GRC1 reeded-rim carinated bowl. Flavian–Trajanic. Context 6093. Fig.13:16.

17. GRA1 small jar with a continuous wave design at shoulder. Context 6093. Fig.13:17.

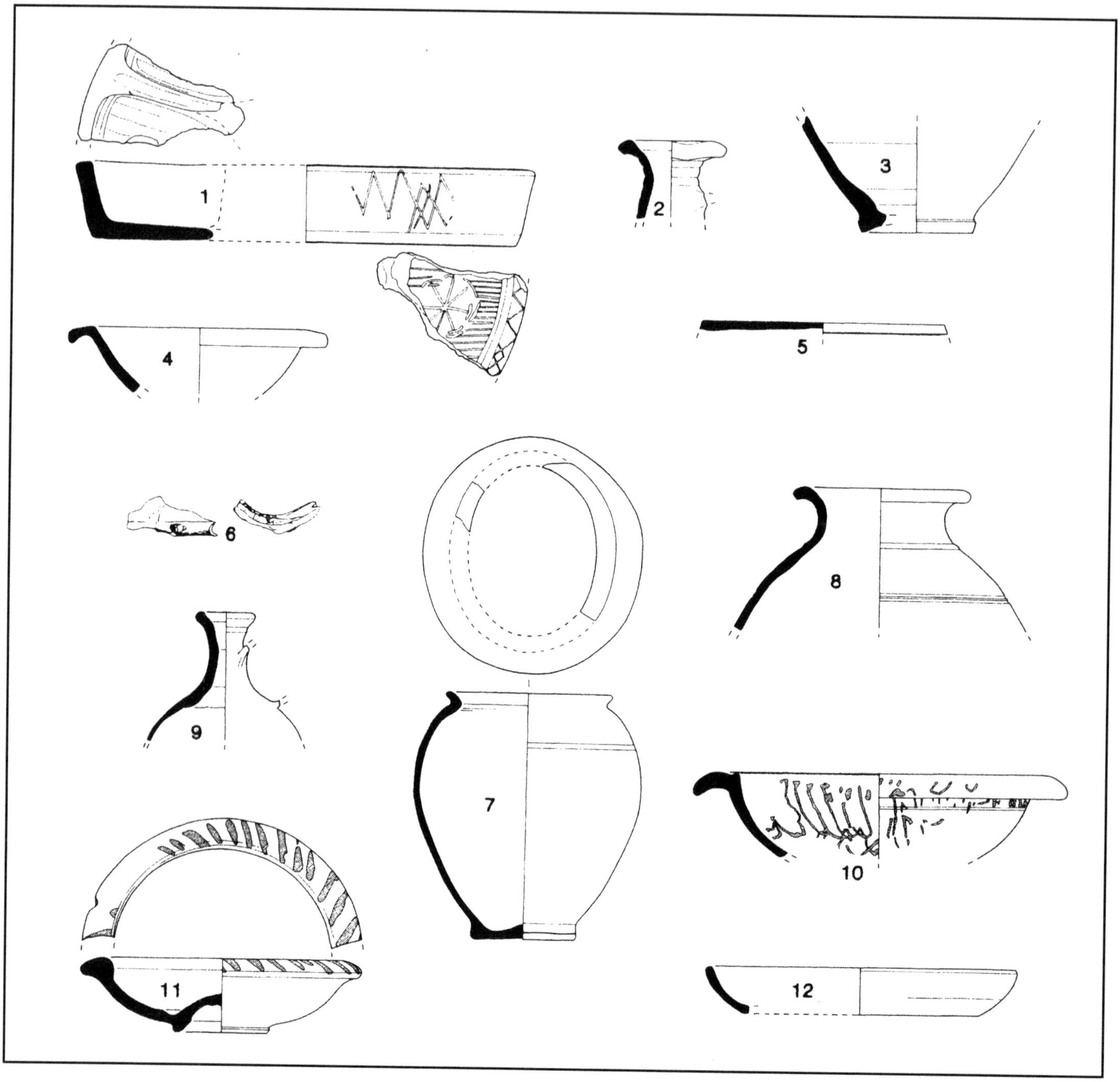

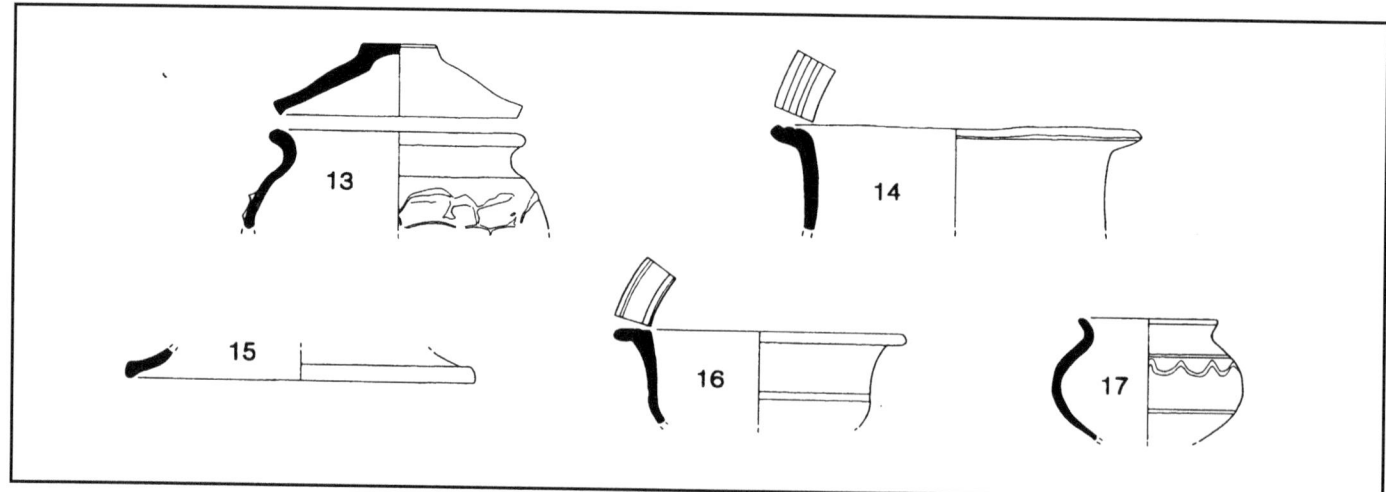

Fig. 12 Roman coarse pottery : vessels 1–12 (Scale 1:4)

Fig. 13 Roman coarse pottery : vessels 13–17 (Scale 1:4)

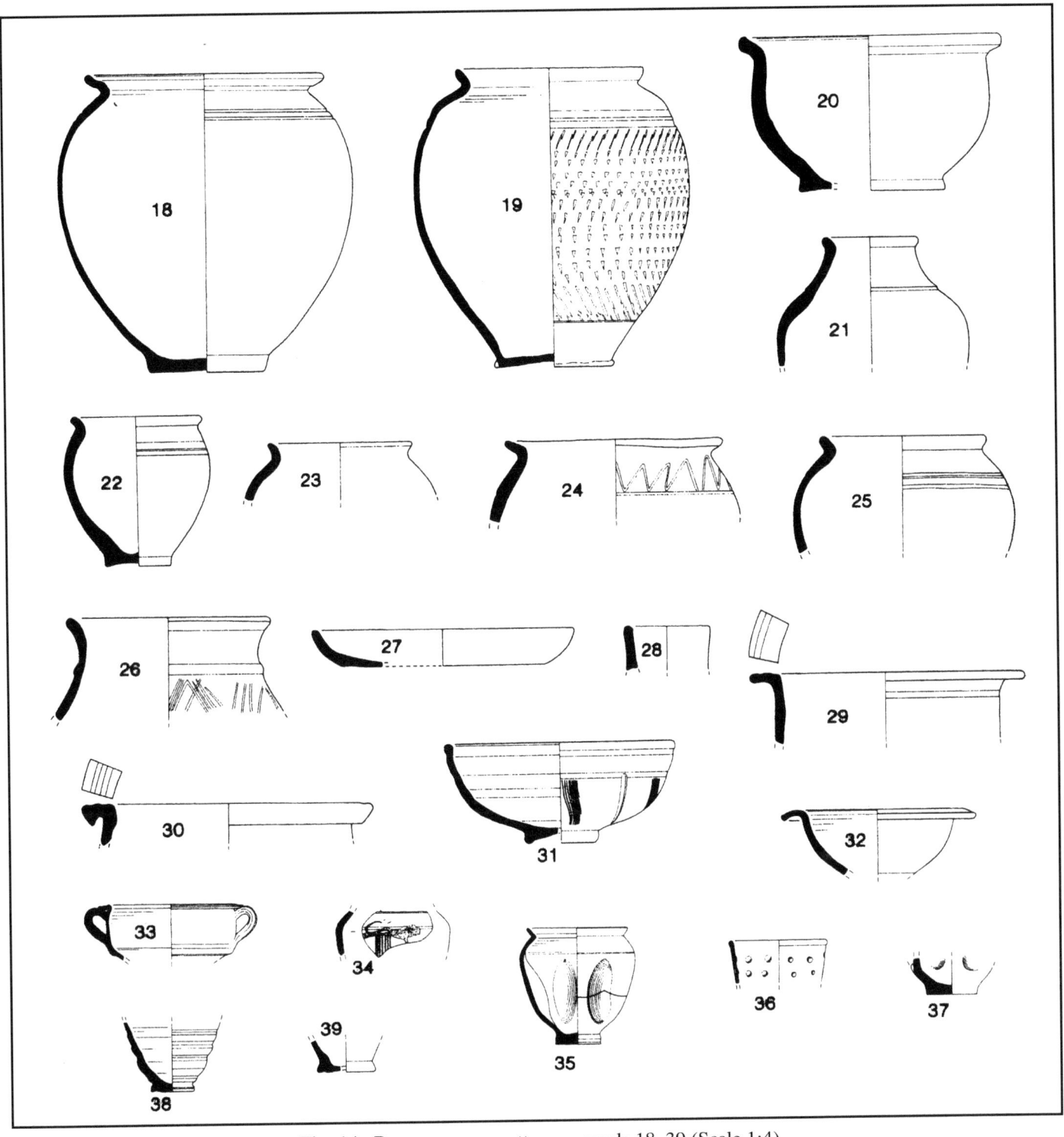

Fig. 14   Roman coarse pottery : vessels 18–39 (Scale 1:4)

Northern Enclosure (Enclosure 1) Re-cut Ditch: F609

18. GRA1 lid-seated jar. Context 6099. Fig.14:18.

19. OBB1 high-shouldered beaker with rouletted decoration, similar to an example from Chesterfield dated to the early second century (Anderson 1989, 23:61). Context 6078. Fig.14:19.

20. GRA1 everted-rim bowl, like form CF1 which was produced during the mid-second century AD at Derby (Dool *et al.* 1985, fig.44:142). Context 6085. Fig.14:20.

21. GRA1 narrow-mouthed jar. Context 6099. Fig.14:21.

22. OAB3 everted-rim jar. Context 6099. Fig.14:22.

23. GRA2 everted-rim jar. Context 6098. Fig.14:23.

24. GRA1 everted-rim bowl. Context 6078. Fig.14:24.

25. GRA1 everted-rim jar with a distorted rim and wavy, irregular, burnished decoration at shoulder. Context 6078. Fig.14:25.

26. GRA1 beaker with irregular, burnished decoration. Context 6078. Fig.14:26.

27. OBB1 dish, similar to an example from well deposits in the Roman industrial settlement at Derby, assigned a Hadrianic to Antonine date (Dool *et al.* 1985, fig.81:182). Context 6070. Fig.14:27.

28. GRB1 small cup. Context 6098. Fig.14:28.

29. GRA1 reeded-rim bowl. Similar forms have been recovered from Derby (Kiln Group 5), with an abandonment date in the mid-second century (Brassington 1980, fig.14: 393, 394). Context 6098. Fig.14:29.

30. GRC2 reeded-rim, possibly carinated, bowl, similar to an example from Derby with an early second-century date (Brassington 1980, Fig.12: 366, 24–25). This form has also been found during previous excavations at Rocester (Leary 1996, fig.25: 102). Context 6098. Fig.14:30.

31. GLZ1 bead-rim bowl with vertically applied ribs interspersed with combed decoration. Context 6078. Fig.14:31.

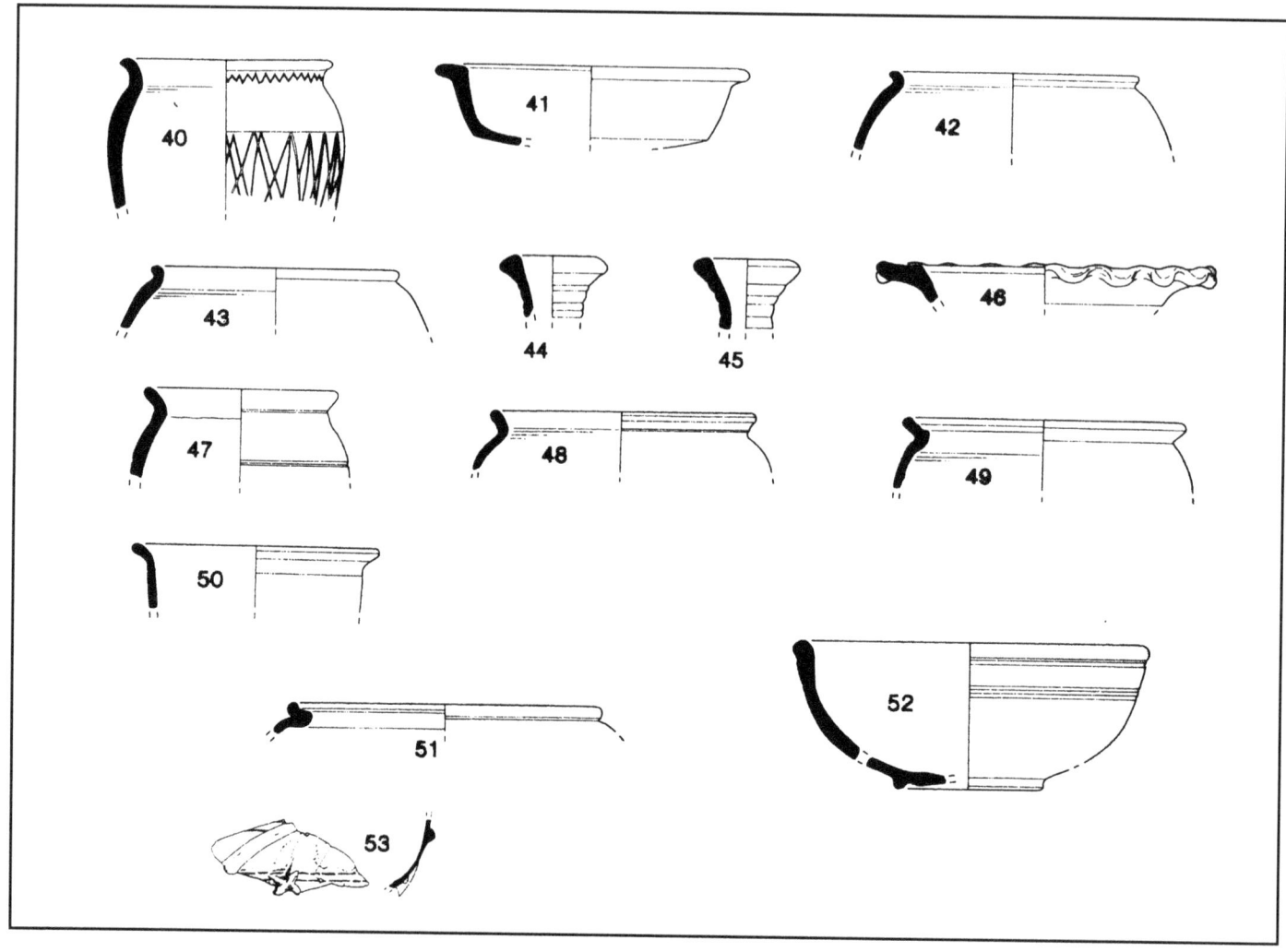

Fig. 15   Roman coarse pottery : vessels 40–53 (Scale 1:4)

32. GLZ1 flange-rimmed bowl. Context 6078. Fig.14:32.

33. GLZ3 handled cup. Context 6078. Fig.14:33.

34. GLZ1 beaker with linear decoration at shoulder and irregularly applied glaze. This style of linear decoration was applied to lead-glazed vessels from a first-century context at Margidunum (Brassington 1971, fig.11:277, 281). Context 6078. Fig.14:34.

35. GLZ1 indented beaker. Context 6078. Fig.14:35.

36. GLZ1 cup with decoration in the form of small impressed circles. Context 6079. Fig.14:36.

37. GLZ1 cup or beaker with decoration in the form of large impressed circles. Context 6078. Fig.14:37.

38. GLZ1 cordoned beaker. Context 6078. Fig.14:38.

39. GLZ1 cup or beaker. Context 6078. Fig.14:39.

Northern Enclosure (Enclosure 1) Pits (F726/F727)

F726

40. BB1 jar, similar in form and design repertoire to a Type 2 BB1 jar from Period 6 at Greyhound Yard, Dorchester, dated to AD 100–200, (Seager Smith and Davies 1993, fig.140:117, 265). Other contexts in the north probably place this form as Hadrianic or later (Jeremy Evans pers. comm.). Several similar vessels were recovered from a quarry ditch (F60) in the Roman industrial settlement at Derby with a terminal date in the second half of the second century (Dool *et al.* 1985, fig.82: 224–229). Context 6613. Fig.15:40.

41. BB1 flat-rimmed bowl, undecorated, a similar form to an example of a Type 22 flat-rimmed bowl from Period 6 at Greyhound Yard, Dorchester, dated to AD 100–120.(Seager Smith and Davies 1993, fig.139: 100, 263). Other contexts in the north probably place this form as Hadrianic or later (Jeremy Evans pers. comm.). Context 6595. Fig.15:41.

42. BB1 developed or 'pulled' bead-rim jar, Type 8 at Greyhound Yard, Dorchester where it was mainly found in Period 6 deposits dating to AD 100–120 (Seager Smith and Davies 1993, fig.122, 230–231), but the general form has been dated to the first century, possibly continuing until the later third century (Gillam 1976, 67). Other contexts in the north probably place this form as Hadrianic or later (Jeremy Evans pers. comm.). Context 6613. Fig.15:42.

43. BB1 bead-rim jar, Type 7 at Greyhound Yard, Dorchester (Seager Smith and Davies 1993, fig.122, 230–231), a type which originated in the first century BC and 'ceased to appear in the north before the end of the second century' (Gillam 1976, 67). Context 6595. Fig.15:43.

44. FLA1 ring-necked flagon. Late first to early second century (Jeremy Evans pers. comm.) (For later similar examples see Dool *et al.* 1985, Figure: 16, table 8, early to mid-Antonine; Leary 1996,21:45,46). Context 6595. Fig.15:44.

45. FLA1 ring-necked flagon. Late first to early second century (Jeremy Evans pers. comm.) (For later similar examples see Dool *et al.* 1985, 93, Figure 16, table 8, early to mid-Antonine, Leary 1996,21:45,46). Context 6595. Fig.15:45.

46. FLA1 flanged bowl with frilled rim, with a close parallel among residual Phase 3 (mid-Antonine) pottery from the north-west sector excavations at Derby (Dool *et al.* 1985, fig.42:78, 98–99). Context 6613. Fig.15:46.

47. GRA3 everted-rim jar, similar to a greyware vessel from previous excavations at Rocester (Leary 1996, fig.25:111). Context 6613. Fig.15:47.

48. GRA1 everted-rim jar, similar to an example from Derby dated to the first quarter of the second century (Brassington 1980, fig.11:338). Context 6595. Fig.15:48.

49. GRA4 lid-seated jar, a common vessel type in the assemblage from the Little Chester kilns which were abandoned in AD 110–20 (Brassington 1971, fig.10:205). Context 6595. Fig.15:49.

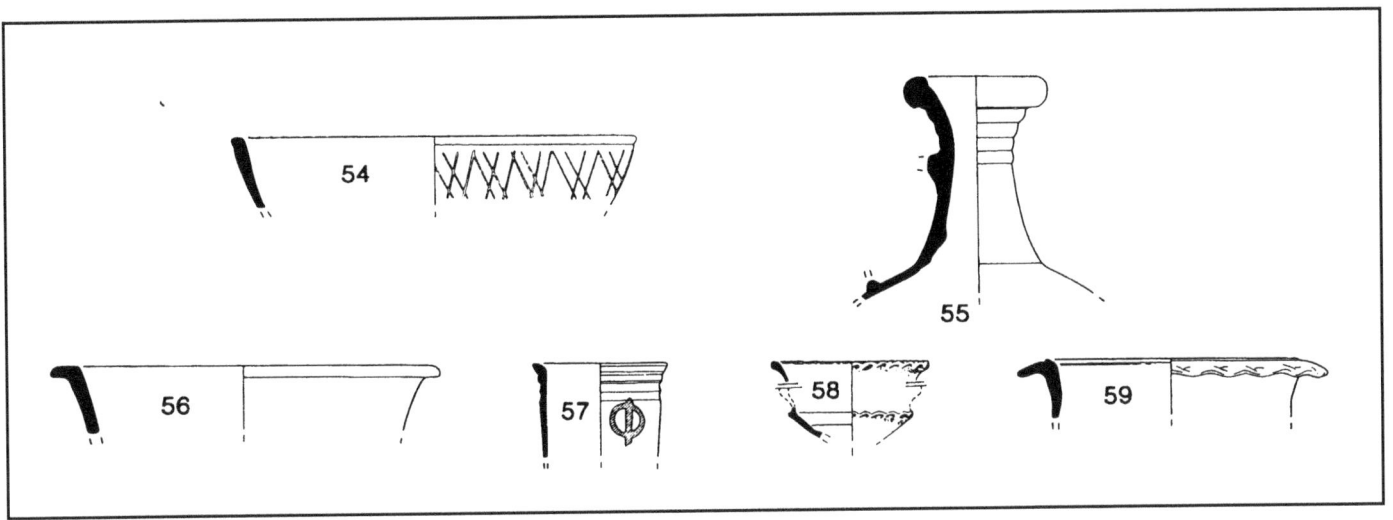

Fig. 16   Roman coarse pottery : vessels 54–59 (Scale 1:4)

50. GRB1 carinated bowl, dated Flavian to mid-second century at Derby (Dool *et al.* 1985 fig.88:60–62, Leary 1986, fig.23:75). Context 6613. Fig.15:50.

F727

51. GRA1 lid-seated jar, a common vessel form with parallels from the kilns at Derby (Kiln Group 5) with an abandonment date in the mid-second century (Brassington 1980, fig.17: 497), and at Little Chester, with a general abandonment date of AD 110–120 (Brassington 1971, fig.11: 238). Context 6596. Fig.15:51.

52. OAA1 bead-rim bowl. Possibly a Dr.37 copy. A similar vessel was identified from Derby (Kiln Group 5), with an abandonment date in the mid-second century (Brassington 1980, fig.18:520). Context 6596 Fig.15:52.

Southern Enclosure (Enclosure 2) Ditch: F704

53. OAB2 face pot, with minimal traces of barbotine decoration in the form of the corner of an eye beneath a prominent, high-arched brow or hairline. An abraded area is shaped like a missing 'ear', the placing of which, below the level of the eye, is not unusual in face pots. Despite the small size of the fragment and the lack of identifiable features, the face is likely to be female, especially if the prominent ridge is considered as part of a rolled hairstyle or headdress, such as the example worn by the female carved head from Birrens (Allason-Jones 1989, fig.40, 114–115). Although this fragment is too small to relate successfully to published material (Braithwaite 1984) the appliqué technique used for the eye is similar to that employed on a greyware face pot from Derby (Brassington 1980, fig.13: 370). Context 1005. Fig.15:53.

Southern Enclosure (Enclosure 2) Ditch: F705

54. BB1 bead-rim dish with open diamond lattice, similar in form to a previous example from Rocester dated to the third century (Leary 1996, fig.24:89; Gillam 1976, No.74), though this example is probably Hadrianic–mid-Antonine (Jeremy Evans pers. comm.). Context 6530. Fig.16:54.

55. FLA1 ring-necked flagon, of Antonine type (Gillam 1970, No. 5 dated AD 110–50, Dool *et al.* 1985, fig.39:16, Table 8, early–mid-Antonine; Leary 1996,21:45,46). Context 6530. Fig.16:55.

Southern Enclosure (Enclosure 2) Ditch: F706

56. BB1 flat-rimmed bowl, an undecorated version of a previous Rocester find which was dated to the mid- to late second century (Leary 1996, fig.21:50). Context 6563. Fig.16:56.

57. FLA1 beaker with circular motif executed in brown slip. Context 6531. Fig.16:57.

58. GRA1 tazza, a form of vessel with 'a wide date range' (Leary 1996, fig.22:60, 47), an example of which was recovered from Kiln 5 at Derby, which had a general abandonment date in the mid-second century (Brassington 1980, fig.17:459). Context 1006. Figure 16:58.

59. GRB3 tazza, a form of vessel with 'a wide date range' (Leary 1996, fig.22:60, 47), an example of which was recovered from Kiln 5 at Derby,

which had a general abandonment date in the mid-second century (Brassington 1980, fig.16:459). Context 6563. Fig.16:59.

Southern Enclosure (Enclosure 2) Pit: F700.

60. GRA1 wide-mouthed jar, possibly Hadrianic–Antonine (Dool *et al.* 1985, fig.79:100). A BBI copy. Context 6511. Fig.17:60.

61. GRA1 wide-mouthed jar, possibly Hadrianic–Antonine (Dool *et al.* 1985, fig.79:113). A BBI copy. Context 6511. Fig.17:61.

62. GRA1 wide-mouthed jar, possibly Hadrianic (Dool *et al.* 1985, fig.79:101). Context 6511. Fig.17:62.

63. GRB1 wide-mouthed jar, possibly Hadrianic (Dool *et al.* 1985, fig.79:109). Context 6511. Fig.17:63.

64. GRA2 narrow-necked jar with grooves at neck and shoulder. Context 6516. Fig.17:64.

65. GRA2 narrow-necked jar with grooves at neck and shoulder. Context 6511. Fig.17:65.

66. GRB3 lid. Similar lids, many in grey fabrics, were recorded at Derby, especially from the well (F24B) dated to the Hadrianic/Antonine periods, terminating during the latter (Dool *et al.* 1985, fig.81:193–198). Context 6511. Fig.17:66.

67. GRB3 lid. Similar lids, many in grey fabrics, were recorded at Derby, especially from the well (F24B) dated to the Hadrianic/Antonine periods, terminating during the latter (Dool *et al.* 1985, fig.81:193–198). Context 3007. Fig.17:67.

68. BB1 lid with decoration in the form of continuous single-line arches (Seager Smith and Davies 1993, fig.132: D19, 245–246). This might be a waster as the profile is irregular and appears sunken. Lids had 'a long lifespan with few morphological changes', but were present in large quantities at Greyhound Yard, Dorchester only up to AD 300 (Seager Smith and Davies 1993, fig.125:26 (lower example, 234–235). This example is Hadrianic or later. Context 3007. Fig.17:68.

69. FLA2 flanged bowl with frilled rim, similar to an example among residual Phase 3 (mid-Antonine) pottery from the north-west sector excavations, Derby (Dool *et al.* 1985, fig.42:78, 98–99), but with an additional, lower, register of frilled decoration. Context 6510. Fig.17:69.

70. GRA3 flanged bowl with frilled rim, with a close parallel among residual Phase 3 (mid-Antonine) pottery from the north-west sector excavations, Derby (Dool *et al.* 1985, fig.42:78, 98–99).Context 6511. Fig.17:70.

71. GRB1 reeded-rim bowl with a grooved exterior. Similar forms have been recovered from Derby (Kiln Group 5), with an abandonment date in the mid-second century (Brassington 1980, fig.14: 393, 394). Context 3007. Fig.17:71.

72. GRA1 reeded-rim bowl. Similar forms have been recovered from Derby (Kiln Group 5), with an abandonment date in the mid-second century (Brassington 1980, fig.14: 393, 394). Context 6511. Fig.17:72.

73. GRB3 reeded-rim jar. Context 3007. Fig.17:73.

74. GRA1 reeded-rim bowl. Similar forms have been recovered from Derby (Kiln Group 5), with an abandonment date in the mid-second century

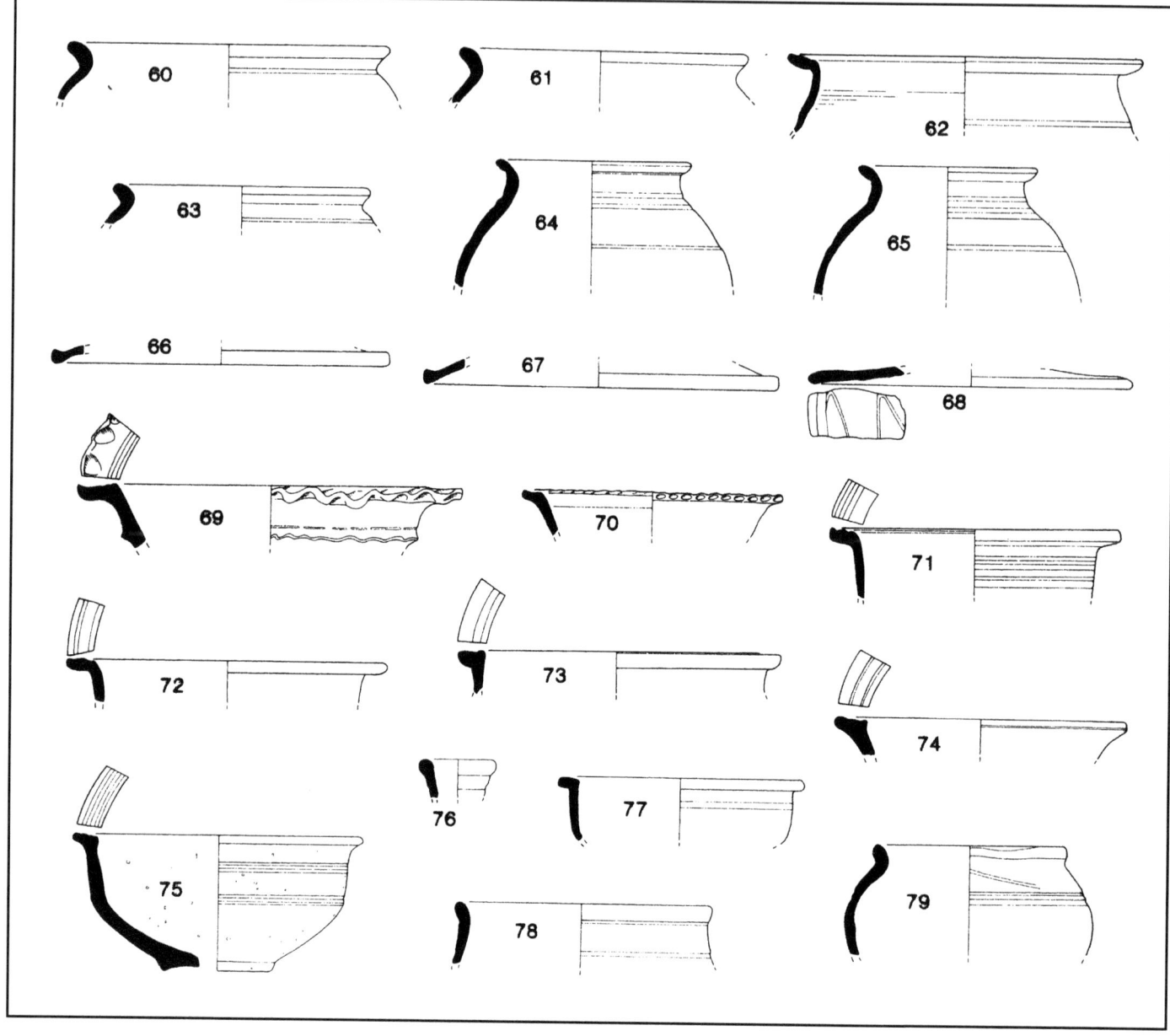

Fig. 17   Roman coarse pottery : vessels 60–79 (Scale 1:4)

(Brassington 1980, fig.14: 393, 394). Context 3007. Fig.17:74.

75. OAA2 reeded-rim, carinated bowl with two registers of grooves on the body of the vessel. Context 3007. Fig.17:75.

76. FLB1 ring-necked flagon, of Antonine type (Gillam 1970, No. 5 dated AD 110–50, Dool *et al.* 1985, fig.39:16, Table 8, early–mid-Antonine; (Leary 1996,21:45,46). Context 6516. Fig.17:76.

77. GRA2 flat-rim dish. Context 3007. Fig.17:77.

78. FLA2 beaker. Context 6516. Fig.17:78.

79. GRB1 rouletted jar with a distorted rim, similar to an example of Hadrianic–Antonine date from Derby (Dool *et al.* 1985, fig.83: 238). Context 3007. Fig.17:79.

Southern Enclosure (Enclosure 2) Pit: F701

80. BB1 flat-rimmed bowl with open diamond lattice (Seager Smith and Davies 1993, fig.132:D6, 245–246), similar to a previous Rocester find which was dated to the mid-to late second century (Leary 1996, fig.21:51). Context 6504. Fig.18:80.

81. BB1 bead-rimmed, wide-mouthed jar or dish, date range uncertain but probably second century. Context 3006. Fig.18:81.

82. GRB2 narrow-necked ovoid jar, similar to an example from Derby which has been assigned a late second- to early third-century date (Dool *et al.* 1985, fig. 43:115, 100–101). Context 6504. Fig.18:82.

83. GRB2 bead rim bowl, probably carinated or hemispherical, based upon previous examples from Derby which have been dated to the early to mid-second century (Dool *et al.* 1985, fig.40:48, 94–95). A previous example from Rocester in a similar fabric has been given a possible Flavian–Trajanic date (Leary 1985, fig.21: 44). Context 3006. Fig.18:83.

84. GRA2 cordoned bowl with out-curving rim, a Flavian–Trajanic form, similar to an example from Wall (Leary 1998, fig.13:45). Context 6506. Fig.18:84.

85. GRA1 reeded-rim bowl. Similar forms have been recovered from Derby (Kiln Group 5), with an abandonment date in the mid-second century (Brassington 1980, fig.14: 393, 394). Context 6504. Fig.18:85.

86. GRB2 reeded-rim bowl with a slightly inverted rim. Similar forms have been recovered from Derby (Kiln Group 5), with an abandonment date in the mid-second century (Brassington 1980, fig.14: 393, 394). Context 6518. Fig.18:86.

87. GRA3 reeded-rim, probably carinated, bowl, similar to an example from Derby with an early second-century date (Brassington 1980, fig.12: 366, 24–25). This form has also been found during previous excavations at Rocester (Leary 1996, fig.25: 102). Context 6504. Fig.18:87.

88. OAA2 lid-seated jar, a common vessel form with parallels from the kilns at Derby (Kiln Group 5), with an abandonment date in the mid-second century (Brassington 1980, fig.17: 497), and at Little Chester, with a general abandonment date of AD 110–120 (Brassington 1971, fig.11: 238). Context 6506. Fig.18:88.

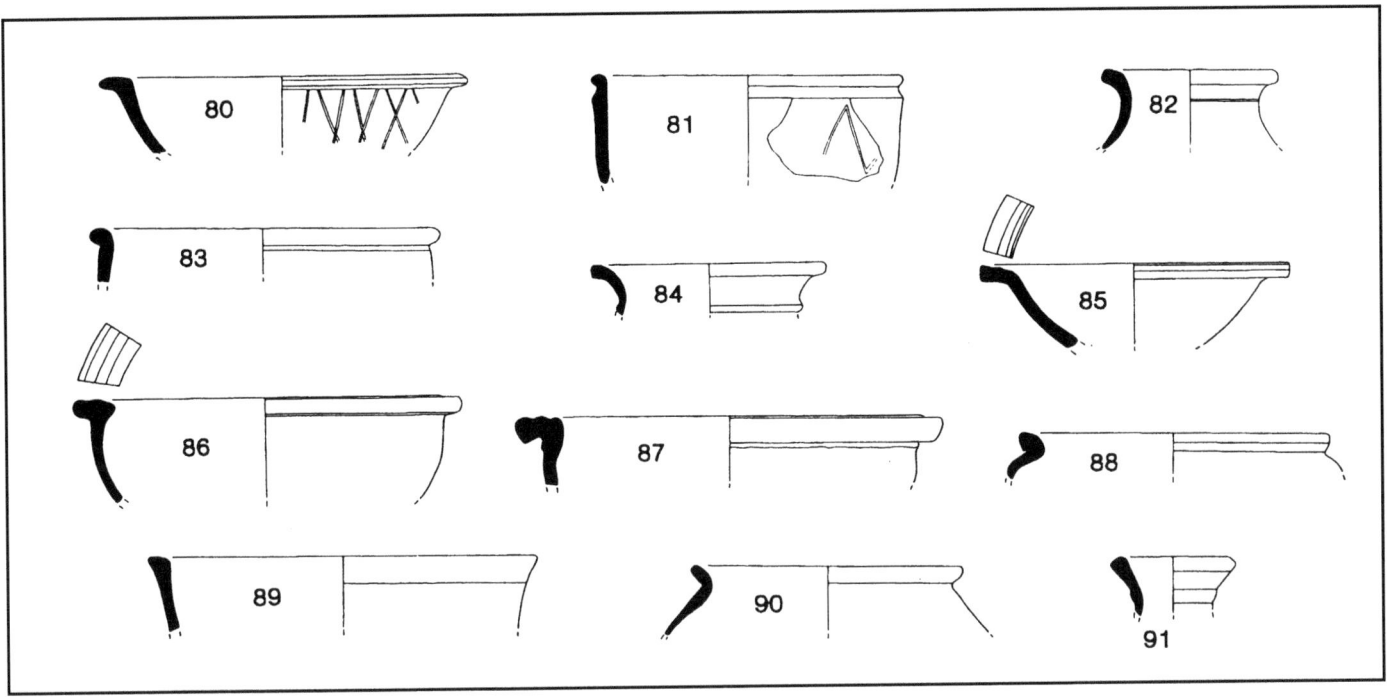

Fig. 18   Roman coarse pottery : vessels 80–91 (Scale 1:4)

89. GRB2 vase-shaped vessel with flaring rim. Context 6506. Fig.18:89.

90. GRB2 everted-rim jar. Context 6506. Fig.18:90.

91. FLA1 ring-necked flagon, of Antonine type (Gillam 1970, No. 5 dated AD 110–50; Dool *et al*. 1985, 93, no. 16, table 8, early–mid-Antonine; Leary 1996, 21:45,46). Context 6507. Fig.18:91.

Discussion

Chronology

The study of the occurrence of pottery fabrics and forms on the site revealed that, though some of the material was in the general Hadrianic to Antonine date range, as with previous work in the area the Orton's Pasture assemblage suggested a slightly earlier floruit of activity here during the Flavian–Trajanic periods. There was some evidence for activity during the Antonine period and later (Leary 1996, 43). This general pattern is supported by the samian evidence (Willis, this volume), there being little Antonine samian present on the site.

Reeded-rim bowls were common in the assemblage (e.g. Nos. 14, 16, 71–75, 85–87). This type of vessel, as noted by Leary (1996, 45), was predominantly Flavian–Trajanic in date, going out of use during the Hadrianic period in the North (Gillam 1970, nos. 214–7), an end-date which accords typologically with the examples previously recorded at Rocester (Leary 1996, nos. 26–27, 14–15, 35, 102). Beaded, flanged and everted rims were also common among the coarsewares, particularly the predominant greywares, especially the latter which suggests on-site manufacture, as observed previously at Rocester at the New Cemetery site (Leary 1996).

Given the presence of good late Flavian–Trajanic groups in feature fills, groups which are unlikely to be residual as they include many near-complete vessels, then Phase 1 would seem to start *c.* AD 95 and continue to *c.* AD 130–150.

Fabric Composition of the Assemblage

The relative percentages by sherd count of the total assemblage are broadly similar to those recorded previously by Leary for the New Cemetery site, Rocester (1996, fig.27, 58), especially with regard to samian, mortaria and BB1, with some changes, notably a significant increase in amphorae from 4.3% to 11.78% and a decrease in Derbyshire ware (DBY) from 8.8% to 4.40%. One of the previously most common fabrics, GRA1, was only slightly reduced in number, at 13.82% of the total assemblage, whereas the fabric GRB1, previously the most common at the New Cemetery, had declined to 4.20% and GRA2, represented only by a small number of sherds, had increased to 9.45%. Collectively, the flagon wares were approximately the same percentage as previously, with slight differences in those fabrics best represented, such as the increase in FLA1 balanced by a decline in FLA2. Similar proportions of oxidised and buff wares were also recorded, with, again, slight differences in the most popular fabrics.

Sources of Pottery

The prevalence of greywares on the site, which constitute over 30% of the overall assemblage, among which are several obvious wasters (e.g. No. 79), together with a high incidence of reeded-rim bowls which Leary noted were much rarer at Derby and Mancetter-Hartshill, suggests local pottery manufacture, reinforcing the view that 'Rocester had its own potters in residence' (Leary 1996, 49). The most common greyware forms produced were everted-rim jars, often with lattice-style decoration imitating BB1 forms, a style of pot that was rare on sites where BB1 predominated, supporting Leary's assertion that local coarsewares dominated the market as much as BB1 ever did (Leary 1996, 50). There is some slight evidence for the production of a local BB1 variant, made from a much coarser-tempered fabric, in the form of a fragment from a segmented bowl or part of a clay stand (No. 1, unstratified), together with some other unstratified fragments from jars (Joyce, this volume). On-site manufacture of mortaria at Rocester has also been noted (Ferguson 1996; Hartley 1996; Bevan and Hartley, this volume).

Oxidised wares were also produced locally, usually in bowl or beaker forms for fabrics OAA1, with flanged and everted rims also occurring in fabrics OAA2 and OAA3 respectively. The bowl forms included imitation samian forms and one unstratified fragment had lattice decoration perhaps in imitation of a BB1 form. As previously noted, other coarseware fabrics found at Rocester included small quantities of various colour-coated and buff wares.

The distinctive Derbyshire ware which is believed to have originated from kilns at Holbrook and Hazlewood in Derbyshire supplied a wide market, expanding into the Midlands and Yorkshire from the Antonine period onwards (Kay 1962). Although the percentage of this fabric in the total assemblage had almost halved, compared with the assemblage from the New Cemetery, again, as previously, both of the main jar forms (Types A and B), distinguished by rim, were present (Leary 1996, 50), although none has been illustrated here.

The green lead-glazed wares discussed below, which were almost exclusively restricted to the re-cut stretch of ditch F609, probably came from kilns in Derby (Leary 1996, 44).

Pottery Groups
Unstratified
The unstratified material, 2224 sherds weighing 70,067 grams, amounted to just under one third (*c.* 32%) of the total assemblage by sherd count. Generally, the composition of the unstratified material reflected that from stratified contexts, with a predominance of coarsewares, especially greywares such as GRA1 and GRA2 which were used for the production of the most popular everted-rim jar forms.

However, some vessels were worthy of publication. Of most interest in the collection is a vessel in a BB1 type fabric, but coarser and probably of local manufacture, nearest in form to a BB1 'dog bowl', but with a segmented interior, irregular, diamond lattice decoration on the exterior, cross-hatching and a crudely formed wheel motif scratched on the underside of the base (Fig.12:1). The basic bowl form conforms to a type dated to *c.* AD 190–340 (Gillam 1970, 329), which was also present at Derby (Dool *et al.* 1985, fig.87:383). The only other examples of segmented vessels, also called 'hors-d'œuvre' bowls (in view of their compartmentalised interiors which suggest that they might have been used for sauces or other accompaniments for foods) are known from the Roman villa at Gadebridge Park, Hemel Hempstead (Neal 1974, fig. 104:241) and the Colchester kilns (Hull 1963, fig. 74:3, 3A). However, neither example is a close parallel in size, form or fabric to the Orton's Pasture bowl since both vessels are approximately twice as large and are in red, rather than in grey, fabrics. The Gadebridge Park vessel has four compartments (Neal 1974, fig. 104:241, 233), as does the Colchester vessel, though the latter has an additional circular compartment in the centre (Hull 1963, Fig74:3, 3A, 134). More recently, a mica-dusted platter with an inner circular compartment was found inverted over a cremation at The Parks, Godmanchester, Cambridge, where it might have originally contained a food offering since eel bones were found mixed with the cremation (Evans, forthcoming). Whether used for ritual purposes or, more mundanely, as tableware to contain condiments or olives, segmented vessels are a rare class of Roman pottery in Britain, and while the purpose of the Orton's Pasture bowl, with its wheel motif, remains unclear, it constitutes a new example of a limited and enigmatic class of vessel.

An alternative interpretation for this unusual object is that it was part of a stand, similar to the Crookham stand. This was made of terracotta, but its form was reminiscent of enamelled bronze stools or stands used for ritual offerings, which were often equipped with a central hole for a candle (see discussion by Martin Henig 1989, 83–85). Although the example from Rocester would have been circular rather than square, and there are no visible depressions on the flat surface, a central hole cannot be ruled out from this small segment. Viewed from above, the cross-hatching and possible wheel motif would have been visible. The wheel motif was a popular symbol during the Roman period, with native antecedents in both the Romano-Celtic wheel god, as well as the classical image of Jupiter (Green 1976, 10). There are examples of pots with wheel motifs from Roman Britain, now in Reading and Norwich museums and from Littlehampton, where a small pot made from smooth, black clay was decorated with wheels imprinted in enamel or glaze (*ibid.* 196, 205 and 219 respectively). Interestingly, the central symbol on the Crookham stand is similarly wheel-shaped (Henig 1989, fig.35:B, 84).

Also present was a ring-necked flagon (Fig.12:2), an obvious waster with a distorted rim, the general form of which is of Antonine date (Gillam 1970, No. 5 dated AD 110–50; Dool *et al.* 1985, fig.39:16, Table 8, early to mid-Antonine; Leary 1996, 21:45,46). Other illustrated sherds comprised a dish (Fig.12:3), similar to a Hadrianic to Antonine example from well deposits in the Roman industrial settlement at Derby (Dool *et al.* 1985, fig.81:182), a flagon base (Fig.12:4) and a flat lid (Fig.12:5).

The Northern Enclosure (Enclosure 1)
Ditches F702 and F715
There were 35 fabrics represented in the overall assemblage from F702, consisting of 908 sherds weighing a total of 31,101 grams, which is dominated by greywares (29%) and BB1 (20%), followed by smaller quantities of amphorae (18%), flagon wares (10%), samian (7%), mortaria (6%) and Derbyshire ware (6%). The remainder of the coarsewares were composed of various oxidised and buff wares. Of most interest in the collection was a fragment from the base of a triple vase (Fig.12:6). A small fragment from another triple vase in a similar sandy fabric was recovered from F704 (6529, not illustrated). Datable material included an everted-rim greyware jar (Fig.12:7), 'the most common jar form of the Flavian–Trajanic period', a form which became more globular in the later period, and which has been found in quantity at Wall where it was difficult to distinguish between earlier and later examples (see Leary 1998, fig.13: 17,18). This particular example is an obvious waster suggestive of on-site manufacture. The assemblage also included a narrow-necked greyware jar with an out-curving rim and grooves at the base of the neck and upper body (Fig.12:8), 'a long-lived type' with many examples from Wall (Leary 1998, fig.13: 34, 30 and 32), and among a Hadrianic to Antonine assemblage from a well (F24C) at Derby (Dool *et al.* 1985, fig.79:117). Amphorae fragments included five rims, one of which was a Gauloise 4 form (Fig.21:3), two of which have been dated to the late first to early second century AD and the remaining two to the late first century, to *c.* AD 175 (Williams, this volume, Context 6539, not illustrated). A large amphora bodysherd with a *graffito* (see Tomlin this volume) was also recovered (Fig.21:5) and two stamped handles (Contexts 6024, 6555, not illustrated, see Williams this volume).

The assemblage from F715, which consisted of 358 sherds weighing a total of 6,266 grams, comprising 28 fabrics, was again dominated by greywares (45%), although the amounts of BB1 (11%) and amphorae (4%) were significantly less than in F702. The proportion of flagon wares was slightly higher (14%), but the other fabrics were proportionally similar. Whereas greywares and Derbyshire wares remained constant through time, the proportions of BB1 declines in the later contexts, whereas flagon wares increase with time. An example of a ring-necked flagon of Antonine type (Gillam 1970, No. 5 dated AD 110–50; Dool *et al.* 1985, fig.36:16, Table 8, early–mid-Antonine; Leary 1996, 21:45,46) has been illustrated (Fig.12:9). Painted, flanged bowls were also recovered, including a flanged bowl with trailed, orange-brown slip decoration (Fig.12:10), a form with numerous parallels at Derby, particularly in Kiln Group 5, which was abandoned during the mid-second century (Brassington 1980, fig.15), and also in the industrial settlement where the closest parallel (in terms of fabric and decoration) was assigned a Hadrianic to Antonine date range (Dool *et al.* 1985, fig.40: 36). Another, similar, vessel (Fig.12:11), a flanged bowl with omphalos base and striped white slip decoration on the flange is broadly contemporary (for similar forms see Brassington 1980). A plain-rimmed dish (Fig.12:12) and an amphora rim (Fig.21:1) were also recovered, the latter dated to the late first century, to *c.* AD 75 (Williams, this volume).

Northern Enclosure (Enclosure 1) F608
The pottery assemblage consisted of 60 sherds, weighing a total of 1,135 grams, the majority of which were from grey and oxidised wares, including a rusticated jar with a lid, apparently a pair, since they are well-matched in size and fabric (Fig.13:13) and a reeded-rim bowl (Fig.13:14). Both rusticated wares and reeded-rim vessels have been recovered from Derby, especially from Kiln Group 5 which was abandoned in the mid-second century (Brassington 1980, fig.18:513–516, fig.14: 393, 394). The illustrated forms are typical of the rest of the assemblage which consisted mainly of jars, some with rusticated and rouletted decoration, and flat-rimmed bowls. A distorted lid was also present (not illustrated), suggestive of local, or on-site, manufacture. A single, abraded, green lead-glazed body sherd was recovered (context 6077, not illustrated). The ten samian sherds are all within the date range of AD 70–100 (see Willis, this volume). This would appear to be a Flavian–Trajanic group.

Northern Enclosure (Enclosure 1) F612
The majority of the 105 sherds from F612, weighing a total of 1,824 grams, consisted of various greywares and some samian, with a few Black Burnished and oxidised wares. Datable material included a greyware lid (Fig.13:15), which was similar to lids recorded at Derby, especially those from a well (F24B) dated to the Hadrianic/Antonine periods, terminating during the latter (Dool *et al.* 1985, fig.81:193–198). Other material included a reeded-rim carinated bowl (Fig.13:16) and a small jar with a continuous wave design at the shoulder (Fig.13:17). Perhaps this is a late Flavian–Trajanic group.

Northern Enclosure (Enclosure 1), Re-cut Ditch F609
The range of fabrics represented in this large assemblage of 814 fragments, weighing a total of 34,660 grams, was fairly restricted in its composition, consisting mainly of greywares (65%) and oxidised wares (14%), followed by samian (8%),

amphorae (5%), flagon wares (4%) and green lead-glazed wares (3%), with BB1 sherds and Derbyshire ware accounting for under 1% each of the assemblage respectively.

The pottery from this feature was distinguished from the majority of the assemblage by the unusually large size of many of the fragments which must have been deposited as complete vessels. The average sherd weight was over 42 grams. The two most complete pots were a lid-seated jar (Fig.14:18) and a high-shouldered beaker with rouletted decoration (Fig.14:19), similar to an example from Chesterfield dated to the early second century (Anderson 1989, 23:61). Other forms included an everted-rim bowl (Fig.14:20), paralleled by form CF1 which was produced during the mid-second century at Derby (Dool *et al.* 1985, fig.44:142), a narrow-mouthed jar (Fig.14:21), everted rim jars (Fig.14:22–24), including one with a distorted rim and wavy, irregular, burnished decoration at the shoulder (Fig.14:24), an everted-rim bowl (Fig.14:25), a beaker with irregular, burnished decoration (Fig.14:26), a dish (Fig.14:27), similar to an example from well deposits in the Roman industrial settlement at Derby, of a Hadrianic to Antonine date (Dool *et al.* 1985, fig.81:182), and a small cup (Fig.14:28). Reeded-rim vessels were common (Fig.14:29–30). Similar forms have been recovered from Derby dating to the early to mid-second century (Brassington 1980, fig.14: 393, 394 and fig.12:366, 24–25). An example of the possibly carinated bowl (Fig.14:30) has been found during previous excavations at Rocester (Leary 1996, fig.25: 102).

The most interesting aspect of this assemblage, however, was the high incidence of green lead-glazed wares (31 fragments), representing the remains of nine different vessels, some of which have been illustrated (Fig.14:31–39). Some of the forms are similar to those produced at Derby; for example, the bead-rimmed and flange-rimmed bowls (Fig.14:31–32), although the bead-rimmed bowl (Fig.14:32) is more elaborately decorated, with vertically applied ribs interspersed with combed decoration (Brassington 1971, fig.13:295, 307). The handled cup (Fig.14:33), the only example of the fabric GLZ3, is also a variation on a Derby form (Brassington 1971, fig.13:302). Other forms included a beaker with linear decoration at the shoulder and irregularly applied glaze (Fig.14:34), a style of decoration applied to lead-glazed vessels from a first-century context at Margidunum (Brassington 1971, fig.11:277, 281), an indented beaker (Fig.14:35) and four other beakers and cups with various forms of decoration (Fig.14:36–39). With the exception of the handled cup which was in a finer white fabric (GLZ3), the lead-glazed wares all belonged to fabric GLZ1. As with previously-excavated lead-glazed wares, the common source is believed to be the Derby kilns, where the 'green glazing episode was confined to the Flavian–Trajanic period' (Leary 1996, 44; Brassington 1971, 62–67). Apart from the single body sherd from F608, there were only four other green-glazed sherds from the Orton's Pasture site, one from a topsoil context, two fragments from a carinated vessel from context 6079, and a bowl fragment from context 6003.

This could be a late Flavian–Trajanic group with a few intrusive sherds of BB1.

Two samian sherds bearing *graffiti* were also recovered from this feature (see Tomlin, this volume).

Northern Enclosure (Enclosure 1), Re-cut Stretch: 7000.
The majority of the 113 sherds from this context, weighing a total of 2,745 grams, consisted of greywares (36%), flagon wares (28%), OBC1 buff ware (11%), BB1 (8%), samian (6%), amphorae (4%), and small quantites of mortaria, oxidised wares and rough-cast North Gaulish ware. One stamped sherd of amphora has been assigned a Hadrianic date (see Williams, this volume, not illustrated).

Northern Enclosure (Enclosure 1) Pit Groups: F726 and F727

F726
A total of 173 sherds, weighing a total of 4,885 grams, came from F726, the majority of which were greywares, followed by oxidised and flagon wares in fairly equal quantities and some Black Burnished ware. Datable material included a BB1 jar (Fig.15:40), similar in form and design repertoire to a Type 2 BB1 jar from Period 6 at Greyhound Yard, Dorchester, dated to AD 100–200 (Seager Smith and Davies 1993, fig.140:117, 265). Several similar vessels were recovered from a quarry ditch in the Roman industrial settlement at Derby with a terminal date within the second half of the second century (Dool *et al.* 1985, fig.82: 224–229). Other BB1 forms included an undecorated, flat-rimmed bowl (Fig.15:41), a similar form to an example of a Type 22 flat-rimmed bowl from Period 6 at Greyhound Yard, Dorchester, dated to AD 100–120 (Seager Smith and Davies 1993, fig.139: 100, 263) and a developed or 'pulled' bead-rim jar (Fig.15:42), Type 8 at Greyhound Yard, where it was mainly found in Period 6 deposits dating to AD 100–120 (Seager Smith and Davies 1993, fig.122, 230–231), but the general form has been dated to the first century AD, possibly continuing until the later third century (Gillam 1976, 67). Also present was a BB1 bead-rim jar (Fig.15:43), Type 7 at Greyhound Yard (Seager Smith and Davies 1993, fig.122, 230–231), a type which originated in the first century BC and 'ceased to appear in the north before end of the second century' (Gillam 1976, 67). Other datable material included ring-necked flagons (Fig.15:44–45) of Antonine type (Gillam 1970, No. 5 dated AD 110–50; Dool *et al.* 1985, 93, no. 16, table 8, early to mid-Antonine; Leary 1996, 21:45,46), and, in the same fabric, a flanged bowl with a frilled rim, like a tazza, (Fig.15:46), with a close parallel among residual Phase 3 (mid-Antonine) pottery from the north-west sector excavations at Derby (Dool *et al.* 1985, fig.42:78, 98–99).

The greywares included everted-rim jars (Fig.15:47–48), the first of which was similar to a greyware vessel from previous excavations at Rocester (Leary 1996, fig.25:111), and the second of which was similar to an example from Derby dated to the first quarter of the second century (Brassington 1980, fig.11:338). Other forms included a lid-seated jar (Fig.15:49), a common vessel type in the assemblage from the Little Chester kilns which were abandoned in AD 110–20 (Brassington 1971, fig.10:205), and a carinated bowl (Fig.15:50), dated Flavian to mid-second century at Derby (Dool *et al.* 1985 fig.88:60–62; Leary 1986, fig.23:75).

The samian from the group is Flavian–Trajanic, but the coarse pot might be Hadrianic–early Antonine.

F727
Proportionally, the composition of this small assemblage of 55 sherds, weighing a total of 693 grams, was very similar to that of F726, although on a smaller scale. Forms represented include a lid-seated jar (Fig.15:51), a common vessel form with parallels from the kilns at Derby, Kiln Group 5, which was abandoned during the mid-second century (Brassington 1980, fig.17: 497), and at Little Chester, with a general abandonment date of AD 110–120 (Brassington 1971, fig.11: 238). A bead-rim bowl — a Dr.37 copy — (Fig.15:52) also has a parallel at Derby, Kiln Group 5, which was abandoned during the mid-second century (Brassington 1980, fig.18:520).

The Southern Enclosure (Enclosure 2) Ditches F704, F705 and F706
This feature produced an assemblage of 81 sherds, weighing a total of 2,291 grams, among which 22 fabrics were represented. Amphorae were predominant in the assemblage (17%), followed by the oxidised ware OAB3 (16%) and samian (14.8%), with BB1 and greywares accounting for a further 24% of the assemblage. Of most interest in the assemblage was the fragment from a face pot (Fig.15:53), with minimal traces of barbotine decoration in the form of the corner of an eye beneath a prominent, high-arched brow or hairline. An abraded area is shaped like a missing ear, the placing of which, below the level of the eye, is not unusual in face pots. Despite the small size of the fragment and the lack of identifiable features, the face is likely to be female, especially if the prominent ridge is considered as part of a rolled hairstyle or head-dress, such as the example worn by the female carved head from Birrens (Allason-Jones 1989, fig.40, 114–115). The appliqué technique used for the eye is similar to that employed on a greyware face pot from Derby (Brassington 1980, fig.13:370). Sometimes used to contain cremations, and seemingly associated with the army 'because all known first century examples come from a military context' (de la Bédoyère 1989, 167), face pots are believed to have fulfilled a ritual or votive function, the precise nature of which is not known. The Rocester example might, originally, have been connected with unusual vessels from adjacent ditch F706. A small fragment from a triple vase was also found in F704 (6529, not illustrated).

The assemblage could be Hadrianic–mid-Antonine in date.

F705 and F706
The ditches F705 and F706 produced only small quantities of pottery, 16 and 13 sherds with total weights of 478 grams and 73 grams respectively, consisting of small amounts of BB1, grey and oxidised wares and flagon wares. Nevertheless, some datable material was present, including, from F705, a BB1 bead-rim dish with open diamond lattice (Fig.16:54), similar in form to a previous example from Rocester (Leary 1996, fig.24:89; Gillam 1976, No. 74) and a ring-necked flagon (Fig.16:55), an Antonine type (Gillam 1970, No. 5 dated AD 110–50; Dool *et al.* 1985, fig.39:16, Table 8, early to mid-Antonine; Leary 1996, 21:45,46). Fragments of a tazza came from F3 3012 in the evaluation, believed to be equivalent to F705.

Pottery from F706 included a BB1 flat-rimmed bowl (Fig.16:56), an undecorated version of a previous Rocester find dated to the mid-second century (Leary 1996, fig.21:50), a beaker with circular motif executed in brown slip, which may be the top of a *caduceus* (Fig.16:57), and fragments from two tazzas (Fig.16:58–59). Tazzas are a form of vessel with 'a wide date range' (Leary 1996, fig.22:60, 47), an example of which was recovered from Kiln 5 at Derby, which had a general abandonment date in the mid-second century (Brassington 1980, fig.16:459). Tazzas, pottery incense cups, are generally associated with ritual, whether at a temple or in a domestic context, and might also have been used as open lamps (de la Bédoyère 1989, 163). The potential cultic significance of the tazza is perhaps reinforced by the presence of the painted cup with a motif reminiscent of part of a *caduceus*. These three vessels are suggestive of some kind of ritual behaviour, perhaps connected with the face pot from adjacent F704 (Fig.15:53).

Southern Enclosure (Enclosure 2) Pit Groups: F 700, F701 and F703

When considered as a whole, the pit group, comprising features F700, F701 and F703, with a total assemblage of 599 sherds weighing 19,692 grams, from 15 contexts was heavily weighted in favour of coarsewares, particularly greywares which accounted for some 40%, followed by oxidised wares (16%) and flagon wares (9%), as opposed to the specialist wares, which were dominated by amphorae (16%). Samian and BB1 accounted for only 7% and 2% of the assemblage respectively. Small quantites of other wares (ROX, NG1, MG2, DBY, CTA2/DW, CTA1) each accounted for only 1%. There were some differences in fabric composition between the three pits, which are discussed individually below but the general impression is of contemporaneity between the features, although the dating of some illustrated coarsewares from F700 suggests a somewhat later date (Hadrianic to Antonine) than the Flavian to Flavian–Trajanic date recorded from the diagnostic samian (see Willis this volume) which accords with the dating of some illustrated forms from F701.

F700

Almost half of the assemblage of 351 sherds, weighing a total of 10,234 grams, consisted of greywares (47%), followed by oxidised wares (14%), amphorae (11%), flagon wares (9%), and small quantities of samian (6%), mortaria and various other wares, including CT1 and CT2, BB1, MG1, NG1 and CC2. Datable material included some possibly Hadrianic to Antonine forms, such as a roulleted jar with a distorted rim (Fig.17:79), similar to an example from Derby (Dool *et al.* 1985, fig.83: 238). Four wide-mouthed jars were recovered (Fig.18:60–63), all of which were of possible Hadrianic date (Dool *et al.* 1985, fig.79:100, 101, 109, 113). Other jar forms included two narrow-necked jars with grooves at neck and shoulder (Fig.17:64–65). Several lids were recorded in the assemblage, three of which have been illustrated (Fig.17:66–68), similar lids to Nos. 66–67, many in grey fabrics, were recorded at Derby, especially from the well (F24B) dated to the Hadrianic/Antonine periods, terminating during the latter (Dool *et al.* 1985, fig.81:193–198). The Black Burnished ware lid (Fig.17:68), with decoration in the form of continuous single-line arches (Seager Smith and Davies 1993, fig.132: D19, 245–246), might be a waster, as the profile is irregular and appears sunken. Black Burnished ware lids are difficult to date since they had 'a long lifespan with few morphological changes', but were present in large quantities at Greyhound Yard, Dorchester only up to AD 300 (Seager Smith and Davies 1993, fig.125:26, 234–235).

Two flanged bowls with frilled rims, like tazzas, were present in the assemblage (Fig.17:69–70), a form of vessel similar to an example from residual Phase 3 (mid-Antonine) pottery from the north-west sector excavations, Derby (Dool *et al.* 1985, fig.42:78, 98–99). The larger vessel, in a flagon fabric (Fig.17:69) has an additional, lower, register of frilled decoration, whereas the greyware vessel is smaller and less elaborate (Fig.17:70). Reeded-rim vessels, similar to forms recovered from Kiln Group 5 at Derby, a kiln site abandoned in the mid-second century (Brassington 1980, fig.14: 393, 394), were common in the assemblage. (Fig.17:71–75). The most complete example was a reeded-rim, carinated bowl with two registers of grooves on the body of the vessel (Fig.17:75).

Other illustrated vessels include a ring-necked flagon (Fig.17:76), of Antonine type (Gillam 1970, No. 5 dated AD 110–50; Dool *et al.* 1985, fig.39:16, Table 8, early to mid-Antonine; Leary 1996, 21:45,46), a flat-rimmed dish (Fig.17:77), a beaker (Fig.17:78) and a roulleted jar with a distorted rim (Fig.17:79), similar to an example of Hadrianic–Antonine date from Derby (Dool *et al.* 1985, fig.83:238). Taken as a whole, the assemblage includes much Trajanic material, as well as some Hadrianic.

F701

The pottery assemblage of 101 sherds from F701, weighing a total of 3,914 grams, is dominated by greywares (33%), followed by equal quantities of oxidised (17%) and flagon wares (17%), with smaller quantities of mortaria (11%), samian (8%), amphorae (6%), and very small quantities of other fabrics, including Black Burnished ware (2%), among which were forms such as a Hadrianic–mid-Antonine flat-rimmed bowl with open-diamond lattice (Fig.19:80) similar to a previous Rocester find which was dated to the mid-to late second century (Leary 1996, fig.21:51), and a bead-rimmed, wide-mouthed jar or dish (Fig.18:81) whose date range is uncertain, though it probably dates to the Hadrianic–mid-Antonine period.

Among the greywares, datable material included a narrow-necked ovoid jar (Fig.18:82), similar to an example from Derby with a late second to early third century date (Dool *et al.* 1985, fig. 43:115, 100–101), a bead-rim bowl (Fig.18:83), probably carinated or hemispherical, based upon previous examples from Derby which have been dated to the early to mid-second century (Dool *et al.* 1985, fig.40:48, 94–95). A previous example from Rocester in a similar fabric has been given a possible Flavian–Trajanic date (Leary 1985, fig.21: 44). A cordoned bowl with an out-curving rim (Fig.18:84), is a Flavian–Trajanic form, similar to an example from Wall (Leary 1998, fig.13:45). There was also a number of Flavian–Trajanic reeded-rim bowls, three of which have been illustrated (Fig.18:85–87), with parallels from Kiln Group 5 at Derby, kilns which were abandoned in the mid-second century (Brassington 1980, fig.14: 393, 394). Another Flavian–Trajanic form, a reeded-rim, probably carinated, bowl (Fig.18:87), is similar to an early second century example from Derby (Brassington 1980, fig.12: 366, 24–25). This form has also been found during previous excavations at Rocester (Leary 1996, fig.25: 102). Other material included a lid-seated jar (Fig.18:88), a common vessel form with parallels from Kiln Group 5 at Derby, kilns abandoned during the mid-second century (Brassington 1980, fig.17: 497), and at Little Chester, with a general abandonment date of AD 110–120 (Brassington 1971, fig.11: 238). Other forms represented were a vase-shaped vessel with flaring rim (Fig.18:89), an everted-rim jar (Fig.18:90), and a ring-necked flagon (Fig.18:91), of Antonine type (Gillam 1970, No. 5 dated AD 110–50; Dool *et al.* 1985, 93, no. 16, table 8, early/mid-Antonine; Leary 1996, 21:45,46).

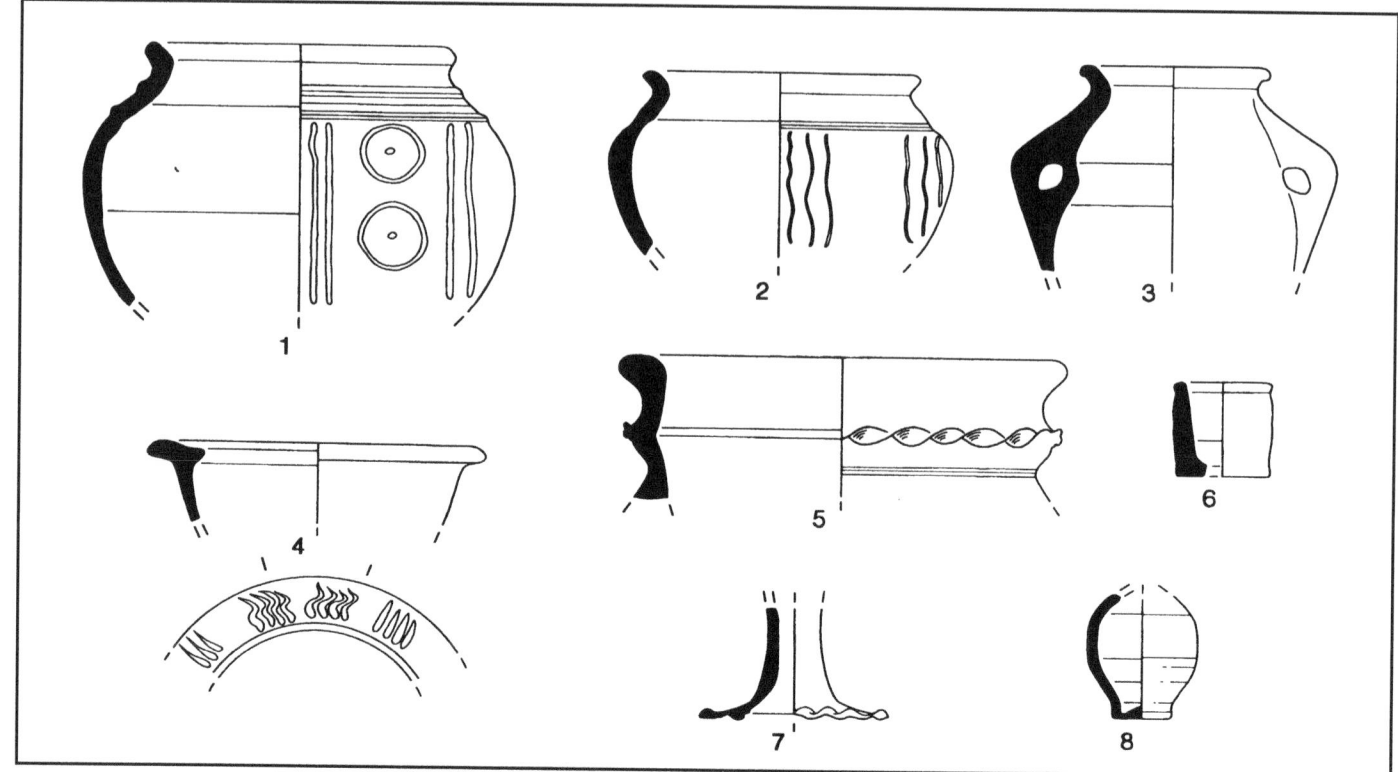

Fig. 19 Unstratified Roman pottery from watching brief (Scale 1:4)

F703

The assemblage of 147 sherds, weighing a total of 5,444 grams, comprised a higher incidence of amphorae (34%) than greywares (27%), followed by oxidised wares (9.7%), and roughly equal quantities of BB1, samian, Derbyshire ware (all under 8% each), with very small quantities of other wares including some mortaria (2.7%).

Romano-British Coarse Pottery from a Watching Brief (by J. Shepherd)

by Tracey Joyce

A total of 300 sherds, weighing 16,241 grams, was recovered during a watching brief and inspection of the site spoilheaps by Mr. J. Shepherd. The material is quantified in Table 2 according to the fabric series devised by Ruth Leary for the New Cemetery site, Rocester (see Appendix One, this volume). A number of small abraded sherds collected by Mr. Shepherd were not included in the quantification.

The assemblage is notable for the presence of a number of complete or near-complete vessels, jars, mortaria and flagons being well represented forms. The additional presence of glazed vessels, including a miniature beaker (No.8), two tazzas (Nos. 5 and 7) and a miniature greyware beaker (No.6) makes the assemblage comparable to the main Orton's Pasture assemblage presented above in terms of this notably high number of specialised vessel forms. Dating parallels suggest contemporaneity with the main assemblage, diagnostic types being early to mid-second century in date.

Catalogue of Illustrated sherds
(Fig. 19)

1. GRB1. Jar with ring and dot decoration. Fig. 19:1.
2. GRB1. Ribbed Jar. Fig.19:2.
3. BB1 (Variant). Jar with pierced lug handle on one, and possibly both

sides. Fig.19:3.
4. CTA1. Bowl with painted rim. Fig.19:4.
5. FLB2. Tazza. Fig.19:5.
6. GRA1. Miniature beaker or cup. Fig.19:6.
7. FLA2. Part of a tazza that appears to have been worked after breaking to turn it into a possible candle-holder or candlestick. Fig.19:7.
8. GLZ1. Miniature beaker. Fig.19:8.

Table 2. Fabrics present in watching brief assemblage by number, weight and relative percentages.

Fabric Code	Quantity	Weight (grams)	% no/weight
AMPH	1	47	>1/>1
SAM	69	1857	23/11.43
MORT	10	4133	3.33/25.44
BB1	60	2036	20/12.53
BB1 (variant)	3	220	1/1.35
CC1	1	98	>1/>1
CTA	8	298	2.66/1.83
DBY	11	138	3.66/>1
FLA1	27	366	9/2.25
FLA2	23	1319	7.66/8.12
FLA3	3	252	1/1.55
FLB1	5	501	1.66/3.08
FLB2	1	126	>1/>1
GLZ1	9	300	3/1.84
GRA1	20	1600	6.66/9.85
GRA2	7	295	2.33/1.81
GRA4	6	284	2/1.74
GRB1	10	1663	3.33/10.23
GRB2	3	73	1/>1
GRB3	3	48	1/>1
GRC2	3	28	1/>1
GTA	4	49	1.33/>1
MG2	2	32	>1/>1
NG1	2	9	>1/>1
0AB2	3	189	1/1.16
0BB1	1	16	>1/>1
0BC1	2	207	>1/1.27
SMST	3	57	1/>1
Totals	**300**	**16241**	

APPENDIX ONE
Rocester Roman Coarse Pottery Fabric Series
by Ruth Leary

GRAI Grey, hard with smooth feel. Smooth fracture. Moderate, fine, well-sorted, sub-angular quartz and sparse, medium-sized, rounded grey/brown oxides. Often micaceous.

GRA2 Grey, hard with smooth feel. Smooth fracture. Moderate, fine, well-sorted, sub-angular quartz and moderate, fine–medium-sized, ill-sorted sub-angular black iron oxides. Often micaceous.

GRA3 Grey, soft with sandy feel. Smooth fracture. Moderate, very fine, well-sorted, angular quartz; sparse–moderate, medium-sized, well-sorted, sub-angular quartz; sparse–moderate, medium-sized, rounded, well-sorted, grey inclusions ?grog; sparse–moderate, medium-sized, well-sorted, rounded, brown oxides.

GRA4 Pale grey with off-white paste, hard with smooth feel. Smooth fracture. Moderate, very fine; well-sorted quartz and sparse, fine, rounded, black oxides. Very similar to a fabric from the Derby Racecourse kilns (samples in Derby Museum).

GRBI Grey, sometimes with dirty buff core. Hard with slightly sandy feel. Irregular fracture. Moderate, medium-sized, well-sorted, sub-angular quartz; rare, medium-sized, well-sorted, sub-angular, black oxides. Sometimes slightly micaceous.

GRB2 Grey/greyish brown. Hard with smooth feel and finely irregular fracture. Moderate, medium-sized, well-sorted, sub-angular, clear quartz; sparse, medium-sized/ coarse, ill-sorted, rounded, buff/orange grog; rare, medium-sized, well-sorted, sub-angular, opaque, white quartz.

GRB3 Grey with orange core. Soft, slightly gritty feel and irregular fracture. Moderate, medium-sized, well-sorted, sub-angular quartz; moderate, medium-sized, well-sorted, laminar vesicles (but only visible in fracture); rare, medium-sized, angular, black oxides. Slightly micaceous.

GRCI Grey, hard with an appearance of very fine 'goosepimples'. Irregular fracture. Abundant, medium-coarse, well-sorted. sub-angular quartz. Possibly a Northamptonshire product, as OBC2.

GRC2 Grey or brown/reddish brown, hard with rough feel. Irregular fracture. Moderate, coarse, ill-sorted, sub-angular quartz and sparse, coarse, rounded, grey, brown and orange grog.

OAAI Fairly bright orange through to pink, usually with self slip. Soft with smooth feel and smooth fracture. Sparse, fine, well-sorted, sub-angular quartz and rare, coarse, rounded, black iron oxides. Often micaceous.

OAA2 Paler orange than OAAI with slightly dark orange slip. Moderate, fine, well-sorted, sub-angular quartz; rare, fine, well-sorted, rounded, red/brown iron oxides; rare, coarse, rounded, black iron oxides.

OAA3 As OAA2 but for distinct reddish slip and lighter red body with moderate, fine, well-sorted, rounded, red/brown, iron oxides.

OABI Pale orange with slightly darker slip. Hard with smooth but slightly sandy feel. Smooth fracture. Sparse, medium-sized, well-sorted, sub-angular quartz; sparse, medium-sized, well-sorted, rounded brown inclusions.

OAB2 Pale orange. Soft with gritty feel and irregular fracture. Moderate, medium-sized, well-sorted, sub-angular quartz; rare, medium-sized, rounded, black inclusions.

OAB3 Pinkish buff. Hard with granular feel and fracture. Abundant, fine or medium-sized, well-sorted, sub-angular quartz; sparse, fine to medium-sized, well-sorted, rounded, brown inclusions.

OBA1 Buff or brownish orange. Soft with very smooth feel and smooth fracture. Sparse, very fine, sub-angular quartz; moderate, fine, rounded, red/brown inclusions. Often micaceous.

OBA2 Pale orange/buff. Hard with smooth feel and finely irregular fracture. Very thin walled. Moderate, very fine, well-sorted, sub-angular quartz; moderate, fine, well-sorted, rounded, black iron oxides. Micaceous.

OBA3 Buff/beige. Very hard fired with smooth feel and conchoidal fracture. Very thin walled. Moderate, very fine, well-sorted quartz; rare, very fine, black inclusions. Micaceous.

OBBI Buff. Hard with gritty feel and finely irregular fracture. Sparse, medium-sized, well-sorted, sub-angular quartz; sparse, medium-sized, black and brown inclusions; sparse, medium-sized white inclusions.

OBCI Buff with grey core. Hard with rough feel and irregular fracture. Moderate, coarse/ medium-sized, ill-sorted, sub-angular quartz; moderate, medium-sized/fine, rounded brown inclusions. *Cf.* pre-Derbyshire ware (Brassington 1971, nos. 226–52).

OBC2 As GRC1 but greyish, off-white. Cf. Wood 1970, 37, fabric A used for painted ware.

GTA Brown. Soft with fairly smooth feel and irregular fracture. Moderate, very coarse, irregular and rounded grog; sparse, fine, angular quartz.

DBY Derbyshire ware as Kay 1962.

BB1 Black Burnished ware category 1 as Williams 1977.

FLA1 White/cream. Hard with smooth feel and smooth, almost conchoidal fracture. Rare, very fine, quartz and red/brown inclusions.

FLA2 Cream or pale yellow. Hard with smooth feel and smooth, almost conchoidal fracture. Slipped, sometimes fired to a darker yellow or a greyish hue. Moderate, fine, well-sorted, sub-angular, clear quartz; moderate, fine, ill-sorted, rounded, red or black inclusions — grog or clay pellets — and red streaks in matrix; rare, fine, well-sorted, sub-angular, black/brown iron oxides.

FLA3 White/cream, occasionally orange. Hard with rough feel and irregular fracture. Moderate, medium-sized, well-sorted, sub-angular quartz; sparse, fine, well-sorted, rounded, brown/black iron oxides.

FLA4 White/cream with pink core. Hard, rough with irregular fracture. Abundant, medium-sized, well-sorted, sub-angular, white translucent and rose quartz; sparse, medium-sized, well-sorted, rounded, black/brown iron oxides. Possibly Brockley Hill product.

FLBI Orange or buff with white/dirty white slip. Soft with smooth feel and smooth fracture. Moderate, very fine, well-sorted quartz; rare, coarse, rounded, black iron oxides.

FLB2 Pale orange or buff with white/off-white slip. Hard with slightly rough feel and fracture. Moderate, medium-sized, well-sorted, sub-angular quartz; rare, medium-sized, well-sorted, rounded, brown/black iron oxides

CTA1 Dull orange, orange or yellowish brown. Soft with smooth, soapy feel and laminar fracture. Abundant, medium-sized, well-sorted, laminar vesicles and white inclusions; sparse, fine, well-sorted, rounded, brown iron oxides.

CTA2 As CTAI but brownish grey. Sometimes in DW Dales ware forms.

GTA Brown. Soft soapy feel and irregular fracture. Sparse, fine, angular quartz; moderate, very coarse, irregular and rounded grog.

NG1 Rough-cast ware in forms hitherto identified as North Gaulish types. Orange through to pale orange/off-white with brown/black colour coat. Hard. Smooth feel and fracture. Moderate fine, well-sorted, sub-angular quartz; sparse, fine, rounded, black/brown inclusions.

CCI Pale buff with pale orange/buff colour coat. Hard with smooth feel and finely irregular fracture. Moderate, fine, well-sorted, sub-angular quartz; moderate, fine, well-sorted, rounded, black inclusions; moderate, rare, well-sorted, rounded, red grog.

CC2 Orange with grey core and dark red/orange colour coat and paint. Hard with smooth feel and fracture. Moderate, fine, well-sorted, sub-angular quartz; sparse, fine, rounded, black/brown inclusions.

NVI Nene Valley-type colour coat. White/off-white with black or brown colour coat. Hard with smooth feel and finely irregular fracture. Moderate, fine, well-sorted sub-angular quartz; moderate, fine, well-sorted, rounded, brown and orange inclusions.

NV2 Nene Valley-type as NVI but with orange colour-coat.

ROX Oxfordshire red-colour-coated ware.

MGI Orange with golden mica slip. Fairly hard with slightly sandy feel and irregular fracture. Moderate, medium-sized, well-sorted, sub-angular quartz; sparse, medium-sized, rounded, brown and orange inclusions.

MG2 Buff with golden mica slip. Soft with smooth feel and fracture. Sparse, medium-sized/fine, well-sorted, sub-angular quartz; moderate, medium to coarse, ill-sorted, rounded, brown and orange inclusions.

MG3 Buff and orange with golden mica slip. Usually with darker brown/red surface. Hard with sandy feel and irregular fracture. Moderate, medium-sized, well-sorted, sub-angular quartz; sparse, medium-sized, rounded, brown and orange inclusions.

GLZI As GRAI but with green glaze.

GLZ2 Pale orange with green glaze. Hard with smooth feel and finely irregular fracture. Moderate, fine, well-sorted, sub-angular quartz; moderate, fine, well-sorted, rounded, red/brown inclusions; moderate, very fine, well-sorted mica.

GLZ3 Buff/off-white with green glaze. Hard with gritty feel and irregular fracture. Moderate, medium-sized/fine, ill-sorted, sub-angular quartz; sparse, coarse, rounded, black inclusions.

—◇—

THE MORTARIA

by Lynne Bevan, with specialist identifications by Kay Hartley

The site produced a total of 124 sherds of mortaria with a total weight of 11,230 grams. A minimum number of 85 vessels was represented. Detailed recording by context is contained in the archive. Total numbers and weights appear below by fabric.

Of the 85 vessels, 43 of them can be consigned to local sources (those in the Rocester fabrics and those in the Little Chester fabrics below), 27 are from the Mancetter-Hartshill production area, seven are from either Mancetter-Hartshill or Little Chester, and eight are attributed to other sources (Oxford, Wroxeter and Verulamium).

Rocester Fabrics

Four red fabrics, the most likely source of which is Rocester, were identified in the assemblage:

1. Very hard-fired, deep red fabric with haematite inclusions, a thick yellow slip and translucent and opaque white quartz trituration grits. Rim fragments from two separate vessels were recovered, two of which were joining fragments from an obvious waster (6025, Fig. 20:1), and the other a more substantial rim with a wide, shallow flange (6024, Fig. 20:2) to which a date of AD 100–130 has been assigned (Kay Hartley pers. comm.). Total sherds: 3, total weight: 649 grams, MNV: 2.

2. Very hard-fired, dark red fabric with a reduced, dark grey interior, distinguished from Fabric 3 by frequent white quartz inclusions, evenly distributed throughout the fabric. The trituration grits are composed exclusively of small fragments of opaque, white quartz and a thick, yellow slip has been applied to the surface of the vessel. All three sherds belong to the same vessel, the profile of which has been illustrated (6000, 6036 x 2, Fig. 20: 3), although none of them joins. Total sherds: 3, total weight: 308 grams, MNV:1.

3. Deep red, over-fired, micaceous fabric with a grey core, occasional haematite inclusions and opaque white quartz trituration grits. One overfired rim (6070, not illustrated), has been assigned a late first- to early second-century date range, between *c.* AD 70–100 to possibly AD 120. Other sherds comprised an abraded rim/spout fragment (6500), two body fragments (6500, 6089), and part of a base (6089). Total sherds: 6, total weight: 546 grams, MNV:3.

4. Only one sherd, a stamped rim fragment, was recovered (6594, Fig. 20:4). See further discussion (Kay Hartley, this volume No.10). Total sherds: 1, total weight: 200 grams, MNV: 1.

Rocester/Little Chester Fabrics

Two fabrics might have originated from *either* Rocester or Little Chester. These are described below:

1. Fairly hard-fired fabric ranging from a pale cream to sandy yellow, and occasionally pink, in colour, with a fabric characterised by occasional white quartz and red-brown inclusions, and opaque white and brown quartz trituration grits. One stamped rim fragment is discussed by Kay Hartley (this volume No.8). One substantial rim fragment (6555, not illustrated), was identical in form to that of a published rim (in a Little Chester fabric) dated to *c.* AD 100–130 (Hartley 1996, fig.30:23, 66, 69). Fragments from two other rims (6000, 6519, not illustrated), dated to *c.* AD 100–130 (Kay Hartley pers. comm.), also have a published parallel (Hartley 1996, fig.30:22, 66, 69). Only one sherd, an abraded rim fragment dated to between *c.* AD 70–100 (6555, not illustrated), is possibly earlier than the general AD 100–130 date range proposed for the collection as a whole. There is also evidence that one abraded rim fragment (6563, not illustrated), dating to the late first to early second century, was a low-quality imitation of a Verulamium mortaria form (Kay Hartley pers. comm.). Other sherds in the same fabric were recovered from contexts 6007, 6501, 6011, 6511, 6504, 6506, 6555, 6569, and 7000. Total sherds: 19, total weight: 1959 grams, MNV:13.

2. Very coarse, bright orange fabric, occasionally with a grey core, containing abundant quartz and sparse haematite inclusions, with occasional voids from burnt-out organic inclusions. The trituration grits are composed of large fragments of white quartz, red and brown grog, and a red sandstone. Some fragments have retained traces of a thick yellow slip. This fabric is very similar to red, locally made fabrics recovered from previous excavations in Rocester (Hartley 1986; Ferguson 1996, 63). Several rim sherds originated from the same vessel (6595, 6001, and 6028, Fig. 21:5), to which a date range of AD 100–140 has been assigned (Kay Hartley pers. comm.). Another rim (6024, not illustrated) is similar in form to a published example, also from a workshop at either Rocester or Little Chester, which was dated to the late first or early second century (Hartley 1996, fig. 29:9, 65, 67), although in this case the latter date is more likely in view of the similarity with the rim (Fig. 20:5). Additional sherds were recorded from contexts 6025, 6011, 6506, 6525 (x 2), 6535 (x 2), and 6554. Total sherds: 18, total weight: 952 grams, MNV: 10.

Little Chester

1. Cream fabric, often with a pinkish core, containing occasional brown quartz and smaller dark brown particles, with predominantly dark brown and grey quartz trituration grits. One rim sherd (6520, not illustrated), with a published parallel also in a Little Chester fabric (Hartley 1996, fig. 30:16, 66, 68), was dated within the range of *c.* AD 100–140 (Kay Hartley pers. comm.). Some of the sherds end at *c.* AD 120 (6507, 6532), but the remaining datable sherds (contexts 6501 (x 2), 6506, 6518, and 6569) fall into the same date range (*c.* AD 100–140) as the aforementioned rim (6520, not illustrated). Additional undated fragments were recovered from the following contexts: 6031, 6500, 6525, 6596 and 6613. The sherds were generally very abraded and quite small in size within this fabric group, and although several of them might have originated from the same vessels, this could not be demonstrated by cross-fitting. Total sherds: 13, total weight: 850 grams, MNV: 13.

Little Chester/Mancetter-Hartshill

Previously, two similar 'creamy white to yellowish buff fabrics with small red-brown and black inclusions and some quartz' were identified at Rocester where they were believed to be the product of either the Little Chester or the Mancetter-Hartshill

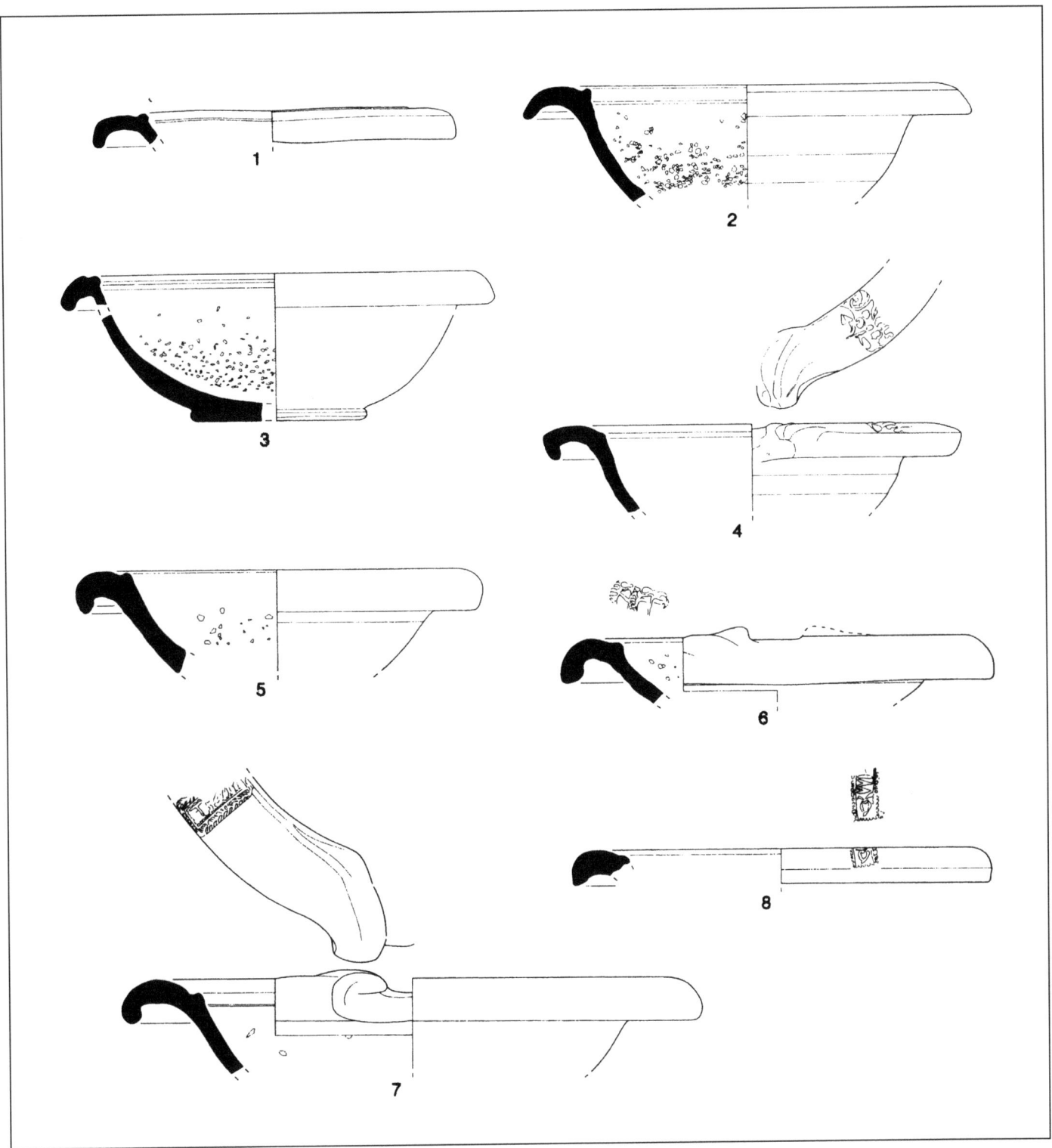

Fig. 20   Mortaria (Scale 1:4)

kilns (Ferguson 1996, 62). The fabrics were distinguished purely on the basis of their slightly different trituration grits, which consisted of 'angular black and red grog, flint, sandstone, white and clear quartz' (Fabric 1), and 'densely scattered white quartz' (Fabric 2). While it was possible to equate both fabrics with fabrics from the Little Chester kilns, they also bore a close resemblance to Mancetter-Hartshill products, although the latter are usually finer and less commonly slipped (*ibid.*). For these reasons, a common group of potentially mixed origin was established, a group which is still apparent among the more recent material discussed here. In addition to the stamped mortaria fragments discussed by Mrs. Hartley (this volume), other datable fragments were identified among this fabric group, including three fragments from a grey, over-fired rim dated to the early second century, between AD 100–130 (Unstratified, not illustrated) and a rim sherd dated to between AD 100–140 (6040). Part of an undated base was also recovered (6025). Total sherds: 10, total weight: 1242 grams, MNV: 7.

Mancetter-Hartshill

1. Fine-textured creamy-white fabric, often very hard, with inclusions of fine quartz and occasional red-brown and white particles gritted with either quartz and red-brown sandstone (on earlier specimens) or abundant red-brown or black

angular grits. Description adapted from Tyers (1996, 123).

In addition to the stamped mortaria fragments discussed in Mrs. Hartley's report (this volume), several other datable fragments were identified in the collection, including fragments from three mortaria with multi-reeded, hammerhead rims (6001, 6020, 6504), none of which has been illustrated. The earliest has been dated from the mid-second to the third century (6020), and the others to the third century (Kay Hartley pers. comm.). Other datable sherds include a badly finished base and body sherd from the same vessel which were dated to the second half of the second century (6042), a body sherd with the same general dating (6014), a fragment from a 'bead through spout' type of mortaria dated to between AD 200–260 (6509), three probably third-century body sherds from different vessels (6020, 6537 x 2), a third-century, post-AD 230, rim (6039), and a rim dated to between AD 170 to 210 (6007). Additional sherds came from contexts 5003 (x 3), 6000 (x 5), 6001 (x 5), 6036, 6511 (x 2), and 6554. Total sherds: 43, total weight: 3246 grams, MNV: 27.

Other Sources

1. One rim sherd of an Oxfordshire mortarium, weighing 117 grams, was found (2041, not illustrated), a late form of mortarium with an upstanding rim and a wide, thin flange which has been dated to between AD 240 to 300 (Young 1977, fig. 22:M20.02, 75–76).

2. A rim sherd with a spout from Wroxeter (6025, not illustrated), weighing 153 grams, was also found. The fabric is very pale, brownish-cream with a tinge of pink in the core and inclusions in the form of fairly frequent, tiny to small, pinkish and transparent quartz and opaque orange-brown and rare grey material, with rare larger orange-brown and grey material. The type of spout used is typical in every way for mortaria attributed to the vicinity of Wroxeter in the period AD 90–130, and made by such potters as Docilis 1 (Kay Hartley pers. comm.).

3. Six sherds from as many vessels of Verulamium mortaria were recovered, weighing a total of 1008 grams. The sandy fabrics were cream, some with a pinkish tint, with, when visible, trituration grits in the form of small fragments of flint, quartz and brown sandstone. One very abraded base (7000) was dated to *c.* AD 70–130, two badly damaged rim fragments (6506 and 6501) to AD 70–90 and AD 80–120 respectively, and a body fragment from the side of a vessel (6504) to AD 90–120 (Kay Hartley pers. comm.). The remaining sherds comprised a small rim fragment (6070) and a small base fragment (6506). Due to the high incidence of fragmentation and abrasion, none of the Verulamium fragments has been illustrated.

Stamped Mortaria

by Kay Hartley

1. **5003** (Not illustrated) 35 grams Fragment with incomplete rim-section, in self-coloured, cream, fairly fine-textured fabric. Inclusions are fairly frequent, ill-sorted, transparent and pinkish quartz, with some sparse red-brown and black material. The fragmentary, left-facing stamp, preserves the last two letters, [......]VS with part of the lower border of large dots, of a stamp of Gratinus from one of at least ten dies used by him. No trituration grit survives.

One of his kilns and an area where he probably had a second kiln, have been excavated at Hartshill, Warks. (unpublished), and there is no reason to doubt that the whole of his activity was in the Mancetter-Hartshill potteries. Over 70 mortaria stamped by Gratinus have been noted from occupation sites in the north and Midlands of England, and ten to eleven from sites in Scotland. His general date is clear from his mortaria in Antonine Scotland, including five from sites on the Antonine Wall. His rim profiles, the trituration grit used, and his kiln all suggest optimum productivity *c.* AD 130–150. This is the second mortarium of Gratinus recorded from Rocester (Esmonde Cleary and Ferris 1996, 70, No. 31).

2. **6000** (Fig. 20:6) 220 grams. Fragment with incomplete rim-section, overfired to grey in the flange and a drab cream in the body with darker surfaces. Inclusions are fairly frequent, mostly tiny, and mostly transparent quartz with few orange-brown and vesicular black particles. The trituration grit included quartz, opaque orange-brown and black material. The broken, two-line stamp shows V[.....] in the lower line. This is a stamp of Vitalis 4; only one of the two lines of letters has registered properly. In better impressions, the upper line is almost identical to the lower one. The A in the upper line is always blind, that in the lower line normally has a diagonal bar; LI appear in the top line as two downstrokes, in the lower line as a lambda L followed by a single downstroke. The best impressions show a slight but complete cross-bar to the T in the lower line but in the upper line only half of the cross-bar is ever registered. Vitalis 4 has two known die-types, differing from each other only in detail, and possibly made from the same matrix.

One kiln plus an area where he probably had a second kiln have been excavated at Hartshill, Warks. (unpublished). Over 60 of his mortaria have been found on occupation sites in the Midlands and north of England, but significantly, only one has been recorded from Scotland. His rim-profiles and the general distribution of his mortaria are typical for a pre-Antonine potter working in the Mancetter-Hartshill potteries. His working life must certainly have been within the period AD 115–145. Stamps on six different mortaria of his have now been recorded from Rocester (Esmonde Cleary and Ferris 1996, 64, No. 3 and 67, No. 10, both stamps published upside-down, plus two old finds, and No. 6 below). No stamps of Vitalis have been found in association with kilns at Little Chester, but Nos. 2 and 6 are in fabrics which one might expect to have been produced there rather than in the Mancetter-Hartshill potteries, though the latter is not impossible. The other mortaria of his from Rocester are in the cream fabric mainly associated with early second-century production in the Mancetter-Hartshill potteries, but possibly also produced at Little Chester.

3. **6001** (Fig. 20:7) 468 grams. Diam. 43 cms (17%) Hard, cream fabric, probably self-coloured, with frequent but ill-sorted inclusions, mostly transparent quartz, few orange-brown and rarely black or grey. Most of the trituration grit has been worn away, what remains is mostly quartz with a few red-brown grits. The broken, left-facing stamp is from a die, giving FECIT retrograde, used by G. Attius Marinus. Three mortaria of his have now been recorded from Rocester (including Esmonde Cleary and

Ferris 1996, 67 and fig. 30, No. 13, stamp published upside-down; plus an old find). G. Attius Marinus began stamping mortaria at Colchester in the late first century, and after what was probably a brief period at Radlett, moved to the Midlands, where his major production occurred within the period AD 100–130. He almost certainly spent most of this time in the Mancetter-Hartshill potteries. The distribution of his stamps is in keeping with this source, but some activity at Little Chester cannot be ruled out. The fabric of both of the Rocester mortaria fits well with production in the Mancetter-Hartshill potteries. The detail in the border of the stamp suggests that it was impressed early in the life of the die, while the rim-profile is very reminiscent of his work at Radlett. This suggests that this mortarium was a very early product of his midland activity.

4. **6025** **i.** (Not illustrated) 416 grams. About a third of a worn mortarium with incomplete rim-section in fine-textured, hard cream fabric with darker cream slip and inclusions consisting of fairly frequent, tiny and small, mostly transparent and pinkish quartz, with some opaque orange-brown and rare black material. There is abundant trituration grit up to *c.* 2cms below the bead, consisting of quartz, orange-brown (including sandstone), and black material. The broken, left-facing stamp, ICO[.....] retrogradee, is from one of the nine dies of Icotasgus who can be attributed to the Mancetter-Hartshill potteries. A total of seven stamps from probably six mortaria is now recorded from Rocester and at least four dies are represented (includes Esmonde Cleary and Ferris 1996, 69, and fig. 31, No. 29, published upside-down). Over 90 of Icotasgus's mortaria are known from sites in Britain, including at least five from Scotland and excluding 20 stamps from the production site at Mancetter. Icotasgus has a typical distribution for a Mancetter potter active in the Antonine period, but many of his mortaria show pre-Antonine characteristics in the rim-form and spout, and he may always have used a range of trituration grit which went out of use at these potteries *c.* AD 150. A date of AD 120–150 could fit his work.

5. **6025** **ii** (Fig. 20:8) 120 grams. Diam. 29 cms, (15%). Flange and bead of a mortarium in hard, fairly fine-textured, cream fabric, probably with cream-buff slip. Inclusions consist of moderate to fairly frequent, tiny, transparent quartz and opaque orange-brown material with rare dark red-brown ?slag and very white (non-reactive) material (?quartz sandstone). The stamp shows a leaf stop followed by MI retrograde; this is the first example of this stamp which preserves all the borders clearly enough to indicate that the stamp is complete as it stands. There is a slight shadow of a possible second vertical stroke giving MII for ME. This stamp always occurs in conjunction with another stamp which gives the rest of the name, a very unusual practice. The second stamp reads either TTIIS or TILIS retrograde. Clearer stamps will remove the uncertainties in this potter's name, but the possible interpretations appear to be MITTES, MITILIS, METTES and METILIS. The two stamps were usually impressed close together, but on this occasion they were probably on opposite sides of the rim.

His mortaria have now been found on the following sites: Caersws; Leicester (3–4); Mancetter (pottery-making area);

Northwich (1–2); Rocester (2, including Esmonde Cleary and Ferris 1996, 70, not illust. 1119); and Wasperton. His work would best fit with manufacture in the Mancetter-Hartshill potteries within the period AD 100–140.

6. **6032** (Not illustrated) 50 grams. Diam. 27 cms (12%). Flange fragment in very hard, fine-textured, buff-brown fabric with pale grey core and inclusions in the form of fairly frequent, very ill-sorted, red-brown (?chert); quartz, black vesicular (?slag), soft, opaque white, calcareous material, and clusters of quartz grains in a black matrix. The fragmentary stamp reads [ ]TA[ ], A with diagonal dash. This is a stamp of Vitalis 4 on a second mortarium (see No. 2 above).

7. **6050** (Not illustrated) 95 grams Fragment with incomplete rim-section in hard, fine-textured, cream fabric with thick pinkish core; self-coloured. Inclusions consist of moderate, ill-sorted, transparent and pinkish quartz and orange-brown material, with some voids. The trituration grit is worn away, except for a few fragments of quartz. The fragmentary stamp may begin in V[...], but cannot yet be identified. This mortarium was rather crudely made and the wall is notably thick; there is enough surviving to show that the flange and spout were notably higher than the bead. Its characteristics clearly point to a date very early in the second century. Although the fabric would fit well with production in the Mancetter-Hartshill potteries, production at Little Chester or Rocester is a possibility. See discussion.

8. **6060** (Not illustrated) 100 grams Fragment with incomplete rim-section in self-coloured, hard, drab cream fabric and inclusions in the form of moderate, ill-sorted, sub-rounded, mostly transparent quartz with a few orange-brown fragments. The trituration grit consists of pebbly quartz and brown or grey material (?sandstone) up to 5mm in size. The internal surface (not the flange) is coarsely scored and both grit and scoring are worn smooth towards the bottom of the vessel. The border of a stamp survives, and, although it cannot yet be identified, enough survives for future identification. The wall and flange of this mortarium are notably thick and the flange is rising slightly above the bead. This fabric is not likely to be from Mancetter or Hartshill; it is much more likely to have been made at Little Chester or Rocester. All the characteristics together, especially the scoring, point to a date in the early second century.

9. **6555** (Not illustrated) 70 grams Diam. 28 cms (13.5%). A flange fragment in hard, fine-textured cream fabric with moderate, ill-sorted and random inclusions, mostly rounded quartz with some opaque orange-brown and rare opaque black. Slightly singed before fracture. The fragmentary stamp preserves parts of the last three letters, [.........]NVS, of a stamp of Septuminus, who had workshops, perhaps at different times, in the Mancetter-Hartshill potteries and at Little Chester (Brassington 1971, 53–53). His mortaria have now been recorded from Bucknall, Staffs.; Coleshill, Warks.; Leicester; Hartshill; Little Chester (3); Mancetter (4); Metchley; Ribchester; Rocester (2); Staden, near Buxton; Wall; and Vindolanda. The abandonment of the Little Chester kilns is consistent with a date about AD 110–120, his rim-profiles must fall within the period AD 100–130. His optimum date is AD 100–120+. The fabric

of this example fits best with manufacture in the Mancetter-Hartshill potteries.

10. **Area C 6594** (Fig. 20:4) 200 grams Diam. 27 cms (18%). A mortarium, probably self-coloured, in fairly fine-textured, orange-brown fabric, with drab cream core and inclusions in the form of fairly frequent, but very random, and ill-sorted, quartz, orange-brown, rare black material and cream clay pellets up to 3mm in size. The trituration grit is virtually worn away but it included quartz (with hackly fracture) and orange-brown material.

The right-facing stamp is from a very crudely made die which is otherwise unknown. It is possible to read the stamp, especially if the letters are incuse, as OACV? in the upper line with the possibility of an M in the lower line, but clearer examples are needed to clarify it, though it appears, at best, to be semi-legible. There is just a possibility that the die belonged to a potter whose semi-legible stamp was found at Little Chester (Brassington 1980, 41, fig. 21, No. 564).

The fabric is not especially identifiable as one produced at Little Chester and it seems more likely that it was made at Rocester. The rim-profile leaves no doubt that this potter was working in the tradition favoured by G. Attius Marinus and Vitalis 4 (Kenyon 1948, fig. 58, Nos. 2C and 19) and a date within the period AD 100–130 is certain.

Discussion

The stamped mortaria found at Rocester over the years show some distinctive and unusual features and this sample, small though it is, is entirely representative.

Links in the production of mortaria at Hartshill, Mancetter, Little Chester and Rocester in the early second century.

It has been known for nearly thirty years that mortaria were being made in the early second century at Hartshill, Mancetter and at Little Chester. There was also some pottery found at Rocester in the 1960s by Fiona Sturdy, which caused me to believe that mortaria and flagons were being made at Rocester, in the late first century from *c.* AD 80+ to a date in the early second century. There is now firm evidence of production at Rocester in the form of an unusable distorted and twisted mortarium waster attributed to the early second century (Bevan, this volume Fig. 20:1). The fabric linked with this production is in the orange- to red-brown range.

The distribution of stamps for some of the potters represented at Rocester would also fit with production there. A semi-legible stamp has now been recorded from Brough-on-Noe; Little Chester (Brassington 1980, 41, fig. 21, No. 564); Melandra Castle; and on four different mortaria found at Rocester (Esmonde Cleary and Ferris 1997, 68 1052ii (not illust.) and 70, 1119iii (not illust.), and fig. 31, No. 24, 1081 and, (not published), 1018). If the stamp from context 6594 (see above) was also by this potter, five of his seven recorded mortaria would be from Rocester. This potter has previously been attributed to Little Chester, but production at Rocester is at least as likely, and activity at both sites is not impossible. At least three other potters whose mortaria have been found at Rocester could well have worked there, for example a potter probably called Vitalis who stamped VITALF. Six of his mortaria have been recorded, four of them from Rocester (Esmonde Cleary and Ferris 1997);

fig. 31, No. 28 and p. 69, No. 28 (1430); 69, not illust. 1248i & 1052; 70, u/s not illust.; and ROFS 85 6005, 1172, 6032 *et al.*, not published). One fragmentary, two-line stamp, [.....]/[....]VS.F, is unpublished (ROFS 85 1072), and, for another, a semi-legible stamp, see Esmonde Cleary and Ferris 67, No. 9, 1447 + 1485 and fig. 29, No. 9 ?QCIOS.

We also have sufficient evidence to indicate that Septuminus had workshops at both Little Chester and Mancetter, and perhaps at Hartshill. There has always been some element of doubt about whether any of his products at Little Chester were in a cream fabric similar to that produced at the same period at Mancetter and Hartshill, because the only mortarium of Septuminus in cream fabric at Little Chester was in the clay kiln-pedestal where repeated firing of the kiln could easily cause distortion and cracking. Certainly the vast majority of the sherds which can be associated with the kilns found at Little Chester are in orange-brown and grey fabrics, including large numbers of segmental bowls whose equivalents in the Mancetter-Hartshill potteries were always made in the cream fabric used for mortaria.

Moreover, mortaria do not appear in large quantities at the Little Chester kilns and the extremely small number in a fabric which can be described as cream tends to be somewhat greyish or have a grey core. The evidence at present available from Little Chester suggests that any output in cream fabric was limited. Only further discoveries will show whether such fabrics were also produced at Rocester, but the four mortaria with semi-legible stamps mentioned above (Esmonde Cleary and Ferris 1997, fig. 31, no.24) are in this type of fabric, as is also No. 8 above. The evidence from Hartshill and Mancetter shows that the mortaria produced there in fair quantity in the early second century (*e.g.* kilns of Cevanos, Surus, Victor and Vitalis 4) are in cream fabrics of variable quality which are sometimes very gritty, but they are rarely greyish and are unlikely to have grey cores. In general, one can say that the orange-brown fabrics are typical for mortaria made at Little Chester and at Rocester and that mortaria in cream, often drab greyish, or with a grey core were made in limited quantity. The reverse is true for the Mancetter-Hartshill potteries where the major production was in cream fabric, sometimes varying in quality or grittiness but very rarely with a grey core, while production of mortaria in orange-brown fabrics was very limited. Nevertheless, similarities, or possible similarities, in fabric can make it difficult to attribute some early second century mortaria with certainty.

The difficulty in knowing what the exact proportion of the Little Chester output was in cream fabric and the lack of certainty about which potters, other than Septuminus and perhaps Aesticus (see below), had workshops there as well as in Hartshill and/or Mancetter is largely the result of so few kilns having been excavated at Little Chester. Unfortunately the evidence from Mancetter and Hartshill is also fairly limited for the early second century, partly because of the destruction of kilns in antiquity to make further use of the sites in the second to fourth centuries, and also because production extended over a very wide area, much of which has been quarried away and much of which remains unexcavated. The discovery of further kilns at these three sites could resolve some of these problems.

There are potters attributable to Little Chester who never worked in the Mancetter-Hartshill potteries and the distribution of their mortaria may indicate the market served by the Little Chester workshop better than the distribution for Septuminus whose

Little Chester and Mancetter products may be confused. Many of the stamps found at the Little Chester kilns have not been recorded elsewhere, but one exception is a trademark (Brassington 1980, 41, fig. 21, No. 566), now recorded from Carlisle, Little Chester (3), and Templeborough. This is the only potter who appears to have worked solely at Little Chester, and who has any distribution outside Little Chester, so this evidence also suggests that the workshops at Little Chester were catering for a local market. The production of mortaria there is dated to the period AD 100–130 with perhaps some in the late first century.

Septuminus certainly worked at Little Chester at some point and it seems likely that Aesticus did so too (Brassington 1980, 41, fig. 21, No. 562). G. Attius Marinus and Vitalis 4 may have worked at Little Chester at some point, but their considerable and wide distributions are typical for potters in the Mancetter-Hartshill potteries. The only known kilns of Vitalis 4 are at Hartshill and the circumstantial evidence for G. Attius Marinus working there is strong.

G. Attius Marinus came to the Midlands from Radlett (Page 1898) and in theory one would expect him to have found the clays at Manduessedum and Hartshill before any supposed activity at Little Chester. But, it is also fair to assume that the military activity in the Peak District could have acted as a magnet to a potter coming to the Midlands at just the right time. If the small number of products in cream fabric, at present attributable to Little Chester (or Rocester), is any guide, then one would assume that any activity there by potters also associated with the Mancetter-Hartshill potteries was short-lived. Only the discovery of further kilns at these three sites could resolve some of these problems. What is certain is that a very small number of the early second century potters working at Mancetter and Hartshill were also active in a small workshop at Little Chester. It is even possible that their workshops at Hartshill and/or Mancetter were active at the same time as that at Little Chester (see Breeze forthcoming for evidence of subsidiary workshops). There were other contemporary potters at Little Chester whose markets were almost entirely local; some of these potters could have had contemporary or near contemporary links with a pottery workshop at Rocester.

The Number of Stamped Mortaria at Rocester and their Date

The total number of stamped mortaria recorded from Rocester is at least 76, a very high number for an occupation which was probably always fairly small, and it is certainly higher than the totals known for Lincoln and for Chester, while perhaps the more comparable site at Wall has only 54. Forty-eight of the 76 stamped mortaria from Rocester are earlier than AD 130, and very few of these could be earlier than AD 90. Twenty more mortaria stamped by potters who are more difficult to date closely can be attributed to the first half of the second century, and many of these will be much earlier than AD 150. Seven can be dated to the mid-second century and one only to the period AD 150–170. Despite the constraints which difficulties in dating impose, the heavy bias to the early second century is clear, as well as the rarity of potters whose activity began much later than c. AD 130. Few sites have this kind of bias, the most obvious being Holditch, Staffs., whose fifteen stamped mortaria are closely comparable. The 64 stamped mortaria from Little Chester are much more evenly spread in date, up to c. AD 170+ when the practice of stamping ceased in the Mancetter-Harthill potteries.

Sources of Mortaria Found at Rocester

The survey by Rowan Ferguson (Esmonde Cleary and Ferris 1997, 61–63) shows all the main sources of the mortaria at Rocester and their relative importance, but it is worth pointing out that there is a surprising number of mortaria from unexpected sources which were not supplying mortaria to this area on a trading basis. These were presumably carried to Rocester by soldiers or other individuals. They include at least one late first-century to early second-century mortarium from Colchester[1] (Viator, *ibid.*, 68, 17) and a second-century mortarium from north-eastern England, probably the Catterick area (Esmonde Cleary and Ferris 1997, 68, No. 18). The unstamped sherd (6025) from the potteries supplying Wroxeter in the late first and early second centuries is from a relatively close source, but Rocester and Holditch, which has a Wroxeter stamp dating c. AD 110–150, are not in their normal marketing area as the rest of the pottery clearly shows. Six mortaria from the New Cemetery site were attributed to the lower Nene Valley. These are dated within the period AD 230–400 and the number, although very small, could perhaps indicate more than casual 'carries'; nevertheless, this is an unusual source for such an inland site.

[1] Seven unmarked stamped mortaria in Stoke-on-Trent museum are old finds believed to be from Rocester. These include a mortarium of Sextus Valerius C[....], believed to date within the period AD 60–100 and a second-century mortarium with herringbone stamp (Hull 1963, fig. 60, no.37), dated AD 140–170.

THE AMPHORAE
by D F Williams

Introduction

The amphorae were classified by fabric and form, and in order to consider the material quantitatively were then weighed and counted. The classification of the forms is based on Dressel (1899), the Camulodunum series (Hawkes and Hull 1947), Laubenheimer (1985) and with descriptive terms suggested by Peacock (1971). The dominant amphora type present is the southern Spanish olive-oil vessel Dressel 20, with lesser amounts of Gauloise 4, Beltran I or II (southern Spanish) and an undesignated sherd. Brief notes on the origins and chronological span of the amphorae are given below.

Table 3 Percentage total of each fabric

Quantification	% by count	% by weight (grams)
Dressel 20	820 / 98.91	87,930 / 97.82
Gauloise 4	7 / >1	1,404 / 1.56
Beltran I or II	1 / >1	140 / >1
Camuldonum 186 sp	1 / >1	123 / >1
Undesignated	1 / >1	285 / >1
Totals	**830**	**89,882**

Discussion

The vast majority of this group of amphorae sherds belongs to the Spanish globular Baetican Dressel 20 olive-oil amphora, which was made in the valley of the River Guadalquivir and its tributaries between Seville and Cordoba in the Roman province of Baetica (Peacock and Williams 1986, Class 25). This form of amphora is the most common type found on Romano-British sites during the first three centuries AD, as well as being present in some numbers during the late Iron Age (Williams and Peacock 1983). On the evidence of several rim sherds and handle stamps, most of this material can probably be dated to the period from the later first century AD to the middle of the second century AD. Of the 70 amphora sherds previous reported on from the New Cemetery site at Rocester, 69 were from the Dressel 20 form, the rim fragments suggesting a mid-second-century date (Williams 1996) and five of the published forms have been identified in this assemblage (Williams 1996, fig. 32: 1–5).

Seven sherds listed in the above table belong to the flat-bottomed southern French wine amphora Gauloise 4, including a complete rim (Laubenheimer 1985). Dressel 20 olive-oil and Gauloise 4 wine amphorae are commonly found together on a range of British civil and military sites from the later first century AD to the third century AD However, the paucity of Gauloise 4 vessels on many forts in the northern frontier district suggests that the supply system for wine may have been different there and that barrels could perhaps have been used instead of amphorae (Bidwell and Speak 1994, 214).

Also present is a small fragment of handle from a Beltran I or II amphora: it is not possible to say which particular variety of form it belongs to (Peacock and Williams 1986, Classes 17, 18 and 19). These types of amphora were made along the southern Spanish coast, *tituli picti,* suggesting that the main product carried was fish-based. The date range covered by these forms taken as a whole, is from the late first century BC until about the mid-second century AD One Camulodunum 186sp part

handle was also identified. This form was produced along the southern Spanish coast, notably in the Cadiz region, and was used to carry fish-based products, especially fish sauces such as *liquamen* and *muria* (Beltran 1970; Peacock 1971; 1974). It is not possible to say to which variety of form the Rocester sherd belongs, which could fall anywhere in the period from the late first century BC to the early second century AD (*ibid*).

One of the amphora sherds from Orton's Pasture, consisting of a joining rim and handle, cannot at present be paralleled. However, the petrology suggests that it may have originated from perhaps Italy or the eastern Mediterranean region.

Catalogue of Dressel 20 Rims and Stamps

All of the Dressel 20 rims from Rocester can be paralleled with examples from Augst, illustrated by Martin-Kilcher (1983) in her scheme for the development of the Dressel 20 rim. The majority of the Rocester rims appears to fall within the period from the late first century AD to just after the middle of the second century AD

1. Rim dated to late first century AD to AD 175 (*ibid.,* no.32), similar to a form previously identified at the New Cemetery, Rocester (Williams 1996, fig. 32:1). F715 6564. Fig. 21:1.

2. Rim dated to late first century AD to AD 175 (*ibid.,* no.30), similar to a form previously identified at the New Cemetery, Rocester (Williams 1996, fig.32:4). F617 6108. Fig. 21:2.

3.–6. Four rims

    a. dated late first century AD to AD 175 (*ibid.,* no.30 or 32), and similar to a form identified at the New Cemetery, Rocester (Williams 1996, fig.32:1).

    b. late first century AD to early second century AD (*ibid.,* no.17), and similar to a form previously identified at the New Cemetery, Rocester (Williams 1996, fig.32:5).

    c. and d. abraded fragments from two different rims, dated to late first century AD to AD 175 (*ibid.,* no.30), and similar to a form previously identified at the New Cemetery, Rocester (Williams 1996, fig.32:4). 6025. Not illustrated.

7. Rim dated to the late first century AD to early second century AD (*ibid.,* no.20), and similar to a form identified at the New Cemetery, Rocester (Williams 1996, fig.32:2). F707 6558. Not illustrated.

8. Two fragments from one rim dated to the late first century to AD 175 (*ibid.,* no.32), similar to a form previously identified at the New Cemetery, Rocester (Williams 1996, fig.32:1). Area B. F702 6539. Not illustrated.

9. Rim. Part of the top section with neck and handle. The shape of the rim is similar to no.65, dated AD 70–110, in Martin-Kilcher's typology of stratified Dressel 20 rims from the Swiss forts at Augst and Kaiseraugst (Martin-Kilcher 1987). F701 6518. Not illustrated.

Stamped Handles

The individual stamps are positioned towards the summit of the handle. In the first three examples the stamp reads downwards from the summit, while on the fourth handle it reads up towards the summit.

C (or F) I ....   A reading of this stamp is very difficult as it is faint and much worn. It is possible that it may be one of the stamps used by *G. Iulius Albinus,* though this is by no means certain. His *figlinae* were situated at Malpica and Valbuenas on the River Genil and seem to have been producing amphorae at some stage during the period from the latter part of the first century AD until just after the mid-second century AD (Callender 1965, no.333; Carreras and Funari 1998, 238). F602 6054.

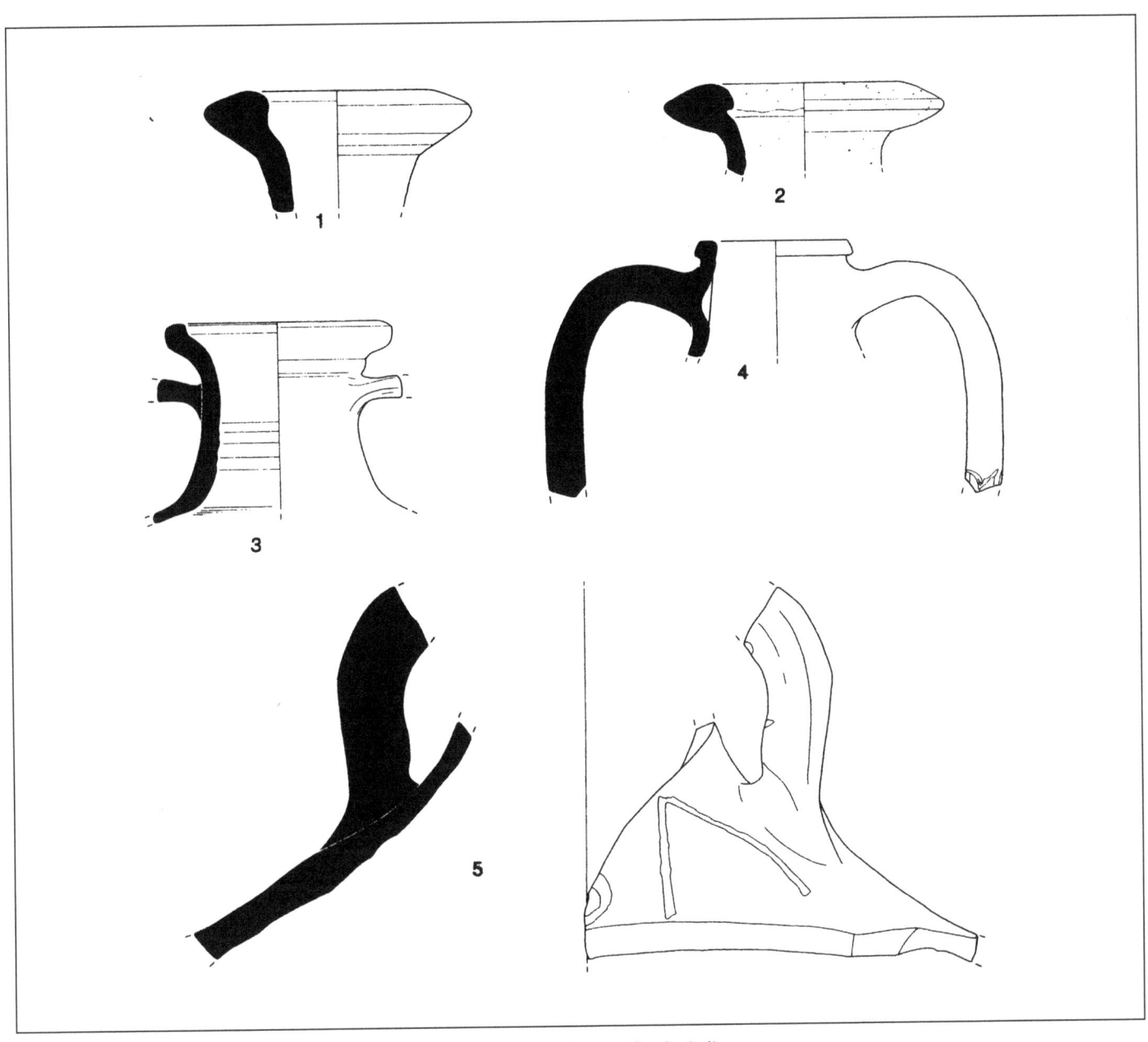

Fig. 21   Amphorae (Scale 1:4)

C.S.L   (the S is reversed and there are rounded stops positioned between the letters). Examples of this stamp are dated to the Hadrianic period (Callender 1965, no.470; Carreras and Funari 1998, no.427). 7000.

.C A ....   A partially legible stamp. F702 6024.

?S ?C A .. G R   (complete handle joined onto the body.) This stamp is difficult to parallel. F702 6555.

Gauloise 4

Rim:
Unusually for this type the sherd is a dark grey colour. This might be due to an accidentally reduced firing or perhaps it is evidence of burning. F702 6509. Fig. 21:3.

Bodysherds:
6000 (with rivet hole), 6001 (2), 6081, 6555 (2).

One Camulodunum 186sp part-handle and one Dressel 20 bodysherd. Context 1005.

Undesignated

Rim and Handle:
This is part of the top section of an amphora with a joining flat-topped rim and short oval-shaped handle. The fabric is hard and smoothish, light buff in colour throughout (Munsell 7.5YR 8/6). A thin section shows that the paste contains small pieces of volcanic rock, grains of green and colourless pyroxene, felspar and quartz. It is at present difficult to find an exact parallel for the form. However, the petrology suggests an origin in an area of volcanic rocks, perhaps Italy or the eastern Mediterranean region. F602 6032. Fig. 21:4.

Graffito

Handle and body fragment with a partial *graffito* (see report by Tomlin below). F702, 6555. Fig. 21:5.

THE SAMIAN POTTERY
by Steven Willis

Introduction

A total of 740 sherds of samian, weighing 9.8kg (EVE, by rims:19.83), was recovered from Orton's Pasture. Of this total, 401 sherds came from post-Phase 1 contexts and topsoil or were unstratified (see archive); these items have been examined but are not reported in full, being residual or not usefully stratified. The remaining 339 sherds from Phase 1 (Table 4) cover a date range from *c.* AD 70 to around AD 150, with the large majority of items being later Flavian and early second-century to *c.* AD 120 or 130. This chronological pattern is reflected amongst the samian from the later deposits and topsoil, amongst which there are few items which date to after *c.* AD 150.

The catalogue below follows a consistent format: it gives the context, the sherd type, vessel form (where identifiable) and quantitative data (with weights in grams), the source, and an estimate of the date of the sherd (*i.e.* the date range of deposits with which like pieces are normally associated). LG = La Graufesenque, the South Gaulish production centre. Two methodological problems exist. First, assigning vessels to the Drag. 18 or Drag. 18/31 categories is not always straightforward, especially when only the rim and/or wall of the vessel is represented, as these types are part of a form continuum; others might classify more items as 18/31 than this author has. Second, there is some general discrepancy in assigning South Gaulish vessels to the Flavian–Trajanic period: the literature demonstrates that it is more frequent for decorated vessels to be assigned to a date bracket ending at AD 110 than it is for South Gaulish plain wares which are not normally dated beyond AD 100.

Table 4: Quantities of Samian from Phase 1 Contexts

Feature	Weight (Grams)	Number of Sherds	EVE (by Rims)	Average Sherd Weight (Grams)
F602	311	24	0.36	12.9
F603	199	12	0.61	16.5
F604	276	12	0.41	23.0
F605	113	8	0.31	14.1
F608	129	10	0.35	12.9
F609	965	70	2.01	13.8
F612	213	17	0.50	12.5
F700	245	12	0.40	20.4
F701	121	28	0.65	4.3
F702	732	62	1.50	11.8
F704	147	10	0.20	14.7
F706	1	1	–	1.0
F707	40	3	0.07	13.3
F708	12	3	0.08	4.0
F711	192	20	0.18	9.6
F713	36	10	–	36.0
F715	167	15	0.27	11.1
F718	27	2	–	13.5
F719	91	8	0.11	11.4
F726	418	12	0.13	34.8
Totals:	**4435**	**339**	**8.14**	**13.1**

Catalogue of Samian from Phase 1

The catalogue is laid out in feature number order, and by context under each feature. A discussion of the material by feature groups follows.

F602

6020: 1 body sherd, Drag. 18/31R, 18g, Central Gaulish, *c.* AD 120–150.

6020: 1 body sherd, Drag. 37, 5g, LG *c.* AD 70–100.

6030: 1 rim, Drag. 18, 2g, RE: 0.06 Diam 160mm, LG, Flavian.

6030: 1 rim, Drag. 37, 15g, RE: 0.05 Diam 210mm, Central Gaulish, possibly first century micaceous Lezoux ware.

6030: 1 body sherd, Drag. 37, 5g, Dec: badly blurred ovolo, Central Gaulish, second century.

6030: 1 base, bowl, 14g, BE: 0.22 Diam 60mm, LG, first century.

6030: 1 body sherd, 1g, LG, first century.

6031: 2 conjoining rim sherds, Drag. 18, 12g, RE: 0.07 Diam 200mm, Les Martres-de-Veyre, *c.* AD 100–120.

6031: 1 rim, Drag. 27, 19g, RE: 0.08 Diam 130mm, Central Gaulish, *c.* AD 100–150.

6031: 1 body sherd, Drag. 30 or 37, 3g, Dec: ovolo of Potter X-6, with slanting corded tongue ending in a petalled rosette bent to the left (Stanfield and Simpson 1958, 148, type 2 Plate 75 Nos 13–22), Central Gaulish, *c.* AD 125–150.

6031: 1 base sherd, cup (perhaps from the same vessel as the Drag. 27 rim) 5g BE: 0.21 Diam 50mm Central Gaulish, second century.

6031: 1 body sherd, 1g, Central Gaulish.

6032: 1 rim, probably Drag. 18, 3g, RE: 0.05 Diam 180mm, LG, *c.* AD 60–100.

6032: 1 base sherd, Drag. 18/31R, 56g, BE: 0.17 Diam 110mm, Central Gaulish, *c.* AD 120–150.

6032: 1 body sherd, Drag. 37, 4g, Dec: vestige of basal wreath, Central Gaulish.

6032: 1 base sherd, Drag. 37, 95g, BE: 0.65 Diam 78mm, South Gaulish *c.* AD 80–110. Not stamped.

6032: 1 body sherd, 6g, Central Gaulish, second century.

6054: 1 base sherd, Drag. 18/31R or 31R, 19g, BE: 0.10 Diam 100mm, Central Gaulish, *c.* AD 120–150.

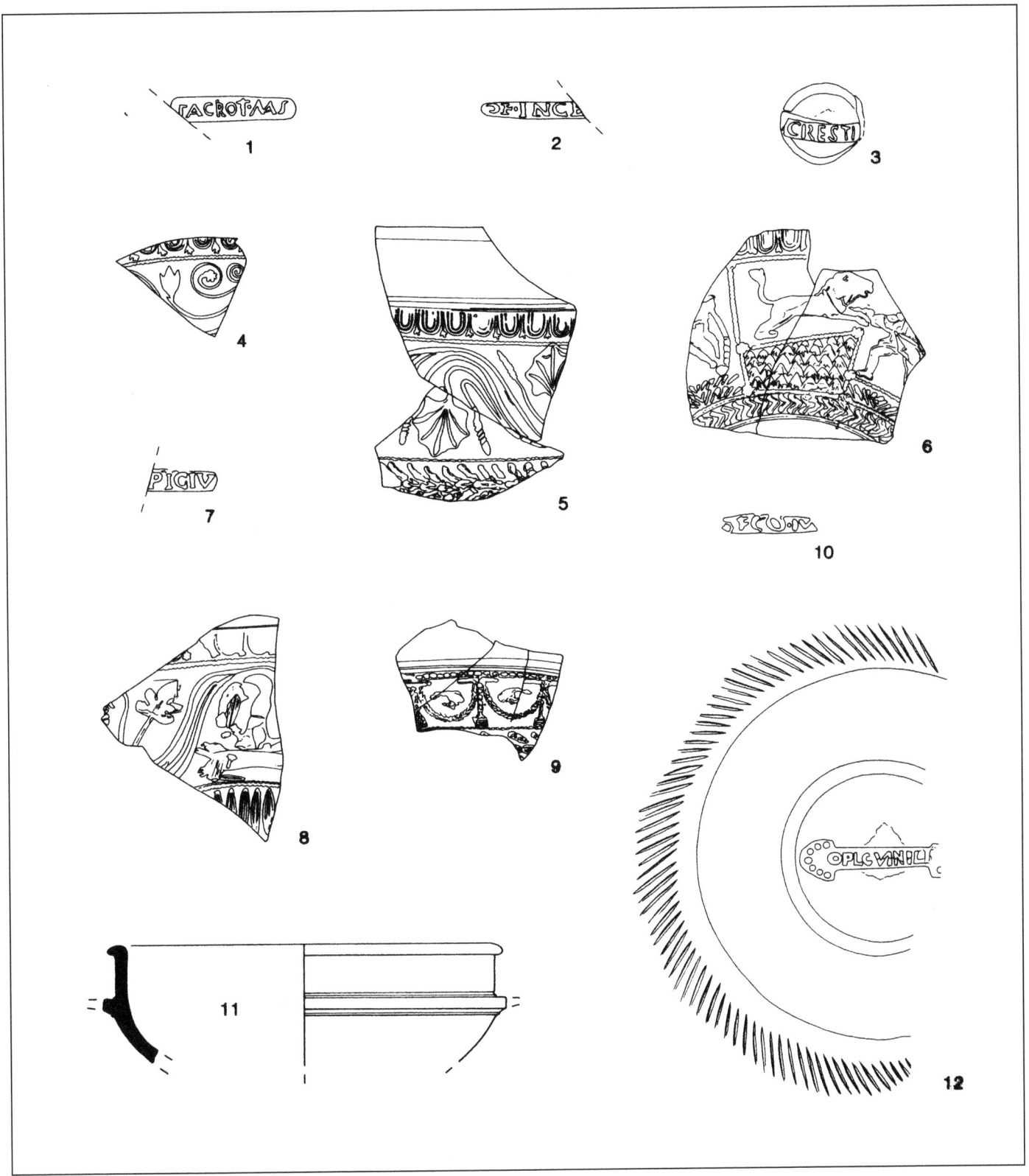

Fig. 22   Samian (Stamps, Scale 1:1, Others Scale 1:2)

6054: 1 body sherd, Drag. 33, 10g, Central Gaulish, second century. *Graffito* on underside of floor reads: '[...] M'.

6054: 1 body sherd, Drag. 37, 10g, Dec: isolated gladiator's shield to right of the type used by Potter X-3, G.I. Vibivs or Gelenvs (Stanfield and Simpson 1958, 11–13, fig. 4 No. 17), the ovolo, tongue and wavy line border are of the style of G.I Vibivs or Gelenvs, Central Gaulish, *c.* AD 120–140.

6054: 1 body sherd, Drag. 37, 6g, Dec: feet and lower costume of Diana with deer (Oswald 1936–7, No. 104B; Atkinson 1914, 61, Pl. 15 No. 76), above basal wreath, Les Martres-de-Veyre, *c.* AD 100–120.

6054: 1 body sherd, 1g, Central Gaulish.

6096: 1 rim, Drag. 33, 6g, RE: 0.10 Diam 120mm, Central Gaulish, second century.

F603

6033: 2 conjoining body sherds, Drag. 18, 10g, Les Martres-de-Veyre, *c.* AD 100–120.

6033: 1 rim, Drag. 33, 8g, RE: 0.11 Diam 130mm, Central Gaulish, second century.

6033: 1 base sherd and 1 body sherd, rouletted plate, 15g, BE: 0.10 Diam 100mm, LG, *c.* AD 70–100.

6033: 1 rim, bead-rimmed vessel, 2g, RE: 0.03 Diam uncertain, LG, *c.* AD 70–100.

6033: 1 body sherd, 1g, LG, *c.* AD 70–100.

6033: 1 body sherd, 4g, LG, *c.* AD 70–100. Abraded.

6033: 1 body sherd with scar where footring has become detached, 5g, Central Gaulish, probably first century micaceous Lezoux ware.

6033: 1 rim and 1 body sherd (probably from the same bead-rimmed vessel), 6g, RE: 0.04 Diam uncertain, Central Gaulish, second century. Both sherds have been drilled for repair.

6097: 1 profile, Drag. 18 (different vessel to sherds from 6033), Fig. 22:1. reads: SAC<u>IR</u>OT<u>MA</u>S, Sacirotus, 148g, RE: 0.43 Diam 176mm, BE: 0.57 Diam 80mm, Les Martres-de-Veyre, *c.* AD 100–120. A stamped Drag. 18/31 of this potter was recovered from the New Cemetery site (Hartley 1996, 89, No. 30).

F604

6052: 1 rim, Drag. 18/31 or 31, 6g, RE: 0.05 Diam 200mm, Central Gaulish, *c.* AD 140–190. Abraded.

6052: 1 body sherd, decorated form, 1g, Central Gaulish, ? *c.* AD 140–190. Abraded.

6094: 1 base sherd, Drag. 18, Fig. 22:2, reads: ? OFI[?<u>AV</u>]CE, 101g, BE: 0.52 Diam 80mm, LG, *c.* AD 70–110.

6094: 1 rim, Drag. 18 or 18/31, 7g, RE: 0.08 Diam 180mm, LG, *c.* AD 80–110.

6094: 1 rim and 1 base from the same Drag. 27g, Fig. 22:3, reads: CRESTI, Crestus, 42g, RE: 0.07 Diam 100mm, BE: 0.49 Diam 50mm, LG, *c.* AD 80–110.

6094: 1 body sherd, Drag. 37, 15g, Dec: the ovolo and tongue are somewhat blurred, but the latter is long and slants to the left, ending in four prongs, LG, *c.* AD 70–90.

6094: 1 body sherd, Drag. 37 (a sherd from the same vessel, from 6061, F 605), 1g, Central Gaulish, *c.* AD 120–150.

6094: 1 body sherd, 3g probably Central Gaulish.

6095: 1 base sherd, Drag. 18/31, 30g, BE: 0.20 Diam 100mm, Central Gaulish, *c.* AD 120–150.

6095: 1 rim, Drag. 37, 39g, RE: 0.17 Diam 170mm, Dec: chevron festoons containing spirals to the right, LG, *c.* AD 80–100.

6095: 1 rim, Drag. 37, 31g, RE: 0.04 Diam uncertain, Dec: worn mould, figures within panels, style of Libertvs, including figure illustrated by Stanfield and Simpson (1958, Pl. 55 inverted), Central Gaulish, *c.* AD 100–120.

F605

6061: 1 rim/wall sherd, Drag. 37 (a sherd from the same vessel from 6094, F 604), 51g, RE: 0.02 Diam uncertain, Dec: rather blurred, Donnavcvs style, half medallion (*cf.* Stanfield and Simpson 1958, Fig. 11 No.23) with hare below, Central Gaulish, before *c.* AD 150, perhaps Trajanic.

6065: 3 rim and 2 body sherds, Drag. 18, 38g, RE: 0.29 Diam 160mm, LG, *c.* AD 80–110.

6065: 1 body sherd, Drag. 37, 11g, Dec: stylistically similar to that of vessels from the Pompeii hoard of AD 79 (Atkinson 1914), scroll with large bud and rosette, with ovolo and thin tongue terminating in four prongs, turned slightly to the right, perhaps the work of M. Crestio or Crucuro, an apparently identical ovolo occurs in the group from the Carlisle annexe ditch of 1990 (Dickinson 1992, 53–7, fig. 5 Nos 1 and 9, where instances are cited; the item from Orton's Pasture resembles No. 9 more closely than No.1) dated *c.* AD 84, LG, *c.* AD 75–100. Fig. 22:4.

6065: 1 body sherd, Drag. 37, 13g, Dec: basal wreath of short s-shaped gadroons, panelled above with part of a tendril, and, more extant, a hound running to the left closely similar to that on a Drag. 37 from the recently excavated Period 1 ditch at Vindolanda (Birley 1994, fig. 8) though the latter runs to the right, LG, *c.* AD 80–100.

F608

6077: 2 rim sherds from the same Drag. 18, 20g, RE: 0.17 Diam 170mm, LG, *c.* AD 70–100.

6077: 1 rim and 3 conjoining body sherds, Drag. 29 (sherd from same vessel from 6010, F 609), 25g, RE: 0.04 Diam uncertain, Dec: festoon with tendrils and pomegranate buds, LG, *c.* AD 70–85. Thick wall.

6077: 1 base sherd and a body sherd from the same Drag. 30, 50g, BE: 0.37 Diam 70mm, LG, *c.* AD 70–100.

6077: 1 rim sherd, different Drag. 30 (adjoins sherd from 6089, F 609, while sherd from 6099 is also from the same vessel), 31g, RE: 0.09 Diam 150mm, Dec. (with sherd from 6089): scroll with large leaf and tassel, ovolo and tongue which terminates in three prongs turned to the right; the scroll is similar to the design on a Drag. 37 from Inchtuthil (Hartley 1985, 320, fig. 98 No. D18), LG, *c.* AD 70–100. Fig. 22:5.

6077: 1 rim, Drag. 30 or 37, 3g, RE: 0.05 Diam 170mm, LG.

F609

6010: 1 rim, Drag. 18, 5g, RE: 0.03 Diam uncertain, LG, *c.* AD 70–100.

6010: 1 body sherd, Drag. 29 (same vessel as 4 sherds from 6077, F608), 9g. See above under 6077. Abraded.

6010: 1 footring sherd, 5g, BE: 0.18 Diam 90mm, LG.

6016: 1 rim, Drag. 18, 16g, RE: 0.07 Diam 260mm, LG, *c.* AD 70–100.

6070: 1 rim, Drag. 18, 6g, RE: 0.06 Diam 190mm, LG, *c.* AD 70–100.

6070: 4 rims, 3 conjoining, Drag. 18/31, 29g, RE: 0.20 Diam 180mm, LG, *c.* AD 90–110.

6070: 1 rim, Drag. 18/31 or 18/31R, 12g, RE: 0.06 Diam 220mm, LG, *c.* AD 90–110.

6070: 1 body sherd, Drag. 27, 2g, LG, *c.* AD 70–110.

6070: 1 body sherd, Drag. 27, 4g, LG, *c.* AD 70–110.

6070: 1 base sherd, Drag. 27g, 12g, BE: 0.30 Diam 40mm, LG, *c.* AD 70–100. *Graffito* on exterior of lower curve: Fig. 23:1.

6070: 1 body sherd, Drag. 37 (adjoins 'eagle and hare' sherd from 6085), 11g, See below under 6085.

6070: 1 body sherd, Drag. 37 (adjoins 'lion and *bestiarius*' sherd from 6078), 24g. See below under 6078. Fig. 22:6.

6070: 1 base sherd and a body sherd, Drag. 37, 100g, BE: 0.23 Diam 100mm, Dec: panelled, including St Andrew's Cross motif similar to that of a Drag. 37 amongst the Pompeii hoard (Atkinson 1914, Pl. 16 No. 78), above a trifid bud basal wreath, LG, *c.* AD 70–100.

6070: 2 conjoining rim sherds, Drag. 37, 30g, RE: 0.14 Diam 230mm, Dec: the ovolo is that described by Atkinson as belonging to the potter of the large rosette (1914 Pl. 7–10), ovolos of this type were employed by Frontinus, Paullus and M. Crestio, LG, *c.* AD 70–90.

6070: 1 body sherd, Drag. 37, 26g, Dec: the decoration is in comparatively high relief, in panels and a festoon, with wavy line borders, the 'skirt' of a costumed figure is represented LG, *c.* AD 70–100.

6070: 1 rim, small Drag. 37 or 30 lacking internal groove, 11g, RE: 0.11 Diam 150mm, Dec: very blurred ovolo, LG, *c.* AD 80–110.

6070: 1 rim, Drag. 37, 13g, RE: 0.07 Diam 220mm, Dec: very blurred ovolo, LG, *c.* AD 80–110.

6070: 1 body sherd, decorated form, 2g, Dec: ? hound, LG.

6070: 1 body sherd, Dech. 67, 3g, Dec: legs and feet of hoofed creature, LG, *c.* AD 80–100.

6070: 2 conjoining base sherds, plate, 33g, BE: 0.27 Diam 80mm, LG, *c.* AD 70–100.

6070: 1 body sherd, plate, 16g, LG, *c.* AD 70–100.

6070: 1 footring sherd, 2g, BE: 0.01 Diam uncertain, LG.

6070: 1 body sherd, 6g, LG. Thick walled; burnt.

6078: 1 profile and an adjoining rim, Drag. 15/17 (same vessel as sherds in 6085 and 6089), Partial Stamp, Fig. 22:7, reads: [...]PICIV, 125g, RE: 0.41 Diam 150mm, BE: 0.51 Diam 80mm, LG, *c.* AD 70–90. Cursive *Graffito* on underside, within footring. Fig. 23:2.

6078: 1 rim, Drag. 18, 20g, RE: 0.07 Diam 200mm, LG, *c.* AD 70–100.

6078: 1 base sherd, Drag. 37, 42g, BE: 0.29 Diam 80mm, LG, *c.* AD 70–100.

6078: 1 body sherd, Drag. 37 (same vessel as sherds from 6085 and 6089 with blurred ovolo from worn mould), 3g. See below.

6078: 1 body sherd, Drag. 37, 2g, Dec: part of ? small tailed creature, perhaps lion, LG, *c.* AD 70–110.

6078: 1 body sherd, Drag. 37 (adjoins 'lion sherd' from 6070), 28g, Dec. (with sherd from 6070): *bestiarius* (Oswald 1936–7, No, 1102) with lion similar to (or the same as) Oswald's 1497 (Oswald 1936–7); ovolo blurred. LG, *c.* AD 70–110. Fig. 22:6.

6078: 1 rim sherd, Drag. 37, 12g, RE: 0.06 Diam 190mm, Dec: blurred ovolo with three pronged tongue, bead border and part of spiral, LG, *c.* AD 70–90.

6080: 1 base sherd and a conjoining body sherd, Drag. 18 (2 sherds from same vessel in 6085), 35g, BE: 0.26 Diam 90m, LG, *c.* AD 70–100.

6080: 1 body sherd, Drag. 27, 7g, LG, *c.* AD 70–100. Trimmed and smoothed at junction of the two curves to create an adapted vessel.

6080: 1 rim, Drag. 30, 31g, RE: 0.15 Diam 140mm, Dec: ovolo with somewhat blurred three pronged tongue, below bead border is the front part of a boar, running to the left, similar to Oswald's types 1671 and 1686 (Oswald 1936–70) and a boar on a Drag. 29 from the Pompeii hoard (Atkinson 1914, Pl. 3 No. 12), LG, *c.* AD 70–90.

6085: 1 rim, Drag. 15/17 (adjoins sherd from 6089), 5g, RE: 0.07 Diam 150mm, LG, *c.* AD 70–90.

6085: 1 rim, Drag. 15/17, 4g, RE: 0.06 Diam 160mm, LG, *c.* AD 70–90.

6085: 2 rims, Drag. 18 (same vessel as 2 sherds from 6080), 6g, RE: 0.06 Diam 170mm, LG, *c.* AD 70–100.

6085: 1 rim, Drag. 27, 4g, RE: 0.10 Diam 130mm, LG, *c.* AD 70–100.

6085: 1 rim and 2 body sherds, Drag. 37 (another rim from this vessel occurs in 6089), 40g, RE: 0.07 Diam 180mm, Dec. (with sherd from 6089): worn mould; palisade of straight thin leafs, above which is an inhabited scroll, including pomegranate bud, lower lobe contains an eagle, head to left over and inverted hare, upper lobe contains foliage with leaf similar to one appearing on a Drag. 37 from the Period 1 ditch at Vindolanda (Birley 1994, fig. 8), the general design is similar to that on a 37 amongst the Pompeii hoard of AD 79 (Atkinson 1914, Pl. 13 No. 72) upon which occurs an identical eagle, perhaps the work of Frontinus, LG, *c.* AD 70–110. Fig. 22:8.

6085: 2 body sherds, Drag. 37 (1 adjoins sherd from 6089), 15g. See below under 6089.

6085: 1 body sherd, Dech. 67 (adjoins sherd from 6089, this feature and 6093, F612), 5g, Dec: festoon containing geese motifs alternatively to left and right, a similar festoon with identical birds is known from Exeter on a Drag. 29 (Dannell 1992, 40–2, fig. 1 No. 12; the geese are in Oswald 1936–7, Nos 2244 and 2286) dated as Neronian, but they also occur on vessels from Flavian contexts, as for instance the annexe ditch at Carlisle (Dickinson 1992), LG, *c.* AD 65–90. Fig. 22:9.

6087: 1 rim, Drag. 18, 6g, RE: 0.11 Diam 150mm, LG, first century. Perhaps partially burnt.

6087: 1 base sherd and conjoining body sherd, Drag. 37, 71g, BE: 0.20 Diam 90mm, Dec: basal wreath of s-shaped gadroons, above which is a simple tendril and rosette design, all rather blurred, LG, *c.* AD 80–110.

6089: 1 profile sherd, Drag. 15/17 (adjoins sherd from 6085), 62g, RE: 0.18 Diam 150mm, BE: 0.25 Diam 80mm. See 6085. Together with sherd from 6085 this item comprises an exact quarter of this vessel.

6089: 1 body sherd, probably Drag. 18, 1g, LG, first century.

6089: 1 rim, Drag. 18, 3g, RE: 0.04 Diam uncertain, LG, *c.* AD 65–100.

6089: 1 rim, small Drag. 27, 1g, RE: 0.10 Diam 80mm, LG, *c.* AD 70–100.

6089: 1 body sherd, Drag. 30 (adjoins sherd from 6077, F 608, while a sherd from 6099 is also from this vessel), 13g. See above under 6077. Fig.22:5.

6089: 1 rim, Drag. 37 (same vessel as 3 sherds from 6085), 11g, RE: 0.12 Diam 180mm.

6089: 1 body sherd, Drag. 37 (same vessel as 2 sherds from 6085), 14g, Dec: lower frieze is a vegetal scroll with a cordate leaf and in the extant lower lobe is a crudely executed lotus flower above a hound of the same type as that on a Drag. 37 from 6065 (above), LG, *c.* AD 80–110.

6089: 1 body sherd, Dech. 67 (adjoins sherd from 6085, another sherd in 6093, F 612), 3g. See above under 6085. Fig. 22:8

6089: 1 rim, bead-rimmed vessel, 1g, RE: 0.02 Diam uncertain, LG, *c.* AD 70–100.

6099: 1 rim, Drag. 30 (same vessel as sherds from 6077, F608 and 6089, this feature), 12g, RE: 0.06 Diam 170mm. See above under 6077. Fig. 22:5.

6099: 2 conjoining body sherds, Drag. 37, 6g, Dec: ? festoon, ovolo and tongue with fist-like terminal, LG, *c.* AD 70–110.

F612

6088: 1 rim, Drag. 37, 19g, RE: 0.05 Diam 220mm, Dec: very blurred ovolo above wreath, LG, *c.* AD 80–110.

6090: 1 profile, Drag. 18/31, 91g, RE: 0.09 Diam 160mm, BE: 0.45 Diam 80mm, LG, *c.* AD 90–110.

Herringbone and dot *graffito* on underside of base, within footring, consisting of a short spine with three pairs of ribs pointing outwards from the centre of the vessel; two dots occur on the outer side approximately in alignment with the end of the ribs.

6090: 1 body sherd, Drag. 30, 9g, Dec: parts of a festoon, panel zonal and elaborate basal wreath, LG, *c.* AD 70–100.

6090: 1 body sherd, Drag. 37, 9g, Dec: chevron panel and basal wreath, LG, *c.* AD 70–110.

6093: 1 rim, Drag. 18, 15g, RE: 0.11 Diam 170mm, LG, *c.* AD 80–110.

6093: 1 body sherd, Drag. 18 or 18/31, 3g, LG, *c.* AD 80–110.

6093: 1 body sherd, prob Drag. 18/31R, 9g, LG, *c.* AD 90–110.

6093: 3 rim sherds and 2 body sherds from the same Drag. 27, 29g, RE: 0.08 Diam 160mm, LG, *c.* AD 70–100.

6093: 2 rim sherds, Drag. 37, 13g, RE: 0.17 Diam 190mm, LG, *c.* AD 70–110.

6093: 2 body sherds probably from the same Drag. 37, 12g, LG, *c.* AD 70–100. One sherd, burnt

6093: 1 body sherd, Dech. 67 (from same vessel as sherds from 6085 and 6089, F 609), 4g. See above under 6085. Fig. 22:9.

F700

6511: 3 rim sherds, Drag. 18, 28g, RE: 0.16 Diam 170mm, LG, *c.* AD 80–110.

6511: 3 rim sherds and 3 base sherds, Drag. 18/31, Fig. 22:10, reads: OFCOS.IV, ? Cosius Julius, 204g, RE: 0.24 Diam 160mm, BE: 0.70 Diam 80mm, LG, *c.* AD 90–110. *Graffito* on underside, within footring. Fig. 23:3.

6511: 1 body sherd, Drag. 27, 1g, LG, first century.

6511: 1 body sherd, Drag. 30 or 37, 6g, Dec: heavily abraded ovolo, LG, *c.* AD 70–100.

6516: 1 body sherd, Drag. 29, 6g, Dec: head of a deer, to right, Oswald's type 1699 (Oswald 1936–7), LG, *c.* AD 60–80.

F701

6504: 1 rim, Drag. 18 (same vessel as Drag. 18 represented by 2 sherds from 6506 and body sherd in 6507; the rim from 6518 is probably the same vessel), 6g, RE: 0.05 Diam 170mm, LG, *c.* AD 80–110. Abraded

6504: 1 base sherd, Stamp, abraded, reads: [...]CVM[...], 17g, BE: 0.15 Diam 90mm, LG, *c.* AD 70–100.

6506: 2 rims, Drag. 18 (adjoining sherds from 6504 and 6507, probably same vessel as rim from 6518), 10g, RE: 0.11 Diam 170mm. See above under 6504.

6506: 1 rim, Drag. 18, 7g, RE: 0.08 Diam 180mm, LG, *c.* AD 70–100. Abraded.

6506: 1 rim, Drag. 18, 5g, RE: 0.03 Diam uncertain, LG, *c.* AD 70–100. Abraded.

6506: 1 rim, Drag. 18, 2g, RE: 0.07 Diam 170mm, LG, *c.* AD 70–100. Abraded.

6506: 1 rim, Drag. 18, 3g, RE: 0.03 Diam uncertain, LG, *c.* AD 70–100. Abraded.

6506: 2 rims, Drag. 27, 4g. RE: 0.12 Diam 110mm, LG, *c.* AD 70–100. Abraded.

6506: 1 body sherd, Drag. 37 (different vessel to sherds from 6518), 7g, Dec: completely blurred ovolo, LG, *c.* AD 90–110.

6506: 1 body sherd, Drag. 37 (different vessel to sherds from 6518), 2g, Dec: ovolo heavily abraded, LG, *c.* AD 70–110.

6506: 2 body sherds (probably from same Drag. 37 as sherds from 6518), 4g, LG. Abraded.

6506: 1 base sherd, cup, 4g, BE: 0.15 Diam 60mm, Probably LG, first century.

6506: 1 body sherd, 1g, LG. Excoriated.

6507: 1 body sherd, Drag. 18 (adjoining sherds from 6504 and 6506, probably same vessel as rim from 6518), 14g. See above under 6504.

6507: 1 body sherd, Drag. 27, 2g, LG, first century. Abraded.

6507: 1 rim, Drag. 27, 3g, RE: 0.07 Diam 160mm, LG, *c.* AD 70–110. Abraded.

6507: 1 body sherd, decorated form, 3g, LG, *c.* AD 70–110. Abraded.

6507: 1 rim, bead-rimmed vessel, possibly a Drag. 18/31, 5g, RE: 0.07 Diam 180mm, LG, *c.* AD 90–110. Abraded.

6518: 1 rim, Drag. 18 (probably same vessel as rims from 6504 and 6506), 6g, RE: 0.02 Diam 170mm, LG, *c.* AD 70–110. Abraded.

6518: 3 body sherds (probably from the same Drag. 37), 9g, Dec: large lanceolate leaves, ovolo and tongue with abraded terminal resembling an inverted heart, LG, *c.* AD 80–110. Abraded.

6518: 1 body sherd, 1g, LG.

6518: 1 body sherd, 1g, LG. Abraded.

6518: 1 body sherd, 5g, LG. Abraded.

F702, S2

6503: 1 body sherd, Drag. 30, 3g, Montans, *c.* AD 80–100.

6505: 1 body sherd, Drag. 27, 2g, LG, first century.

6505: 1 rim, Drag. 30 or 37, 10g, RE: 0.04 Diam uncertain, LG, *c.* AD 70–110.

6505: 1 body sherd, Drag. 37, 2g, Dec: only a vestige of the upper part of the ovolo is represented; internal grooves level with the top of the external decoration *cf.* Drag. 30, LG, *c.* AD 70–110.

6505: 1 body sherd, 4g, LG, *c.* AD 70–110.

6505: 1 body sherd, 3g, micaceous Lezoux ware, first century.

6505: 1 flake, 1g, LG.

F702, S3

6527: 1 rim, Drag. 18, 6g, RE: 0.03 Diam uncertain, LG, *c.* AD 70–100. Heavily abraded.

6527: 1 rim, Drag. 18/31, 26g, RE: 0.13 Diam 180mm, micaceous Lezoux ware, *c.* AD 90–120.

6527: 1 base sherd, 13g, BE: 0.08 Diam 130mm, LG, *c.* AD 70–100. Burnt and heavily abraded.

6527: 1 body sherd, 1g, LG, first century.

6527: 1 body sherd, 2g, LG, first century.

6527: 1 rim, bead-rimmed form, 8g, RE: 0.03 Diam uncertain, Central Gaulish, second century. Heavily abraded.

F702, S4

6525: 1 body sherd, Drag. 18 or 18/31, 6g, LG, *c.* AD 70–110.

6525: 1 rim, Drag. 18 or 18/31, 7g, RE: 0.07 Diam 170m, Les Martres-de-Veyre, *c.* AD 100–130.

6525: 1 profile, Drag. 18/31, 94g, RE: 0.27 Diam 180mm, BE: 0.23 Diam 80mm, LG, *c.* AD 90–110.

6525: 1 body sherd, Drag. 37, 4g, Dec: long thin ovolo with tongue terminating in a club shape, Les Martres-de-Veyre, *c.* AD 100–130.

6525: 1 body sherd, Drag. 37, 4g, Dec: small area of blurred decoration, tongue is three pronged and slants to the left, LG, *c.* AD 90–110.

6525: 1 body sherd, Drag. 37, 9g, Dec: indistinct, LG, *c.* 70–110. Heavily burnt and damaged.

6525: 1 base sherd, from cup, 4g, BE 0.16 Diam 50mm, LG, *c.* AD 70–100.

6525: 1 body sherd, 2g, ? Central Gaulish.

6525: 1 rim, bead-rimmed form, 2g, RE: 0.04 Diam uncertain, LG, first century.

6525: 1 rim, bead-rimmed form, 5g, RE: 0.07 Diam 200m, Les Martres-de-Veyre, *c.* AD 100–130.

6526: 1 body sherd, from a bowl, 6g, LG, *c.* AD 70–100.

6526: 1 fragment from a footring, 1g, LG, first century.

6526: 1 body sherd, 2g, LG, first century.

F702, S5

6520: 1 base sherd, bowl, probably Drag. 37, 13g, BE: 0.26 Diam 80mm, LG, *c.* AD 70– 100.

F702, S6

6571: 1 body sherd, probably Drag. 37, 4g, Dec: spiral and tendril decoration, LG, *c.* AD 80–110.

6571: 1 body sherd (probably from the same vessel as the item above), 6g, LG, *c.* AD 80–110.

6571: 1 body sherd, 1g, LG, first century.

6571: 1 rim, bead-rimmed vessel, 4g, RE: 0.04 Diam uncertain, Central Gaulish, second century.

6572: 1 rim and two joining body sherds, Drag. 37 (probably the same vessel as the two sherds from 6571), 38g, RE: 0.12 Diam 200mm, Dec: ovolo with three or four pronged tongue, hindquarters of a ? lion, LG, *c.* AD 80–110.

F702

6509: 1 base sherd, Drag. 18/31R, 32g, BE: 0.07 Diam 80mm, LG, *c.* AD 90–110.

6509: 1 base sherd, Drag. 27, 9g, BE: 0.20 Diam 40mm, Les Martres-de-Veyre, *c.* AD 100–130.

6509: 2 conjoining rims, Drag. 36, 19g, RE: 0.12 Diam 180mm, LG, *c.* AD 70–100.

6509: 3 body sherds, Drag. 37, plus another body sherd probably from this vessel, 55g, Dec: trifid basal wreath, panelled decoration, LG, *c.* AD 80–110.

6509: 1 body sherd, Drag. 37, 6g, Dec: part of winged ? cupid figure, LG, *c.* AD 70–100.

6509: 1 base sherd, Drag. 37, 19g, BE: 0.17 Diam 90mm, Dec: vestige of basal wreath, LG, *c.* AD 70–100.

6509: 1 base sherd, bowl, 14g, BE: 0.10 Diam 90mm, LG, *c.* AD 80–110.

6509: 1 rim, bead-rimmed vessel, 13g, RE: 0.03 Diam uncertain, Les Martres-de-Veyre, *c.* AD 100–130.

6519: 1 flange sherd, Curle 11, grooved, 6g, Central Gaulish, *c.* AD 100–150.

6519: 1 rim, bead-rimmed vessel, 4g, RE: 0.06 Diam 180mm, LG, *c.* AD 70–100.

6537: 1 body sherd, 1g, LG, first century.

6555: 1 body sherd, Drag. 15/17R or 18R, 8g, LG, *c.* AD 70–100.

6555: 1 rim, Drag. 18 or 18/31, 11g, RE: 0.10 Diam 160mm, LG, *c.* AD 80–110.

6555: 2 rim sherds from the same Drag. 18/31, 49g, RE: 0.18 Diam 160mm, 1 sherd drilled for repair. Probably Les Martres-de-Veyre, *c.* AD 100–130.

6555: 1 body sherd, Drag. 27, 7g, Les Martres-de-Veyre, *c.* AD 100–130.

6555: 1 body sherd, Drag. 30 or 37, 6g, Dec: tiny vestige of ovolo, Les Martres-de-Veyre, *c.* AD 100–130.

6555: 1 body sherd, probably Drag. 30 or 37, 9g, Central Gaulish, *c.* AD 100–130.

6555: 1 body sherd, Drag. 33, 7g, Central Gaulish, second century.

6555: 1 body sherd, Drag. 37, 9g, Dec: St Andrew's Cross motif, badly blurred, LG, *c.* AD 90–110.

6555: 1 base sherd, different Drag. 37, 136g, BE: 0.63 Diam 70mm, Dec: short straight gadroons; not stamped, LG, *c.* AD 70–100.

6555: 1 rim, Curle 11 with bead rim, 15g, RE: 0.05 Diam 140mm, micaceous Lezoux ware, *c.* AD 70–110. Fig. 22:11.

6555: 1 body sherd, possibly from the Drag. 33, represented by another sherd from this context, 3g, Central Gaulish, second century.

6599: 1 rim, bead-rimmed vessel, 3g, RE: 0.04 Diam uncertain, LG, *c.* AD 70–100.

F704

6529: 1 base sherd, Drag. 18/31, 12g, BE: 0.06 Diam 80mm, LG, *c.* AD 80–110. Heavily abraded.

6529: 1 base sherd, Drag. 18/31, vestige of Stamp, reads: [...]V, 44g, BE: 0.20 Diam 90mm, Les Martres-de-Veyre, *c.* 100–130.

6529: 1 body sherd, probably Drag. 18/31R, 11g, Central Gaulish, *c.* AD 120–150.

6529: 1 body sherd, small Drag. 37, 4g, Dec: heavily abraded ovolo, LG, *c.* AD 70–110. Abraded; slightly burnt.

6529: 2 body sherds, bowl, 10g, Central Gaulish, *c.* AD 100–150. Abraded.

6532: 1 rim, from small Drag. 30 or 37, 3g, RE: 0.03 Diam uncertain, LG, *c.* AD 70–110.

6544: 1 rim, Drag. 18, 5g, RE: 0.06 Diam 200mm, LG, *c.* AD 70–100. Abraded.

6545: 1 base sherd, probably 18/31, 36g, BE: 0.30 Diam 100mm, LG, *c.* AD 90–110. Abraded.

6545: 1 rim, large Drag. 33, 22g, RE: 0.11 Diam 170mm, Les Martres-de-Veyre, *c.* AD 100–130. Abraded.

F706

6531: 1 body sherd, 1g, LG, first century. Abraded.

F707

6538: 1 rim, Drag. 18 or 18/31, 31g, RE: 0.07 Diam 190mm, LG, *c.* AD 70–110.

6538: 1 body sherd, Drag. 30 or 37, 4g, LG, *c.* AD 70–100. Abraded.

6538: 1 body sherd, bowl, 5g, LG, *c.* AD 70–100.

F708

6536: 1 rim and a conjoining body sherd, Drag. 18 or 18/31, 10g, RE: 0.08 Diam 250mm, LG, *c.* AD 70–110.

6536: 1 body sherd, from a cup, 2g, LG, *c.* AD 70–100.

F711

6543: 1 body sherd, ? Drag. 18, 2g, LG, first century. Heavily abraded.

6543: 1 body sherd, from a cup, 1g, LG, first century. Heavily abraded.

6543: 3 body sherds, from a bowl, 9g, LG, first century. Flakes; heavily abraded.

6543: 1 body sherd, 3g, LG, first century. Heavily abraded.

6548: 1 base sherd, from Drag. 15/17 or 18, 27g, BE: 0.15 Diam 120mm, LG, *c.* AD 70–100. Abraded; burnt.

6548: 1 body sherd, Drag. 30 or 37, 3g, Dec: ovolo with three pronged tongue slanted to right, LG, *c.* AD 70–100. Abraded.

6548: 1 body sherd, decorated vessel, 4g, LG, *c.* AD 70–100. Heavily abraded.

6548: 1 rim sherd, form uncertain, 1g, RE 0.04 Diam uncertain, Montans first century. Heavily abraded.

6548: 3 body sherds (probably from the same vessel as the 3 body sherds from 6543), 5g, LG, first century. Flakes; abraded.

6548: 1 body sherd, 3g, LG, first century. Excoriated.

6548: 1 body sherd, 3g, LG, first century. Excoriated.

6551: 1 base sherd, from a bowl, 114g, BE: 0.70 Diam 90mm, LG, *c.* AD 80–110. Not stamped; heavily abraded.

6569: 1 rim, Drag. 18, 9g, RE: 0.08 Diam 180mm, LG, *c.* AD 70–100. Abraded.

6569: 1 body sherd, Drag. 27, 6g, LG, first century. Burnt. heavily abraded.

6569: 2 conjoining rim sherds, Drag. 27, 2g, RE: 0.06 Diam 140mm, LG, *c.* AD 70–110. Abraded.

F713

6552: 1 base sherd, Drag. 15/17 or 18, vestige of Stamp reads: [...]TO, 36g, BE: 0.34 Diam 86mm, LG, *c.* AD 70–90. Abraded.

F715

6553: 1 base sherd, Drag. 18 (adjoins sherd from 6559), 42g, BE: 0.20 Diam 90mm, LG, *c.* AD 70–100.

6553: 1 base sherd, Drag. 37, 42g, BE: 0.15 Diam 80mm, LG, *c.* AD 90–110.

6554: 1 rim, Drag. 33, 14g, RE: 0.12 Diam 140mm, LG, *c.* AD 70–100.

6554: 1 body sherd, 3g, LG, *c.* AD 70–100.

6559: 1 base sherd, Drag. 18 (adjoins sherd from 6553), 3g, BE: 0.05. See above under 6553.

6564: 1 body sherd, 1g, LG.

6564: 1 base and a conjoining body sherd, cup, 9g, BE: 0.10 Diam 80mm, Les Martres-de-Veyre, *c.* AD 100–130.

6565: 1 rim, Drag. 18, 30g, RE: 0.11 Diam 140mm, LG, *c.* AD 90–110.

6565: 2 conjoining body sherds, Drag. 27, 8g, LG, *c.* AD 70–110.

6565: 1 fragmentary rim, Drag. 33, 3g, RE: 0.04 Diam uncertain, LG, *c.* AD 70–100.

6565: 1 body sherd, 3g, LG.

6565: 1 base and a conjoining body sherd, bowl, 9g, BE: 0.30 Diam 80mm, LG, *c.* AD 70–110. Thin walled.

F718

6576: 2 conjoining body sherds, Drag. 18/31, 27g, Les Martres-de-Veyre, *c.* AD 100–130.

F719

6577: 1 base sherd, Drag. 18/31, 23g, BE: 0.22 Diam 90mm, Central Gaulish, *c.* AD 120–150. Burnt.

6577: 1 rim, Drag. 27, 3g, RE: 0.03 Diam uncertain, probably Central Gaulish, *c.* AD 100–130.

6577: 1 body sherd, Drag. 29 or 37 (from same vessel as conjoining sherds from 6581), 8g, LG, *c.* AD 70–110.

6577: 1 body sherd, Drag. 37, 8g, Dec: too abraded to be suitable for drawing but certainly the work of the Trajanic potter X-3 whose work is widely distributed in Britain (Stanfield and Simpson 1958), on this sherd appear his warrior (Oswald 1936–7, No. 202a) and basal wreath (Stanfield and Simpson 1958, Pl. 11 No. 137 but to the right), Central Gaulish, *c.* AD 100–120. Abraded.

6581: 2 conjoining body sherds, Drag. 29 or 37 (from same vessel as sherd from 6577), 15g. See above under 6577.

6581: 1 body sherd, Drag. 29 or 37, 4g, LG, *c.* AD 70–100. Heavily abraded.

6581: 1 rim, Drag. 30 or 37, 30g, RE: 0.08 Diam 220mm, Les Martres-de-Veyre, *c.* AD 100–130.

F726

6595: 1 body sherd, Drag. 18/31R (adjoins sherds from 6613), 11g. See below under 6613.

6595: 1 rim, Drag. 37, 6g, RE: 0.04 Diam uncertain, Dec: no ovolo but, on vestigial evidence, a substitute vegetation motif, Les Martres-de-Veyre, *c.* AD 100–130.

6595: 1 rim, Drag. 36, 15g, RE: 0.09 Diam 180mm, LG, *c.* AD 70–110.

6595: 1 base sherd, Drag. 37, 121g, BE: 0.33 Diam 110mm, Dec: panelled, bead borders, Les Martres-de-Veyre, *c.* AD 100–130. Not stamped; Abraded.

6595: 1 body sherd, Drag. 37, 5g, Dec: blurred and indistinct ovolo, below which is a simple spiral festoon common to the Flavian period (*cf.* Hartley 1985, fig. 98 D6, but spiral to right), LG, *c.* AD 70–110. Unusually thin-walled (3–4mm).

6595: 1 base sherd, Drag. 37, 34g, BE: 0.15 Diam 120mm, Dec: trifid basal wreath of Flavian type known from the Pompeii hoard (Atkinson 1914, No. 64) and at Inchtuthil (Hartley 1985, 321 fig. 98 D24), LG, *c.* AD 70–100.

6595: 1 base sherd, Drag. 37, 61g, BE: 0.42 Diam 80mm, Dec: basal wreath of triple poppy-heads to left, these are rather blurred, LG, *c.* AD 80–110.

6595: 1 body sherd, from decorated vessel, 2g, Dec: vestige of ovolo, LG, *c.* AD 70–100.

6595: 1 base sherd, cup (adjoining sherd from 6613), tiny vestige of Stamp, reads: [...]R, 22g, BE: 0.48 Diam 50mm, LG, *c.* AD 80–110.

6613: 1 base sherd and a conjoining body sherd, Drag. 18/31R, Fig. 22:12 reads: OFLCVIRILI, L Cosivs Virilis, (adjoining sherd from 6595), 134g, BE: 0.53 Diam 96mm, LG, *c.* AD 90–110.

6613: 1 body sherd, cup (adjoins base of cup from 6595), 7g. See under 6595 above.

Discussion

The Groups:

Pits to the north of Enclosure 1

Four pits lying to the north of Enclosure 1, in Area A, all contained samian of the first half of the second century AD (together with residual earlier pieces). Within this first half of the second century date bracket there is some difference between these features, however, the recovered groups are small and so the samian evidence certainly needs to be assessed alongside other indices of date. A large proportion of the samian items present in these contexts is South Gaulish. The Drag. 37 decorated bowl is comparatively common amongst this group. The average sherd weight for samian from these pits was above or near to the site mean (*cf.* Table 4).

F602.   As with other features in this area F602 produced an amount of residual South Gaulish samian, but the presence of Hadrianic–early Antonine items amongst its lower fills (*e.g.* 6032 and 6054) suggests that its filling occurred during the second quarter of the second century or later.

F603.   The samian from this feature is of earlier date than that from F602, with nothing necessarily later than *c.* AD 120. Whilst context 6033 yielded a group of consistently small fragments, context 6097 contained an unusually large proportion of a plate (a Drag. 18) approximating to half of a vessel; this had perhaps been deliberately broken (as may also have been the case with the Drag. 15/17 in F609).

F604.   Apart from context 6052, which produced two sherds of Antonine date, the latest samian from the excavated fills of this feature is Hadrianic–early Antonine in date, not necessarily later than *c.* AD 130. Contexts 6094 and 6095 produced sherds which were generally above average weight.

F605.   This feature also contained second century samian, though nothing necessarily later than *c.* AD 120.

Ditch Fills of Enclosure 1
There is a contrast between the date of the samian from the north-east corner and eastern sides of this feature and that from the ditch on the southern side. This difference not withstanding, the average sherd weights from the various sections of the enclosure are closely consistent and cluster around the site mean (Table 4).

Ditch Fills of Enclosure 1: North-East Corner
The samian from these contexts is Flavian or Flavian to early Trajanic. The groups from F609 and F612 have latest pieces dating to *c.* AD 90–110, while the small group from F608 dates to *c.* AD 70–100. Significantly there are no items from Les Martres, indicating that these contexts were deposited before the consumption of this ware at the site, which presumably began, as elsewhere, during the early Trajanic period. Hence the samian evidence suggests that the ditches of Enclosure 1 at this point were filled prior to *c.* AD 110, probably during the late Flavian period.

F608.   Feature F608 produced a small group of Flavian samian, of 'fresh' appearance. Five vessels are represented, including four decorated vessels, one a Drag. 29.

F609.   The samian from the various contexts within this feature forms a sizeable and highly consistent group. It is all South Gaulish and Flavian to early Trajanic; the latest material has a date bracket of *c.* AD 90 –110. The composition of the group by form is indicative of its date, for there are only two Drag. 15/17s represented, one of which appears to have been broken, into a half and two quarters. Similarly the Drag. 29 bowl form is represented by just a single sherd, from a layer across the top of this feature, 6010, immediately below topsoil (this item appears to be residual). There are numerous cross-joins between contexts and little sign of abrasion of the sherds, many of which are large fragments, all of which seems to indicate a rapid sequence of filling. Two vessels display *graffiti*.

F 612.   The samian recovered from F612 is contemporary with that from F609 and in like condition; again it is all South Gaulish. There is at least one cross-join between these groups.

Ditch Fills of Enclosure 1: Southern and South-East Sides

F702.   This feature yielded a varied samian group which, collectively, is comparatively large. South Gaulish ware is prominent, though the Drag. 29 and 15/17 forms are absent and there are Central Gaulish items of second century date.

The modest quantity of samian from F702 S2, dating to *c.* AD 70–110, is at variance with that from the other sections of F702. The samian recovered from other sections (*e.g.* S3, S4 and S6) includes two Central Gaulish pieces from S3, one from S6 and several from S4, all potentially later in date than the samian from the north-east corner of Enclosure 1, F715 and from S2. In sum, since there is a sizeable proportion of material from Les Martres from F702, together with several sherds from Lezoux, it seems certain that this ditch was filled at a later date than the Enclosure 1 ditch elsewhere, perhaps before *c.* AD 130.

F715.   The sample of samian from this feature is more consistent with that from the north-east corner of Enclosure 1 (F608, F 609 and F 612) than it is with that from F702. Bar one item, it is all South Gaulish and Flavian or Flavian–Trajanic. The exception is a cup from Les Martres, represented by two sherds, which is early second century. However, none of the samian needs be later than *c.* AD 110.

Features within Enclosure 1
F707 and F708.   These adjacent pits contained a few sherds of Flavian and Flavian–Trajanic samian, all of which is South Gaulish.

F718.   Only one samian vessel is represented, a Drag. 18/ 31 from Les Martres-de-Veyre, dated *c.* AD 100–130.

F719.   Approximately six samian vessels are represented amongst this group. Two are Flavian or Flavian–Trajanic items, while another is from Les Martres-de-Veyre and of early second-century date; the remaining three vessels are Central Gaulish (Lezoux) belonging to the first half of the second century AD None of the pieces is necessarily later than early Hadrianic and so, on the samian evidence, the filling of the feature may have been contemporary with that of F702 on its southern side.

F726.   Approximately nine vessels are represented amongst this group, seven are Flavian or Flavian–Trajanic South Gaulish items and there are two vessels from Les Martres-de-Veyre of early second-century date.

Ditch Fills of Enclosure 2
The two main groups from this Enclosure boundary have different dates.

F704.   The samian from this feature comprises a modest-sized group of generally small and rather abraded sherds, covering a late first century to second century date range. There is nothing necessarily later than *c.* AD 130.

F706.   This cut contained only one samian fragment, an abraded South Gaulish piece.

F711.   The samian from this ditch cut is entirely South Gaulish, with nothing later than *c.* AD 110. All of the sherds are small fragments, abraded to some degree.

F713.   This cut contained only one samian sherd, an abraded South Gaulish base.

Pits within Enclosure 2

F700. This feature yielded a small group of La Graufesenque samian of Flavian to Flavian–Trajanic date.

F701. This pit also contained only La Graufesenque samian of Flavian to Flavian–Trajanic date. Unlike the contemporary group from pit F700, though, a comparatively large number of vessels is represented, by only one or two sherds in most cases. The average sherd weight is very low (*cf.* Table 4) and most sherds show some degree of abrasion. Six different Drag. 18 plates are represented.

General Points:

Taken as a whole the samian from Phase 1 covers a date range from *c.* AD 70 to around AD 150, with most items being later Flavian and early second century to *c.* AD 120 or 130. This chronological pattern is reflected amongst the samian from the later deposits and topsoil, amongst which there are few items which date to after *c.* AD 150. There are some parallels therefore between this samian assemblage and that from the New Cemetery site (Dickinson 1996) which has an early Roman emphasis, with little material belonging to the Antonine period or later. However, whereas Dickinson (1996, 90) notes that the main *floruit* at the New Cemetery site was in the last two decades of the first century, at Orton's Pasture this may come a decade or so later, and is apparently sustained into the early second century. Typically the groups deposited in the earlier second century contain quantities of South Gaulish material, some of which is likely to be residual. However, it is customary for sites with origins in the first century to yield early second-century samian groups amongst which South Gaulish ware is strongly represented (as at Southwark (SLAEC 1978)), suggesting the continued currency of these earlier vessels into the second century, perhaps the result of a shortfall in new supply (*cf.* Marsh 1978; Willis In Press).

The paucity of Drag. 29 bowls and Drag. 15/17 plates amongst the Orton's Pasture assemblage is telling. There are only two Drag. 29s from Phase 1 (compared to *c.* seven from the New Cemetery site as a whole). As sites founded during the Flavian period demonstrate, the 29 becomes a progressively less frequent find, especially after *c.* AD 85 (*cf.* Dickinson 1992, 52; Hanson *et al.* 1979, 36) and so their infrequency amongst the Orton's Pasture assemblage immediately suggests a start date for occupation later than the mid-Flavian period. On the other hand, Drag. 37 bowls of the late period at La Graufesenque (*c.* AD 90–110), as well as from Les Martres-de-Veyre (*c.* AD 100–120/130), are well represented. The Drag. 15/17 is another form which becomes less common during the later first century (*cf.* Millett 1987; Willis 1997; In Press) as, concomitantly, the Drag. 18 plate becomes more popular; again the list of samian from Phase 1 suggests, on this index, a start date at the end of the first century AD

Three features of the second century samian from the present site mirror patterns noted for the New Cemetery site (*cf.* Dickinson 1996, 91). First, the amount of samian from Les Martres, compared with the quantity from other Central Gaulish sources, is unusually high. Secondly, Trajanic Lezoux ware is comparatively well represented. Finally the range of samian forms characteristic of the second half of the second century is highly circumscribed: the site assemblage as a whole contains no samian gritted mortaria, no examples of form 80, while there are few sherds from the Drag. 31 or 31R. Walters 79R (Central Gaulish) is represented, albeit by one substantial fragment from 6001, and there is also a sherd from a Central Gaulish Dech. 72 beaker with applied decoration, of Antonine date, from context 6500.

The material from Phase 1 includes sherds from two Montans products, one a Drag. 30, and a few sherds of early Lezoux ware (*cf.* Boon 1967; Dannell 1971). Sherds of the latter are also present amongst the pottery from post-Phase 1 contexts; part of a Drag. 18 in this ware was present in 6025, as was a sherd from a Curle 11 with a flattened bead rim. Also present amongst the samian from post-Phase 1 deposits and topsoil are sherds from forms not occurring within Phase 1. These include examples of the following: Drag. 35, probably in Les Martres-de-Veyre fabric (context 6098); Drag. 42, La Graufesenque fabric (6001); and Ritt. 12, La Graufesenque (6025). Part of a Drag. 29 was present amongst the finds from 6003.

Table 5 documents the incidence of repair amongst the samian from this site. The proportion of repaired sherds is just over 1% of the samian assemblage, which is essentially consistent with the pattern observed elsewhere where this aspect has been studied (King and Millett 1993, Table 16.5; Evans 1996a, 89; Evans 1996b, 62).

Table 5: Summary of Repaired Samian items

Context	Form	Fabric	Repair Type
6000	Drag. 37	South Gaulish	Drilled hole
6000	Drag. 37 (different vessel)	South Gaulish	Drilled hole
6001	Drag. 18	Central Gaulish	Dovetail cut
6033	Bead rimmed vessel (2 sherds)	Central Gaulish	Drilled holes
6060	Drag. 18 (2 sherds, same vessel)	South Gaulish	Drilled holes
6555	Drag. 18/31	Probably Les Martres-de-Veyre	Drilled hole

GRAFFITI
by R.S.O. Tomlin

All *graffiti* were made after firing.

Samian

1. F609 (Fig.23:1) 6070 Base sherd of a Drag. 27g cup. Two or three *graffiti* have been scratched in succession on the first wall-curve above the foot ring:

(i) In the vertical axis, T

(ii) Overlying (i), some finer scratches which can be variously interpreted; possibly TR

(iii) In the horizontal axis, the end of a *graffito* whose last letter (S) overlies (i) and (ii): [...]RIS, *[...o]ris*, '(property) of [...]or'.

Victor is much the most likely name in (iii), but there are other possibilities. T and (?)TR in (i) and (ii) would be the abbreviated names of previous owners.

2. F609 (Fig.23:2) 6078 Almost half of a Drag. 15/17 platter stamped [SVL]PICIV. Scratched underneath within the foot ring:

S{.} IINICI, *Senici*, '(property) of Senicus'

S has been scratched over a thick diagonal stroke, and is followed by a 'letter' which can be variously interpreted: it may be part of an earlier *graffito* scratched out (perhaps 'A'), or II (i.e. E) scratched out because it was inadvertently written twice. Whatever the explanation, this 'letter' should be disregarded, since the succeeding letters IINICI are certain, and *Senicus* belongs to the group of *Sen-* names frequent in Celtic-speaking provinces. In Britain, it occurs (as *Senica*) in *RIB* 374.

3. F700 (Fig.23:3) 6511 Base sherd of a Drag. 18 platter apparently stamped SECO·M. Two *graffiti* have been scratched underneath within the foot ring:

(i) A

(ii) TE[...], perhaps TE[R] for *Te[r](...)*, '(property) of Ter...'

The *graffiti* are differently aligned, and A is much larger. In (ii) the alternative reading IE[...] is excluded by the sequence of letters, and the space available would permit only 1–2 more letters, now lost. For other examples of owners' names abbreviated to TER, see *RIB* II.7, 2501.537, and 8.2503, 424. *Tertius* is the most likely, then *Tertullus*, but there are other possibilities.

4. F602 6054 Two sherds, not conjoining, of a Drag. 18/31 R bowl. Scratched on the wall just below the angle: [...]M

The *graffito* may be complete, when it would be the owner's name abbreviated to its initial letter.

5. F609 6090 Base sherd preserving the profile of a Drag. 18/31 bowl. A 'fishbone' pattern has been scratched underneath within the foot ring. This pattern, probably a stylised palm branch, is sometimes found as a mark of identification. For an example, see *RIB* II.8, p. xii.

Amphora and Flagon

Dressel 20; not seen, but described from a drawing (**6**) and flagon from a photograph (**7**) respectively.

6. F702 6555. Sherd from the upper shoulder with part of one handle. Scratched to the left of the handle:

[...]SA[...]

The drawing suggests that the sherd was broken at the handle, so there is no evidence whether or not the *graffito* continued past it, but it probably did. Fig.21:5.

7. No inventory number [in private possession]. Five conjoining sherds from the upper shoulder. Seven scored lines are visible in the photograph, all but the first incomplete, which can be variously interpreted:

(1) At the top are short scratches; possibly P, therefore, but most likely I

(2) and (3): certainly V

(4) and (5): either IL or II (i.e. E, or numeral digits)

(6) :probably I

(7) :the tip of a letter, not quite vertical

If (1) were P, one might read P VIIII, *p(ondo) VIIII*, 'weight 9 (pounds)', but the spacing of the digits is against this. The reading IVILIS is quite possible, but it requires the conjecture that initial C has been lost to abrasion; [C]IVILIS, '(property) of Civilis'.

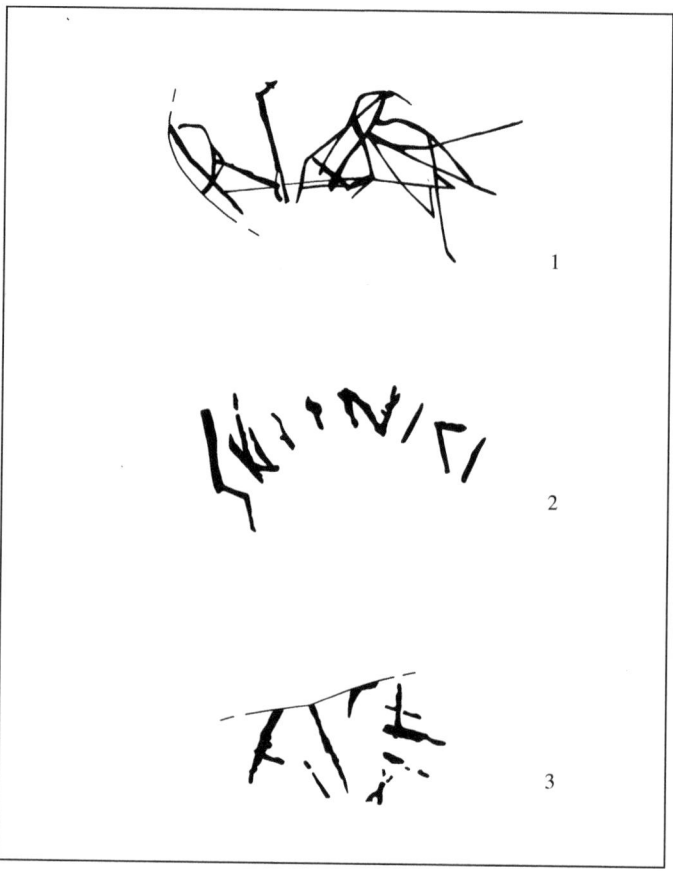

Fig. 23 Graffiti (Scale 1:1)

ROMAN VESSEL GLASS
by Christopher Hewitson

Introduction

The excavations at Orton's Pasture, Rocester produced 89 fragments of Roman vessel glass and three fragments of Roman window glass. The majority of the glass was in good condition, with the exception of a few pieces which had been subject to the effect of heat prior to deposition. However, the majority of the glass was heavily fragmented, with only a few diagnostic pieces surviving. The most noticeable aspect of the assemblage was that for a Roman site of this size it was remarkably small.

The material, virtually all of which can be dated to the late first to second centuries AD, was categorised by type to tablewares (vases, cups, and beakers), and containers (bottles and jars). These were then measured, sorted by colour and catalogued. The more significantly diagnostic pieces were drawn. Analysis of both colour and type, for the glassware, and spatial analysis were carried out.

The Tablewares

Drinking vessels are definitely represented by only two fragments. No.10 (Fig.24:7), a blue/green base fragment of a bowl, is paralleled at Usk (Price 1995, No.63, fig.44) and a closer and more significant parallel from the New Cemetery, Rocester (Cool 1996 No.32/No.17, fig.41) is a tubular-rimmed bowl (Cool and Price 1995, fig.6.3/6.2, 630–691). No.40 (Fig.24:8), a brown/yellow base fragment of a beaker, has no close parallels.

Two other vessels are possibly represented by collections of body fragments. No.11, two joining blue/green fragments, consists of a long curved body fragment which may represent a thin-walled cup, diameter 115mm. No.12 has five associated fragments, possibly representing the side of a large bowl with a diameter of between 200–300mm. The only vessel of a comparable size at this period is the tubular-rimmed bowl. No.13 could less certainly be a cup or beaker, with tool-marking on the side.

As with the excavations at the New Cemetery, globular, and to a lesser extent conical, jugs were present in the assemblage. These were common in the late first to second century AD Three neck fragments (Nos.1, 2 and 3) are all probably from jugs, No.1 (Fig.24:1) being from a globular jug. The form of this neck fragment is not unusual (Cool and Price 1995 Colchester, fig.9.15, 1400/1401). It is, however, remarkably fine, and is misted perhaps due to the effect of heat. No. 2 (Fig.24:2) cannot be ascribed to any particular vessel, but is far more robust than No.1. It is decorated with optic-blown ribs, a technique which involved blowing the glass into a ribbed mould and then swinging, causing the ribs to expand and swirl. They may have extended from the body of the vessel. The closest parallel comes from the Legionary Fortress Baths at Caerleon, where a similar less robust piece exists in yellow-green glass (Allen 1986, fig.40 No.13). No.3 is a less diagnostic piece, but the form and diameter suggest it is from a jug.

The two handle fragments, No.4 (Fig.24:3) in blue/green, and No.39 (Fig.24:6) in brown/yellow, are from jugs, the latter being from a globular jug. Both are decorated with ribbon handles, a common design (Price 1980, fig.15, Cool and Price 1995 fig. 8.4, 8.5, 8.6; Cool 1996, 27, fig.41, No.15) which has variations in the number of ribs, or the number of pinches on the tail. No.4 is best parallelled by a handle from Colchester (Cool and

Price 1995, fig.8.5, 916). No exact parallel can be found for No.39, but the use of pinching on the tail of a single prominent rib is a common technique in the late first and early second centuries (Price 1978: 74). No.5 (Fig.24:4) has been heat crackled, probably from proximity to a fire, and no parallels can be found. However, its fine nature suggests it came from a relatively small vessel. The other two handle fragments, Nos.26 (Fig.24:5) and 34, are undiagnostic. No.34 has been subject to heat distortion and may be recycling waste.

A number of body fragments is almost certainly from jugs (Nos.6, 7 and 8) but these are not identifiable to type.

Other body fragments are insufficiently diagnostic to identify form.

The Containers

Eighteen bottle fragments have been identified, mainly blue/green in colour, of which the majority are from square-bottomed bottles. These are common in first and second century AD contexts but began to fall out of fashion by the late second and early third centuries AD A fragment of a tubular rim (No.14, Fig.24:9) has parallels from Colchester (Cool and Price 1995, fig.11.7, 1841/1847). Three corner fragments from the base, with surviving base rings, occur (blue/green No.15, Fig.24:11, No.16, Fig.24:12, green/yellow No.35, Fig.24:13). The bases of these bottles are not sufficiently large enough to relate to other square bottles, but the use of concentric base rings is common, and several bases of this type were found at the New Cemetery, Rocester (Charlesworth 1959, fig.9; Cool 1996, fig.42). It is highly likely that the bases had more rings than the one or two which are visible, usually with a central spot. There were no examples of the more elaborate moulded base designs commonly found on this type of vessel (Cool 1996, fig. 43, 28–31). A number of body fragments survives, usually with square corners (Nos.19–24). No.17 may be a shoulder fragment and No. 18 (Fig.24:10) represents the corner of a shoulder with the beginnings of a neck. A single fragment of a hexagonal bottle remains (No.25). It is thin walled, so probably represents a small vessel.

No.9, a curved body fragment, is probably the base of a jar. Although other fragments of jars almost certainly did exist there were none of the diagnostic rim sherds which would have allowed identification to type.

Window Glass

There were two sherds of window glass, neither of which had a grozed edge.

Quantification

The problems of quantification of this assemblage are mainly due to its size. It is a relatively small assemblage and therefore certain techniques of quantification cannot be used. Estimated Vessel Equivalents (EVEs) are insufficiently useful on an assemblage of this size. With so few diagnostic fragments it would be impossible to compare fragments from one vessel with another, due to the fact that identification is by a rim for one vessel, and by a base for another. An alternative method is estimation of the minimum vessel numbers (EMN). Although as above, it suffers from the biases of the small nature of the assemblage, it does allow some comparison.

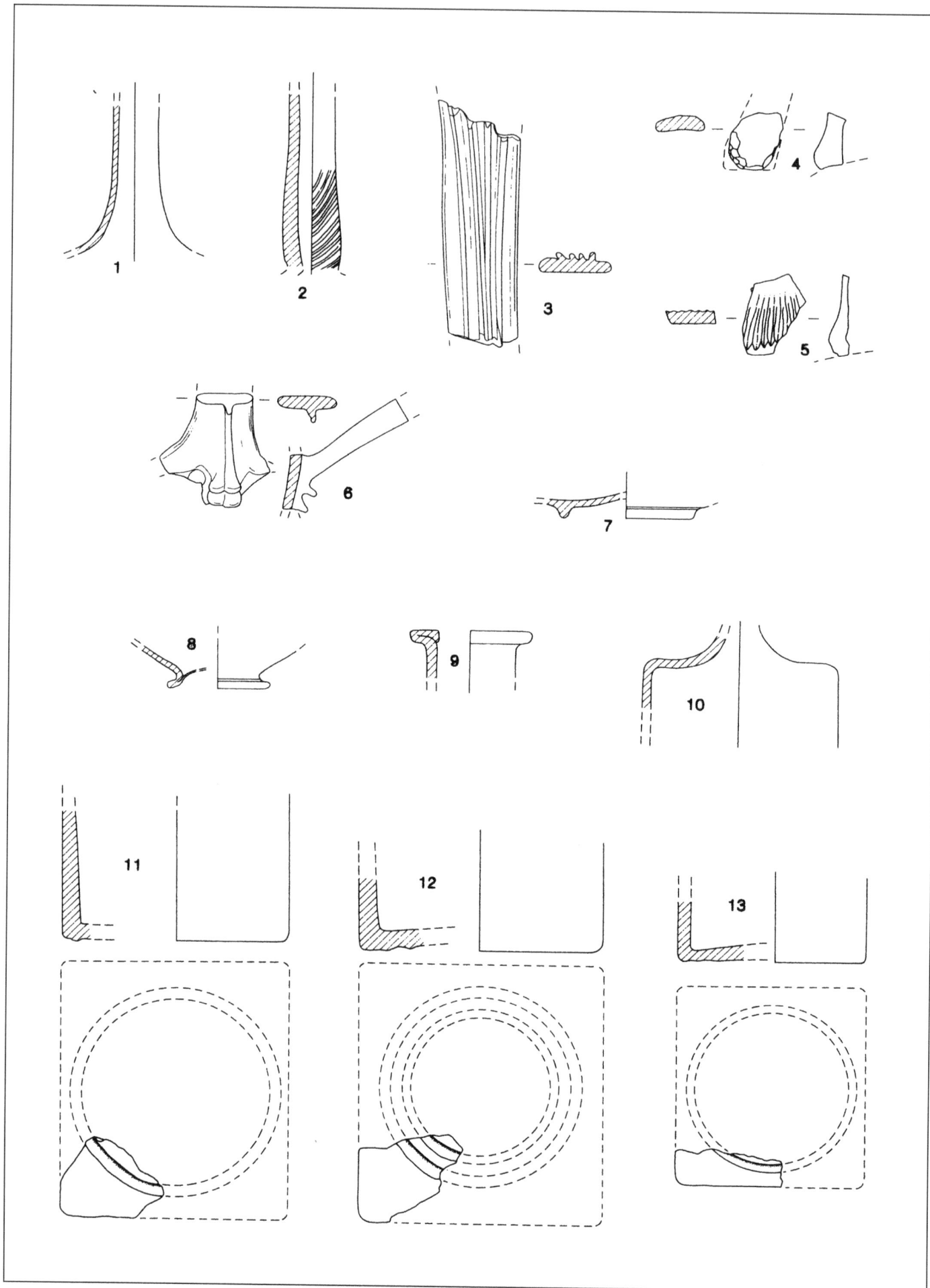

Fig. 24   Glass vessels (Scale 1:2)

Table 6: Estimated Minimum Number of Vessels

Glass type	Glob./ con. jugs	T-R bowls	Other bowls	Sq. bottles	Hex. bottles	Jars	Total
blue/green	3	2	2	2	1	1	11
green/yellow	0	0	0	1	0	0	1
brown/yellow	1	0	0	0	0	0	1
colourless	0	0	0	0	0	0	0
Totals	**4**	**2**	**2**	**3**	**1**	**1**	**13**

Despite the limitations of this technique in terms of quantification, it does indicate that globular or conical jugs are the most common vessel type, followed by bottles. The fact that bottles represent a third of the assemblage is in keeping with the amount expected for a site of this period. The undiagnostic nature of many of these pieces also restricts quantification. Over 55% of the fragments were undiagnostic to type. If the 18 bottle fragments were taken as a percentage of the number of diagnostic pieces they make up 37.5% of the total glass assemblage.

Dating

The glassware dates to the late first and second centuries AD Square bottles were common from the mid-first to the late second centuries but began to go out of fashion and were replaced by mould-blown cylindrical or barrel-shaped bottles (Price 1978, 74). The absence of cylindrical bottles, found in numbers at the New Cemetery, Rocester (Esmonde Cleary and Ferris 1996), suggests the glassware post-dates the Flavian period. At this time, cylindrical bottles were as common as square bottles on sites (Cool and Price 1995, 184), but by the early second century they began to go out of use, and the assemblage is dominated

by square bottles. They did not reappear until the late second century. Absence of evidence, however, is not real evidence and the small nature of the collection suggests it may merely be that cylindrical bottles were absent due to chance.

The globular and conical jugs are late first to early second century AD in date, being of forms Ising 52 or 55 (Cool and Price 1995: 120–130). The handle No.39 (Fig.24:6), light yellow/brown glass in colour, continued into the second century, although the majority of examples were blue/green in colour. The other identifiable tableware, tubular-rimmed bowls, was available throughout the first and early second centuries.

The absence of pillar-moulded bowls, a vessel found at the New Cemetery, Rocester (Esmonde Cleary and Ferris 1996) but absent here, supports the assertion that the assemblage was later first- or early second-century in date. The production of these vessels died out in the late first century, during the Flavian and Trajanic period. Combined with the absence of cylindrical bottles this may suggest the assemblage is later than the earliest phases from the New Cemetery. However, it may be that the size of the assemblage means these pieces are absent due to lack of survival, as opposed to lack of occupation during this period.

Distribution

Table 7: Distribution of Glass by Colour/Type

	Blue/ green	Yellow/ green	Yellow/ brown	Colour-less	Window Glass	Total
Nthn. Enclosure Ditch	12			3		15
Sthn. Enclosure Ditch	2			4		6
Pits	26	3				29
Cess	1					1
Occupation Deposits	2					2
Cultivation Layer	1					1
Unstratified/Cleaning	32		3		3	38
Total	**76**	**3**	**3**	**7**	**3**	**92**

The majority of stratified glass is distributed within the enclosure ditches and the pits within them. As these were the main features within the site this is an unsurprising statistic. Over 42% of the fragments came from unstratified contexts. Noticeably all of

the colourless glass is located within the enclosure ditches. Colourless glass was unusual in the Roman period, with blue/ green glass being the most common.

Table 8: Distribution of Glass by Form

	Jugs	Bowls	Bottles	Jars	Total
Nthn. Enclosure Ditch	1	3			4
Sthn. enclosure Ditch	1				1
Pits	3		6		9
Cess					0
Occupation Deposits			2		2
Cultivation Layer					0
Unstratified/Cleaning	7	2	5	1	15
Total	**12**	**5**	**13**	**1**	**31**

The table above shows the recognisable fragments compared with their locations. Fragments which are clearly associated with one another have been combined as one. Clearly the majority of the assemblage by form was located in unstratified or cleaning layers. The most noticeable statistic to emerge is the prevalence of tablewares in the enclosure ditches, combined with the absence of bottles. The bottles, however, tend to be found within pits or occupation deposits. This would correlate with their different uses. The bottles had a more functional, everyday, domestic purpose, and therefore were found within occupation deposits, but also were discarded into pits. The prevalence of tablewares in the enclosure ditches may relate to a period when tablewares were in more common use.

The location of the pits may be significant. Fragments from at least two jugs, and at least three bottles, came from the pits within the northern enclosure. In comparison there was only one find of an undiagnostic sherd in a pit (F700) inside the southern enclosure. The series of features to the north of the northern enclosure, identified as wells, later in-filled with rubbish, produced a range of sherds, mostly blue/green and undiagnostic due to size. Two heat-affected sherds came from these pits, and the only diagnostic pieces were from two bottles. This correlates with their identification as rubbish pits. They do not contain the tablewares found within the pits of the northern enclosure.

Comparison with other Assemblages

Comparison involving such a small assemblage could be subject to differential survival, and some pieces may be more significantly represented than was the case. Two types of vessel are present in the assemblage in large enough numbers to bear comparison, the square bottles and the conical or globular jugs. Both are common in late first- and early second-century contexts at other sites.

A high proportion of bottle glass is a feature of Roman sites. At Corbridge 380 of the 624 fragments are from bottles, 61% of the assemblage (Allen 1988). At Hayton Roman Fort all except one of the vessels is believed to be a bottle (Charlesworth 1975). Such a high proportion of bottle glass is, however, not present at Orton's Pasture. If the 18 bottle fragments are taken as a proportion of the total diagnostic fragments they make up 37.5%, clearly not as high as other military sites. High proportions of bottle glass are not uncommon even within civil sites at this period. Excavations at Doncaster civil site produced a high proportion of blue/green bottle glass (Allen 1986b, 103).

Tablewares are more difficult to assess, as even with a larger assemblage they do not make up as great a proportion of the assemblage as bottles. However, the presence of conical and globular jugs can be seen at the early settlement at Lincoln (Cool and Price 1988, 42–3), as well as at Doncaster (1986b), and the New Cemetery, Rocester (Cool 1996). The glassware cannot indicate either a civil or military nature to the site. No other diagnostic items are present in significant numbers to allow comparison with other sites.

Catalogue

Abbreviations
PH Present Height; RD Rim Diameter; WT Wall Thickness; ND Neck Diameter; BD Base Diameter; Dim Dimensions. All measurements in mm.

Vessel Glass
Blue/green
Jugs or Jars

1. Unstratified Area A Dim. 65 x 15, ND 17.5, WT 1.5.
   Neck fragment of jug. Elongated bubbles. Strain marks on the neck. Lower part of cylindrical neck with shoulder of a globular jug. Fig.24:1.
2. 6025 PH 76, ND 22–18, WT 4.
   Neck fragment of jug. Some bubbles. Ribbed decoration, spiralling around the neck from the base upward. Optic blown. Constricted at the neck. Fig.24:2.
3. 6581 PH 27, ND 20, WT 4.
   Undecorated neck fragment of jug or flask. Elongated bubbles up the neck.
4. 6001 PH 99, Cross-section 30 x 7, WT 5, Rib height 2.
   Ribbon handle fragment. Four prominent ribs running the full length of the fragment. Probably globular or prismatic jug handle. Fig.24:3.
5. 6543 Dim. 33 x 22, WT 5–6.
   Handle fragment of a jug. Badly decomposed, probably heat crackled. Reeded handle with simple lower attachment. Fig.24:4.
6. 6577 Dim. 18 x 17, WT 6.
   Base of handle. Chipped irregular fragment. Asymmetrical. Flat on inner surface. Curved on outer surface.
7. 6036 Dim. 80 x 20, PH 38, WT 3. Undecorated curved fragment of shoulder of vessel, probably a globular jug.
8. Fragments from jugs or jars.
   6081 Dim. 32 x 21, WT 2.5.
   6088 Dim. 46 x 23, WT 3.
9. 6003
   Dim. 72 x 37, WT 3.5.
   Dim. 31 x 39, WT 3.5.
   2 associated fragments of glass, making up a curved body piece of jug. Small bubbles.

Bowls

10. 6036 Dim. 27 x 27, WT 3, Base Ring 4. Base fragment from a vessel, probably a bowl. Some bubbles. Convex base, slightly out-splayed applied base ring. Fig.24:7
11. 6069
    Dim. 64 x 22, WT 1–1.5.
    Dim. 49 x 20, WT 2.
    Dim. 31 x 22, WT 1.5
    Dim. 35 x 27, WT 1.
    4 curved glass body fragments, probably from a cup or beaker First two are associated and relate to a cup or beaker, possibly a Hofheim cup, diameter 115mm. Some bubbles.
12. 6070
    Dim. 72 x 41, WT 3. Upturned at an angle of 150° at one end.
    Dim. 32 x 23, WT 3. Curved at an angle of 150°.
    Dim. 27 x 18, WT 3.
    Dim. 40 x 30, WT 3.
    Dim. 37 x 22, WT 3.
    Dim. 45 x 19, WT 3.

6 body fragments of a vessel with curved sides. Very few bubbles. First five associated with one another and relate to a tubular-rimmed bowl, approximately 200–300mm diameter.

13. 6089 Dim. 48 x 27, WT 1.

Curved body fragment, almost translucent. Some large bubbles. Tool marks around the curve of the fragment. Probably a fragment of a cup or beaker.

Bottles

14. 6011 RD 48, PH 20, WT 4.

Tubular rim fragment from bottle. Out-turned rim, tubular edge bent out and turned back and in. Flattened on the top. Fig.24:9.

15. 6025 Dim 40 x 29, PH 29, WT 7, Base Ring Diameter 80, 70.

Base corner fragment of square bottle. Many bubbles. Two concentric circular mouldings can be seen. Concave from first moulding. Fig.24:11.

16. 6539 Dim. 43 x 27, PH 49, WT 6. Base Ring Diameter 90.

Corner fragment from the base of square bottle. One base ring present. Some bubbles. Fig.24:12.

17. 6539 Dim. 50 x 22, WT 5.

Curved body fragment at about 90°. Many bubbles. May be a shoulder fragment from a bottle. Broken in modern times.

18. 6596

Dim. 32 x 37, Depth 15, WT 6, Corner Angle 100–110°.

Dim. 35 x 28, Depth 7, WT 5, Corner Angle 120–150°.

2 corner pieces. Both have extensive bubbles. Second is broken at corner. Fig.24:10.

19. 6555 Dim. 63 x 44, PH 25, WT 3.5. Corner of shoulder of square bottle. Beginning of a cylindrical neck. Heavily bubbled.

20. 6596

Dim. 38 x 40, WT 5.

Dim. 47 x40, WT 5–5.5.

2 associated body fragments. Corner piece, and body fragment, slightly upturned at one edge at 90° to the corner, suggesting the beginning of a shoulder. Probably a square bottle fragment.

21. 6039 Dim. 19 x 12, PH 24, WT 5.

Corner fragment of square vessel, possibly a prismatic bottle. Some bubbles.

22. 6050 Dim. 65 x 47, WT 7–11. Undecorated side fragment of prismatic bottle. Broken where it meets the base, but curved corner still remains. Convex, thicker in the centre than the outside. Many bubbles, a few large.

23. 6576

Dim. 38 x 37, WT 5.

Dim. 49 x 29, Deep 13, WT 6.

2 associated flat body fragments. The second is broken at the corner, at less than 90°. Fragments are stress cracked. Heavily bubbled, some large ones. Fragments from a prismatic bottle.

24. Bottle fragment.

6025 Dim. 35 x 22, WT 5–6.5.

6081 Dim. 68 x 22, WT 6.

6596 Dim. 50 x 19, WT 6.

6596 Dim. 30 x 24, WT 4.

25. 6000 Dim. 40 x 27, WT 2.

Flat body fragment. Squared rounded edge, angled at 120°, side edge of prismatic hexagonal vessel. Small vessel due to thin walls.

Jars

26. 6081 Dim.41 x 22, PH 58, WT 7–4.

Curved body fragment at 90°. Base of Oviod Flask. Increase in wall thickness towards the base. Large amount of small bubbles. Fig.24:5.

Undiagnostic

27. Six undecorated body fragments, curved.

6001 Dim. 28 x 21, WT 1.5.

6025 Dim. 35 x 28, WT 3.

6025 Dim. 22 x 24, WT 2.

6050 Dim. 47 x 37. WT 2.5.

6057 Dim. 62 x 29, WT 4.

6511 Dim. 18 x 13, WT 3.

28. Undecorated body fragments, slightly curved.

6001 Dim. 28 x 15, WT 6.

6001 Dim. 26 x 16, WT 6.

6003 Dim. 36 x 25, WT 5.

6025 Dim. 20 x 13, WT 2.5

6025 Dim. 20 x 8, WT 4

6025 Dim. 36 x 16, WT 4.5

6025 Dim. 45 x 10, WT 5.5

6560 Dim. 49 x 35, WT 5.

29. Undecorated curved fragments of shoulder of vessel.

6000 Dim. 64 x 37, WT 6.

6003 Dim. 64 x 39, WT 3.

6058 Dim. 41 x 29, WT 3–2.5.

6070 Dim. 28 x 25, WT 3.

30. Flat undecorated body fragment.

6595 Dim. 18 x 16, WT 2.

6046 Dim. 63 x 43, WT 4.

6501 Dim. 28 x 26, WT 1.5.

6511 Dim. 42 x 26, WT 4–2.5.

6511 Dim. 25 x 17, WT 3.5.

31. Undecorated body fragment.

6036 Dim. 22 x 22, WT 2.5.

6060 Dim. 24 x 21, WT 3.5.

6060 Dim. 41 x 18, WT 4.

6098 Dim. 23 x 15, WT. 3.5.

6506 Dim. 25 x 19, WT 4.

6516 Dim. 21 x 16, WT 4.

6527 Dim. 35 x 14, WT 3.5.

6596 Dim. 19 x 11, WT 2.

6613 Dim. 5 x 12, WT 6.5.

U/S Area B. Dim. 22 x 13, WT 3–4.

32. Fragments heavily bubbled, heat affected or stress fractured glass, of poor quality.

6054 Dim. 31 x 28, WT 4.5–3.

6060 Dim. 35 x 33, WT 6–4.5.

6081 Dim. 27 x 26, WT 7.

33. 6025 Dim. 22 x 7, WT 4.

Body fragment with circular ridges. Mould break. Modern.

Green/Yellow

34. 6613 Dim. 29 x 26, WT 3.

Fragment of handle. Badly distorted. Many elongated bubbles, one large. Single remaining rib. Broken on handle and at join with vessel.

35. 6039 Dim. 39 x 14, PH 23, WT 6, Base Ring Diameter 66.

Base fragment of square bottle. Single base ring visible. Fig.24:13.

36. 6094 Dim. 29 x 10, WT 1.5.

Small undecorated body fragment. Almost translucent. Lightly curved.

37. 6007 Dim. 41 x 17, WT 6, RW 7.

Rim fragment. Edge fire rounded. Folded projection at right angles, out from the rim and 13mm below. Break with body is horizontal with the projection on the interior of the vessel. Suggests a shallow vessel. Post-medieval.

38. 6596 PH 49, ND 19, WT 3.

Neck fragment. Lower neck fragment expanding slightly towards constriction at base. Part of body. Vertical ribs extending from body up onto neck. Small elongated bubbles. Post-medieval.

Brown/Yellow

39. 6025

PH 63, Cross-section 24 x 5.5, Rib Height 4.5, Jug WT 1.5.

Lower handle fragment with part of the body of a globular jug. Single prominent rib on ribbon handle off-set to the right. Clawed attachment to the jug, pinched trail on the rib. Fig.24:6.

40. 6051

BD 38, Body Fragment Extends 15, WT 1.5. Circular base fragment of a beaker. Wide lower body sloping to closed pushed-in base ring. Domed base mostly missing. Small fragments show it to be thin, <1mm. Fig.24:8.

41. 6025 Dim. 23 x 22, WT <1.

Thin curved body fragment. Some bubbles.

Colourless

42. 6070

Dim. 61 x 62, WT 1.5.

Dim. 76 x 35, WT. 1.5–2.

2 associated flat undecorated fragments. Green/Yellow tinge. Elongated bubbles.

43. 6089 Dim. 29 x 10, WT 1.5.

Curved body fragment. Slight Blue/Green tinge. Scratches running horizontally around the body.

44. 6560

Dim. 32 x 25, WT 1.5.

Dim. 31 x 12, WT 1.5.

2 lightly curved body fragments. Blue/Green tinge. Former has large bubble broken at surface.

45. 6569

Dim. 20 x 21, WT 1.5.

Dim. 49 x 35, WT 5.

2 curved body fragments. Blue/Green tinge. Some bubbles. Probably from a cup or beaker.

Green

46. 6001 Dim. 20 x 14, WT 4.

Small curved body fragment. No noticeable bubbles. Modern.

Window Glass

47. 6001

Dim. 46 x 35, WT 3.5.

Dim. 20 x 18, WT 4.5–4.

Flat undecorated Blue/Green tinged fragment.

48. 6025 Dim. 24 x 26, WT 3.

Undecorated flat Blue/Green tinged fragment slightly curved at one edge at about 150°.

—✧—

SMALL FINDS
by Lynne Bevan

Prehistoric Small Finds
Flint
Only five items of human-worked flint were recovered, a blade of translucent beige flint with retouched edges and traces of use-wear, three cores and a waste flake. One of the cores was a blade core of possible Mesolithic date. The blade, which retains scars from previous blade detachments, originated from a long, bi-polar blade core, and is probably of later Mesolithic or earlier Neolithic date. The raw material is of a high quality but would have been obtained from secondary deposits, probably river gravels, in common with most prehistoric worked flint in the Midlands. This small flint collection does not indicate prehistoric settlement or activity of any longevity in the area of the site, despite the discovery of larger and more chronologically varied flint assemblages from previous excavations in Rocester, which attest to 'a long prehistoric occupation covering the periods of the Mesolithic, Late Neolithic and Early Bronze Age' (Barfield and Kalali 1996, 182–183).

Roman Small Finds
Catalogued objects are numbered consecutively. These numbers are retained across the illustrations of the small finds (Figs. 25–30).

Ceramic Lamps

Catalogue
1. Circular ceramic lamp, the base and part of the sides, including the nozzle, of which are now missing. The upper face of the lamp bears a mould-impressed motif enclosed within three concentric circles, the upper two of which form the raised edge of the lamp. The motif consists of a plump,

immature figure of Bacchus, identified by a *thyrsus* which he holds in one hand. In the other hand he holds a vessel *(a cantharus)* from which he appears to be pouring wine, over the poorly defined head of (or into the mouth of) a squatting feline figure on his left-hand side. Bacchus, the feline and the *thyrsus* are all in relief. There is some suggestion of a cloak over the god's left shoulder, but the details are indistinct as the result of a worn die or bad mould pressing. A circular hole for the wick has been impressed to the right of Bacchus' head and the upper face of the lamp has broken just below Bacchus' feet. This particular design is not so far attested among published Romano-British Bacchic material, although several ceramic and copper-alloy lamps featuring other aspects of Bacchic imagery are known from Britain (Hutchinson 1986, 26–27). The closest parallels for this design (featuring the god pouring wine over, or into the mouth of, a small feline) are hitherto known to occur in other media, such as the marble statue of the god from Spoonley Wood Villa and a bronze mount from Chedworth Villa (see Hutchinson 1986 for further discussion).

Although no direct parallels were found in the catalogues of the British Museum lamp collections, there is a number of examples with discus designs featuring Bacchus and his followers, one of which shows Bacchus equipped with both *thyrsus* and *cantharus*, holding the latter above the upturned head of a female panther next to a large vine which extends over the feline's head to the right of the god (Bailey 1980, Q766, 14–15). In this example, Bacchus is leaner and apparently older and he wears a swirling cloak (*ibid.*). Although the origin of this example has not been established, the description of the ceramic fabric, a buff, micaceous clay with a worn red-brown slip (*ibid.* 133), is very similar to that of the Rocester lamp.

Much of the slip on the Rocester lamp has survived, although this has burnt to a dark brown on some areas of the upper face and sides of the lamp as a result of use. That the lamp was well-worn and probably used for a long period is also suggested by some chipping damage to the upper edge. The form of the lamp is difficult to ascertain due to the absence of diagnostic features. It is possible that after breaking, the discus of the lamp was suspended for use as an *oscillum*.

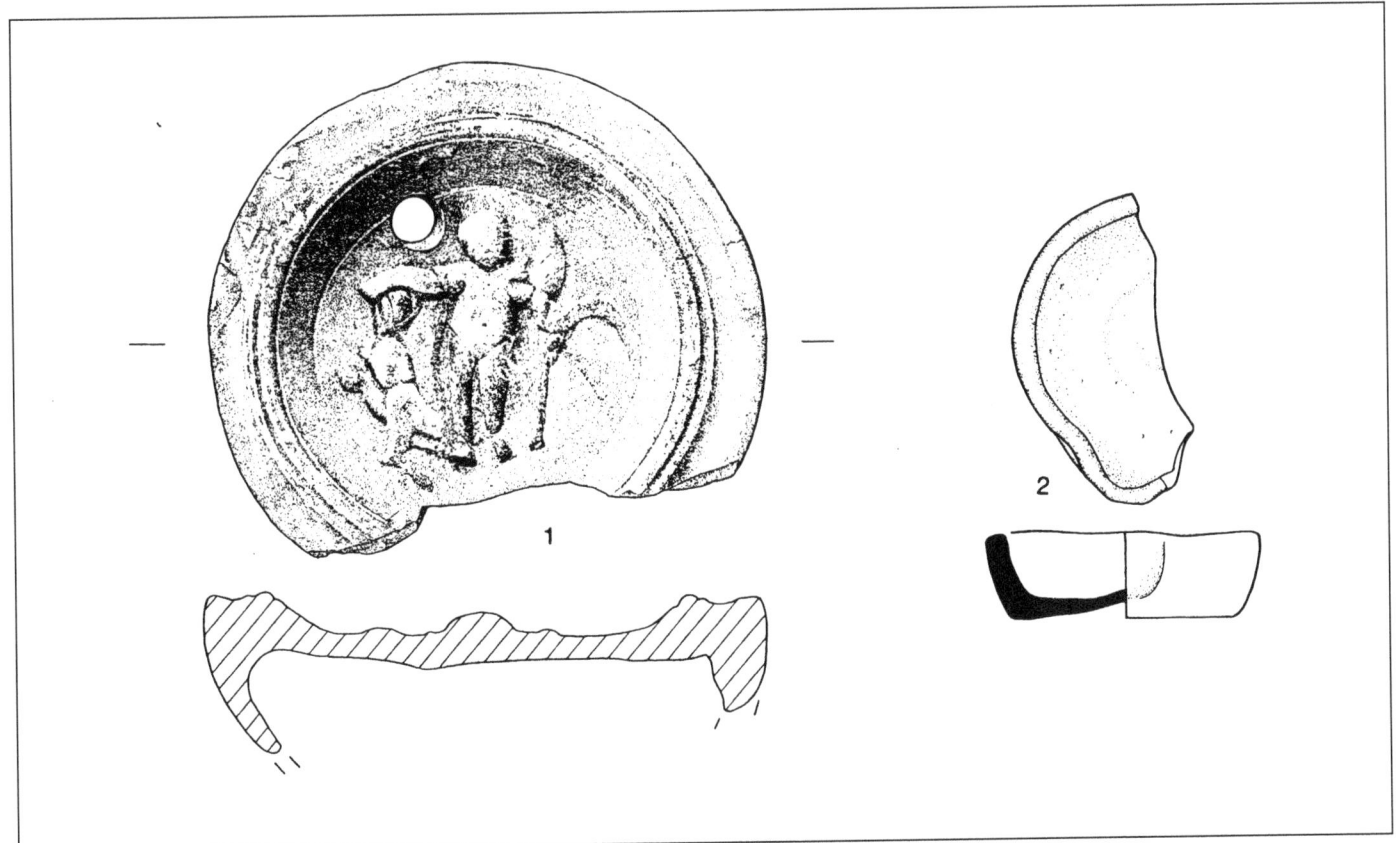

Fig. 25   Ceramic lamps (No. 1, Scale 1:1, No. 2, Scale 1:2)

The rarity of lamps on Romano-British sites has led Toynbee to suggest that in Britain lamps were reserved for use as votives 'in temples or in tombs or in household shrines' rather than representing the 'staple method of lighting' (Toynbee 1964, 432; Hutchinson 1986, 26–27). While Hutchinson was unable to determine whether this was true of the 'Bacchic' lamps found in Britain, she concluded that whether 'cultic or utilitarian' in purpose, 'they should continue to merit serious consideration as "votive Dionysiaca"' (Hutchinson 1986, 27). Although this example was found unstratified from its original context, its presence on a site together with other cultic material such as the Bacchic *patera* handle (Fig. 27), and a number of potentially ritual objects, such as the inscribed vessel/stand (Fig. 13:1), and two triple vases (Fig. 13:6, and 6529, not illustrated), is perhaps, in some way, connected to dealings between mortals and their gods.

Probably a Gaulish product, though it may possibly be Italian in origin.

Diameter: 71mm, thickness: 2–5mm. Context 6500 [Ploughsoil, Area B]. Fig.25:1. Plate 12.

2. Ceramic greyware (fabric GRA2) lamp of a simple, open form, a common type of lamp during the Roman period, and very similar to lamps recovered from Structure 1 at the Derby Racecourse cemetery (Birss 1985, fig.112, bottom right-hand corner). Length: 80mm, width: 33m (original width *c*. 62mm), thickness: 5mm. Context 3002 [Backfill of pit F700]. Fig.25:2.

Bone Objects

Bone objects consisted of a polished bone strip (No.3), part of a decorated knife handle (No.4), a bone pin (No.5), and two pin fragments (Nos.6–7).

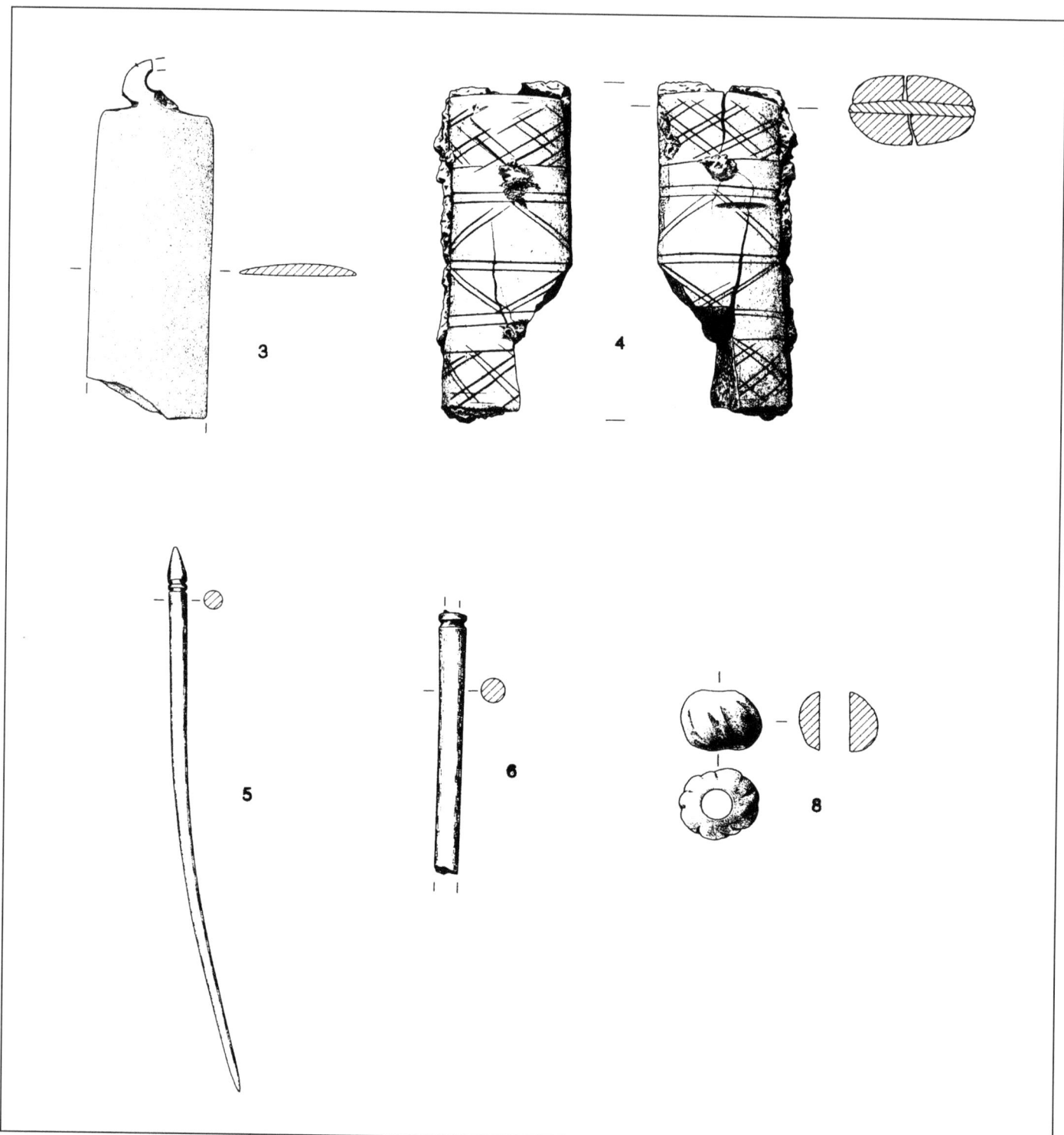

Fig. 26   Objects of bone and glass frit (Scale 1:1)

Catalogue

3. Rectangular segment of rib bone, polished on both sides, and broken at one end, with part of a broken ?suspension loop at the opposite, narrower end. There are many examples of this type of object both in Britain and abroad (for summary see Greep 1998), including some recent examples from Clausentum (V. Allen pers. comm.). The function of these objects is unknown, although the form, which features a perforated oval tab, suggests that they could have been used as some type of label or tag. Greep has classified such items as 'polished bone strips', and dated them to the first century (Greep 1998, fig.124:189–191, 283–285). Length: 64mm, width: 21mm, thickness: 1.5mm. Context 6017 [Ploughsoil] Fig.26:3.

4. Bone knife handle made from a metapodial, with part of the iron tang still visible between the two sides which are held together with two, now corroded, rivets. The polished surface has been decorated with a series of incised lines forming a diamond shape, on the centre of each side, enclosed by trelliswork bands. Similar handles with incised decoration have been recovered from Roman contexts in Colchester, where they have been assigned a generally '3rd- or 4th-century date' (Crummy 1983, 109). Length: 55mm, width: 23mm, thickness: 14mm. Context 6012, SF5 [Upper backfill of F609]. Fig.26:4.

5. Bone pin, complete, with a conical head above a single incised reel, and a slightly bent, tapering shaft. This type of pin conforms to Crummy's Group 5 which has been dated generally to the fourth century AD at Colchester and other contemporary sites (Crummy 1983, 23–24).Length: 96mm. Context 6054 [Dished floor deposit of Phase 2]. Fig.26:5.

6. Bone pin fragment, broken at both ends, with part of a reel visible at the point of breakage from the missing head. Although fragmentary, this pin appears to belong to Group 5 as defined by Crummy (1983, 23–24), the same group to which the complete pin belongs. Length: 45mm. Context 6060 SF20 [Dished floor deposit of Phase 2]. Fig.26:6.

7. Bone pin fragment, broken across lower shaft. The head is globular in shape, with an ovoid section and conforms to Group 3 as defined by Crummy (1983, fig. 19:243, 21–22). Length: 60mm. Context 6033 SF13. Not illustrated [Dished floor deposit of Phase 2].

Melon Beads

A complete turquoise frit melon bead (No 8), and a fragment from a similar bead (No 9) were recovered. A total of 38 complete or fragmentary turquoise frit melon beads was previously found at Rocester, where they vastly outnumbered both clear glass melon beads and all other types of bead (Cool 1996, fig.44, 122). Melon beads were a long-lived bead form in Roman Britain, and 'are normally very common finds on military sites of the first to late second centuries'. They are not necessarily derived from women's necklaces and it has been suggested that they were horse harness decorations (Fox 1940, 132), a theory which is supported by the discovery of such beads decorating a metal neck collar in a horse burial at Krefeld-Gellep (Pirling 1997, 58 Grave 3960).

Catalogue

8. Faience melon bead. Diameter: 12mm. Context 6596 [Backfill of pit F727]. Fig.26:8.

9. Half of an irregularly shaped faience melon bead. Diameter: 23mm, height: 19mm. Context 6007 SF3 [Ploughsoil]. Not illustrated.

Copper-alloy Objects

A total of 39 items of copper alloy was recovered, comprising 219 recognisable objects, three fragments of plate, and 16 other assorted fragments. Recognisable objects included the heavily leaded decorated handle from a *patera* (No. 10), a spoon (No. 11), a lock bolt (No. 12), a broken key (No. 13), a drop handle (No. 14), a waisted fitting (No. 16), two mounts (Nos. 17–18), a coin (see below, p.60), two pins (Nos. 19–20), a dome-headed spike (No. 21), part of a buckle associated with rivetted leather belt fragments (No. 22) seven studs, one of which bears a male portrait (No. 15), and a nail (No. 28).

Catalogue

10. *Patera* handle of heavily leaded copper alloy which terminates in an upward-turned face, possibly that of a 'Bacchic Medusa', an interpretation based upon the two snakes curling upwards from the centrally parted coiffure, their bodies framing the lower face. The face is expressionless and the eyes, one of which is slightly lower than the other, were probably originally inlaid with niello. The reverse of the head is shaped like a fluted shell and separated from the main body of the ribbed handle with banded decoration. There is a roughly chamfered area where the handle once joined the upper side of the *patera,* from which a second decorative motif might have been deliberately removed, perhaps for use as an amulet, since *paterae* and jugs often incorporated other figurative elements associated with the Bacchic cult, such as maenads or felines who were often shown facing inwards over the vessel's rim.

    The handle was once riveted on to the vessel's base through a second decorated area comprising a lion's face (the lower part of which is now missing from below the eyebrows), surmounted by a pair of wings. The closest parallel for this piece comes from Overasselt in the Netherlands and is now in the collection of the Rijksmuseum at Nijmegen. The published catalogue description of this object (Boestard 1956, 26–27) does not allude to any presence of snakes around the head of the female face placed at the end of the handle, rather it refers to her 'wearing a horned cap with wings (?) on top', but otherwise the style and composition of the piece are virtually identical to that of the Rocester example, including the handle attachment in the form of 'a lion's head with a waving mane'. It would seem logical that the Rocester *patera* originated from the same workshop as the Overasselt *patera*, for which an Italian origin has been put forward, and the manufacture of which has been dated to the first or early second century (Boestard 1956, 26). The Overasselt *patera* was found in a burial context together with a jug which also incorporated elements of Bacchic imagery. A similar jug has been recovered from previous excavations at Rocester (Cooper 1996, 134–136), which might have originally formed a pair with the item here discussed. Bacchic iconography and artefactual parallels for both vessels have been discussed in further detail elsewhere (Bevan 1999). Length: 130mm, diameter of handle: 18mm, maximum width of handle attachment: 80mm, thickness of 1–3mm. Context 6007 SF1 [Ploughsoil]. Fig.27. Plate 13.

11. Spoon, with a shallow circular bowl, decorated with a concentric ring 3mm from the inner edge. The handle is broken. Length: 69mm, diameter of bowl: 23mm. Context 6576, SF59 [Backfill of pit F718]. Fig.28:11.

12. Lock bolt, with square and ovoid cut-outs and a protruding spur on the lower edge, similar in design to an undated example from Colchester (Crummy 1983, fig. 136:4136). Length: 80mm, width: 17mm, maximum thickness: 5mm. Unstratified SF57. Fig.28:12.

13. Part of a broken key, possibly from a chest or box, with a fragment of iron corroded inside the looped handle, which terminates in a cut 'V'-shape. Matching shapes have been cut from each side. The key appears to have been a slide key, although the bit is set against the wider, rather than the narrower, side of the handle and all of the teeth are now missing. Length: 30mm, width of handle: 12mm, thickness of handle: 4mm. Context 6061 SF25 [Backfill of pit F605]. Fig.28:13.

14. Drop handle with square-sectioned loop and circular-sectioned terminals, possibly in the shape of birds' heads, but any surface decoration has been obscured by corrosion products. While this could have been attached to a casket or piece of furniture, it is more likely to have been a carrying handle for a military helmet (*e.g.* as at Caerleon, Brewer 1986, 185 No.156). Length: 79mm, maximum thickness: 3mm. Context 6001 SF7 [Ploughsoil]. Fig.28:14.

15. Circular mount with a short, centrally placed rivet on the reverse, partially corroded with part of the outer edge now missing, a male head is visible executed in repoussé decoration within a moulded surround, giving the general appearance of a coin. The male head appears to wear a radiate crown. A similar mount decorated with the face of Vespasian within a laurel wreath was previously found at Rocester (Webster 1996, fig. 49:11, Cat. No. 13, 138 and 141). According to Gunter Ulbert such items were 'decorative features attached to a strap or chain for decorating equipment' (*ibid.* 141; Ulbert 1971). An extended discussion of a similar boss or stud from Caerleon (Brewer in Zienkiewicz 1986, 181–183) provides numerous parallels for such objects post-dating Ulbert's study. There is a great variety of types of head, ranging from those of individual emperors to indeterminate male busts — perhaps of deities — and of attributes represented. No firm date can be placed on these objects as a group, though many examples date to the first and second centuries. Diameter: 21mm, thickness: 0.5mm. Context 6613 SF66 [Backfill of pit F726] (found with Nos.22 and 25, below). Fig.28:15.

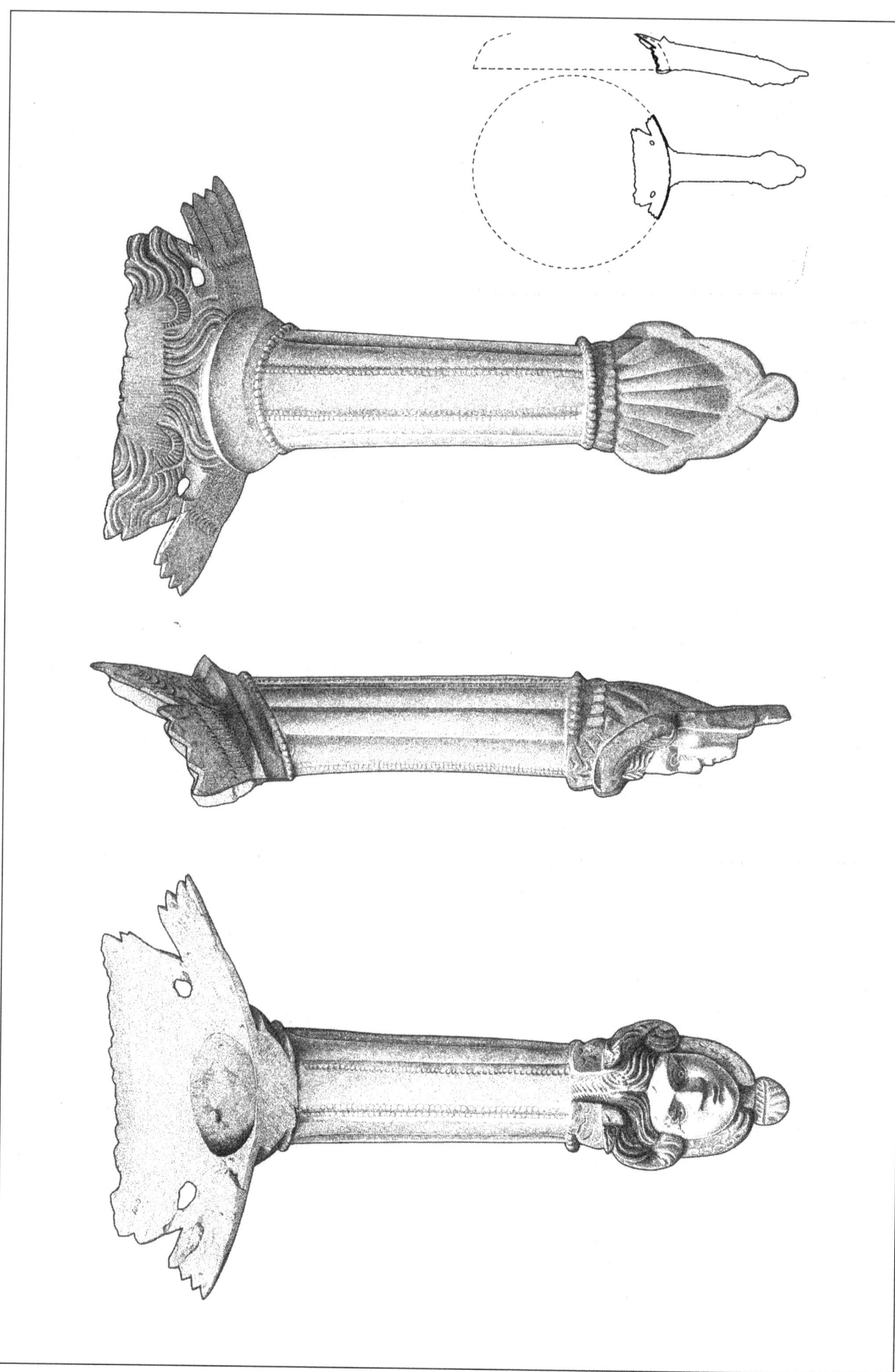

Fig. 27 Decorated copper alloy *patera* handle (Scale 1:1)

The preserved piece of leather strap from the same deposit at Ortons Pasture (No. 22 below) retains parts of two or three pieces of similar studs partially *in situ.*

16. A waisted fitting or toggle of military origin with two circular, perforated terminals for the attachment of domed studs, one of which was probably attached to a clip or other fitting, similar in general shape to a harness clip from Sea Mills (Webster 1958, fig. 7:202, 91, 93), and a broken apron mount terminal previously found at Rocester (*cf*. Hofheim 1913, Taf. XIII, Nos. 16, 17 and 19, Webster 1996, fig. 49.15, Cat. No. 18, 138, 141). Context 6077 SF36 [Backfill of ditch F608]. Fig.28:16.

17. Corroded fragment of copper alloy with an openwork, fretted design. All of the edges are missing but the fragment appears to have been part of the central panel of a rectangular mount of military origin, with a characteristic fretted design which may, according to Webster (1958), 'be later than the mid-first century and probably replaced the solid nielloed plate mount' (Allason-Jones and Miket 1984, 3.771, 224). Length: 35mm, width: 25mm, thickness: 1mm. Context 6078 SF62 [Backfill of ditch F609]. Fig.28:17.

18. Openwork mount or pendant, probably from military equine equipment, roughly heart-shaped with the remains of two rivets on the reverse. While no exact parallels have been found, heart-shaped pendants were not uncommon, and examples with lunate or more elaborate openwork decoration have been found on many sites, including Vindolanda (Allason-Jones *et al.* 1985, Figure 40:16, 119–120). Length: 50mm, maximum width: 29mm, thickness: 1mm. Context 6101 SF67 [Backfill of ditch F613]. Fig.28:18.

19. Conical-headed pin, broken across the shaft. There are grooves beneath the head, which has irregularly spaced incised lines radiating from the point. A similar example from Colchester has been provisionally dated to the second century (Crummy 1983, fig. 31:497, 30–31). Length: 47mm, diameter: 8mm. Context 6030 SF10 [Phase 2 floor]. Not illustrated.

20. Hairpin, with a plain conical head, corroded and broken into two pieces. This unusual type of pin conforms to Group 1 as defined by Crummy, which has been tentatively dated to the second century (Crummy 1983, fig. 26:466, 28). Length: 83mm. Context 6076 SF35 [Backfill of ditch F613]. Not illustrated.

21. Dome-headed spike. Length: 195mm, diameter of head: 4mm. Context 6060 SF19 [Phase 2 floor]. Not illustrated.

22. Two fragments from a leather belt or strap, one of which has two *in situ* copper alloy rivetted bosses while the other fragment has one. A third boss fragment was also recovered. The leather was fairly well-preserved in a waterlogged context. Though the copper-alloy bosses were fragmentary, examination under a microscope revealed that very small portions of embossed design were apparent, suggesting that these bosses were as the more complete example No. 15, described above. Length: 43mm, width: 30mm, thickness: 2mm. Context 6613 [Backfill of pit F726]. Not illustrated.

23. Circular stud, broken, with traces of iron adhering to the inside. Diameter: 13mm, thickness: 1mm. Context 6061 SF30 [Backfill of pit F605]. Not illustrated.

24. Flat, circular stud with an offset shank. Diameter: 17mm, thickness: 1mm. Context 6070 SF38 [Backfill of ditch F609]. Not illustrated.

25. Circular stud, corroded. Diameter: 25mm, thickness: 1mm. Context 6613 SF66 [Backfill of pit F726] (found with Nos.15 and 22, above). Not illustrated.

26. Circular stud. Diameter: 23mm, thickness: 4mm. Context 6519 SF24 [Backfill of ditch F715]. Not illustrated.

27. Two flat, circular studs. Diameter: 14mm, thickness: 1mm. Context 6098 [Backfill of ditch F609]. Not illustrated.

28. Nail with small ovoid head. Diameter of head: 5mm, length of shank: 12mm. Context 6596 [Backfill of pit F727]. Not illustrated.

29. Plate fragment of copper alloy, with a single *in situ* rivet. Length: 27mm, width: 24mm, thickness: 1mm. Unstratified. Not illustrated.

30. Plate fragment of copper alloy with one circular perforated terminal. Context 6070 SF32 [Backfill of ditch F609]. Not illustrated.

31. Plate fragment of copper alloy with a curved, perforated terminal, now very corroded. Length: 15mm, width: 35mm, thickness: 1.5mm. Context 6087 SF52 [Backfill of ditch F612]. Not illustrated.

Copper-alloy Fragments
Context information can be found in the site archive.

Riveted plate: Context 6093 SF60,

Plate fragments:Contexts 3007, 6000, 6001 x 2, 6007, 6061 SF26, 6070 SF41, 6101 x 2, 6109, 6571 SF56, 6089 SF54.

Amorphous lumps: Contexts 6065, 6070 SF33, 6078, 6085, 6098.

Baked Clay Crucible and Metalworking Debris
A fragment from a bowl-shaped ceramic crucible was found. Further evidence for the on-site working of copper alloys came in the form of six globule-shaped fragments of slag, five of which came from one context (Context 6101), and one of which was leaded (Context 6086).

Catalogue

32. Fragment from a ceramic crucible with traces of copper-alloy slag adhering to the inside. Diameter: 45mm, height: 43mm, thickness: 10mm. Context 6089, SF55. Not illustrated.

Lead Objects
Eighteen fragments of lead, weighing a total of approximately 1937 grammes, were recovered. Of these, only three recognisable objects were identified, comprising a washer, a pot cramp with a pottery fragment *in situ*, and a circular disc (Nos. 33–35). Other items consisted of a ?pin-shaped object, perhaps a stopper for a small vessel (No. 36), and various unidentified fragments of strip, rod and plate, as well as two amorphous lumps, one of which included a high level of copper-alloy.

Catalogue

33. Washer. Diameter: 30mm, thickness: 4mm, diameter of central hole: 7mm, weight: 13g. Context 6520, SF44 [Backfill of ditch F702]. Not illustrated.

34. Pot cramp, enclosing a small fragment of oxidised coarseware pottery. The pot cramp is unusually large and unwieldy in view of the small fragment it still holds *in situ*, although its angle of curvature suggests that the vessel it was designed to secure was originally quite broad, and might have been a substantial cooking pot or storage jar. Length of longest side: 83mm, width: 35mm, thickness: 10mm, weight: 194g (including pot sherd). Context 6085 SF49 [Backfill of ditch F609]. Not illustrated.

35. Circular disc of leaded copper alloy with at least two concentric circles around the outer edge (the central area is now obscured by corrosion products), and a small 'post' placed centrally on the underside. This object might have been intended as a mount or decorative rivet. Diameter: 45mm, thickness: 3mm, weight: 35g. Context 6001 SF6 [Ploughsoil]. Not illustrated.

36. ?Pin-shaped object of leaded copper alloy, with a broad, badly cast head, perhaps intended as a stopper for an unguent bottle or flask. Length: 43mm, diameter of head:10mm, weight: 15g.Context 6000 SF63 [Ploughsoil]. Not illustrated.

37. Rectangular lead object with two slightly raised edges. Length: 40mm, width: 37mm, thickness: 18mm, weight: 162g. Unstratified SF46. Not illustrated.

38. Tapering lead strip with central perforation. Length: 120mm, width: 25mm, thickness: 14mm, weight: 82g. Context 6105 [Backfill of pit F614]. Not illustrated.

39. Round-sectioned rod. Length: 170mm, diameter: 18mm, weight: 131g. 6520 [Backfill of ditch F702]. Not illustrated.

40. Amorphous lump of leaded copper alloy. Length: 32mm, width: thickness: 30mm, thickness: 20mm, weight: 33g. 6520 [Backfill of ditch F702]. Not illustrated.

41. Amorphous lump of waste lead. Length: 130mm, width: 70mm, thickness: 15mm, weight: 787g. Context 6500 [Ploughsoil]. Not illustrated.

Lead Sheet Fragments
Context information can be found in the site archive.

Contexts 6001 (163g), 6025 (31g), 6500 x 3 (88g, 25g, 36g), 6532 x 3 (3g, 4g, 6g), 6095 (129g).

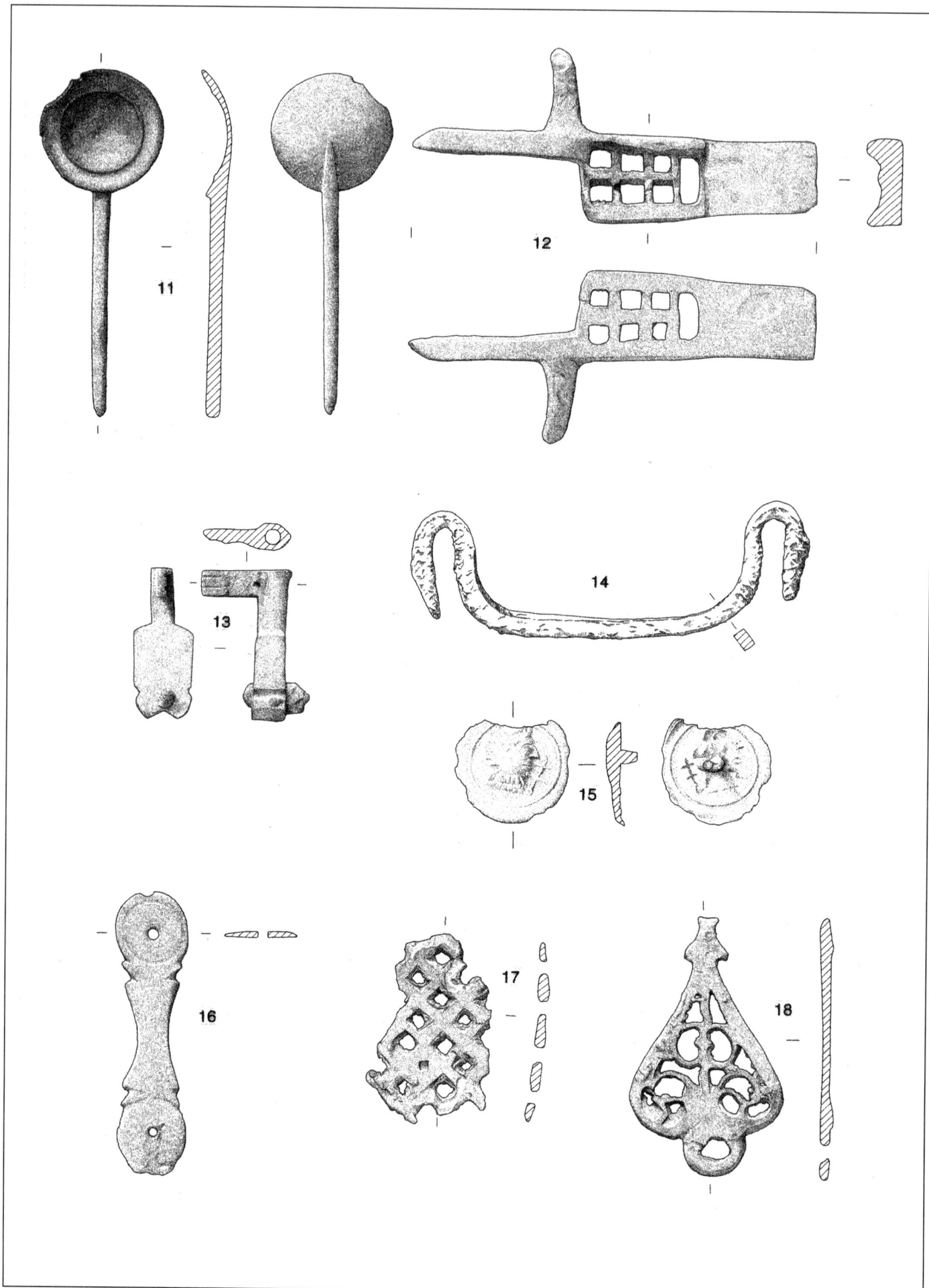

Fig. 28   Objects of copper alloy (Scale 1:1)

Iron Objects

A total of 37 iron objects and 434 nails was recovered. A small quantity of slag from ironworking was also recovered. Although the general condition of the ironwork was poor, with a high incidence of fragmentation and corrosion, several tools and fittings were identified in the collection (Nos.42–59), only one of which, a possible paring chisel (No. 42), was sufficiently complete for illustration.

Parallels for identifiable tools were sought in the corpus of Roman ironwork collected by Manning (1985), but in most cases accurate identification was precluded by the degree of corrosion, so that the object references given are based upon general size and shape rather than diagnostic criteria.

Catalogue

42. Possible paring chisel (Manning 1985, B27, 22, Plate 10). Length: 75mm, maximum width: 17mm, maximum thickness: 2mm. Context 6007 [Ploughsoil]. Fig.29.

43. Blade fragment, very corroded. Length: 60mm, maximum width: 28mm, thickness: 3mm. Context 6595 [Backfill of pit F726]. Not illustrated.

44. Blade fragment, very corroded. Length: 130mm, maximum width: 47mm, thickness: 6mm. Context 6025 [Ploughsoil]. Not illustrated.

45. Strip with perforation at one end. Length: 55mm, maximum width: 22mm, thickness: 1mm. Context 6060 [Phase 2 floor]. Not illustrated.

46. A rectangular-sectioned tapering rod. Length: 148mm, maximum width: 10mm, maximum thickness: 7mm. Context 6028 SF9 [Phase 2 floor]. Not illustrated.

47. Implement shaft or spike, consisting of a circular-sectioned length of iron. Length: 112mm, maximum width: 8mm, maximum thickness: 7mm. Context 6007 [Ploughsoil]. Not illustrated.

48. Possible cross-bar from a two-tined hoe (Manning, 1985, F13,47, Plate 19) or a baling fork (Manning, 1985, F67, 60, Plate 25). Length: 39mm, width: 13mm, thichness: 12mm. Context 6025 [Ploughsoil]. Not illustrated.

49. Bucket handle (Manning, 1985, P13, 102, Plate 47). Length: 175mm, width: 9mm, thickness: 8mm. Context 6001 [Ploughsoil]. Not illustrated.

50. Large wedge-shaped iron block with rectangular section. Length: 107mm, width: 35mm, maximum thickness:27mm. Unstratified. SF64. Not illustrated.

51. Long straight strip, possibly door furniture. Length: 163mm, width: 25mm, thickness: 3mm. Context 6001 [Ploughsoil]. Not illustrated.

52. L-staple with rectangular section. Length: 87mm, width: 17mm, thickness: 7mm. Context 6014 [Ploughsoil]. Not illustrated.

53. Ring, probably from chainlink. Diameter; 35mm, width: 4mm, thickness: 3mm. Context 6000 [Ploughsoil]. Not illustrated.

54. Binding strip with a round perforated end. Length: 86mm, maximum width:17mm, thickness: 3mm. Context 6065 [Backfill of pit F605]. Not illustrated.

55. Possible hinge fragment. Length; 102mm, maximum width: 25mm, thickness: 2mm. Context 6031 [Phase 2 floor]. Not illustrated.

56. A curved strip with a single perforation at one end and a copper-alloy attachment in the centre. This object is now very corroded but the copper-alloy element appears to have been a mount or finial. Length of curved strip: 85mm, width: 20mm, thickness: 8mm, height of copper-alloy attachment: 33mm, thickness: 15mm. Context 6105 [Backfill of pit F614].

57. Fragment of plate, possibly door furniture, with an organic imprint, probably from wood. Length: 38mm, width: 32mm, thickness: 3mm. Context 6065 [Backfill of pit F605].

58. Strip. Length: 110mm, width: 14mm, thickness: 2mm. Context 6001 [Ploughsoil]. Not illustrated.

59. Curved fragment. Length: 95mm, width:8mm, thickness: 8mm. Context 6105 [Backfill of pit F614]. Not illustrated.

Unidentified iron fragments were recovered from the following contexts, details of which can be found in the archive: Context 6001, Context 6014, Context 6046, Context 6066, Context 6078, Context 6105 x 4, Context 6534, Context 6595 x 5.

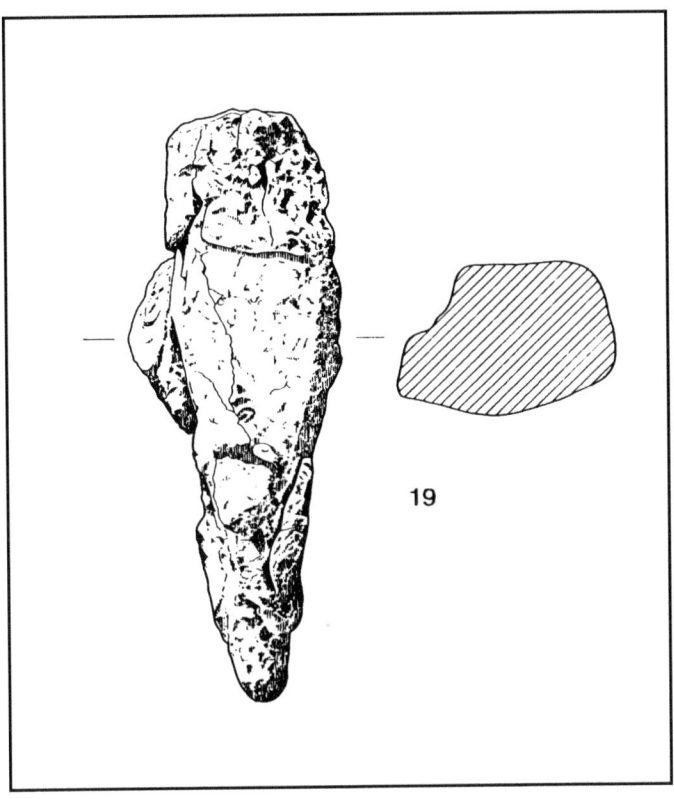

19

Fig. 29   Object of iron (Scale 1:1)

Ironworking Residues

Approximately 25.035kg or iron smithing slag and hearth bottom (not differentiated here) were recovered. The majority of this material came from deposits of Phase 2 (17.426kg), attesting to low-level on-site ironworking in this phase.

Iron nails

A total of 430 nails was recovered, of which 167 were unidentifiable fragments, either corroded heads or broken shanks. The complete nails were related to Manning's typology of Roman nails (Manning 1985, 133). The majority of the nails belonged to the most common nail groups, Group 1a and Group 1b, categorised by relative flatness of head.

With the exception of the large groups of nails from Contexts 6001 (75) and 6050 (44), the majority of nails was found in small groups of under ten and between 10–20 nails.

Type 1a: 107
Type 1b: 153
Type 2: 1
Type 3: 2
Unidentified: 167
Total nails found: 430

The nails are listed below by context, details of which can be found in the site archive:
2041 x 1, 6000 x 2, 6001 x 75, 6002 x 1, 6003 x 3, 6007 x 18, 6010 x 2, 6011 x 12, 6020 x 2, 6025 x 18, 6030 x 6, 6031 x 9, 6032 x 8, 6033 x 14, 6036 x 14, 6038 x 1, 6039 x 2, 6042 x 3, 6046 x 2, 6047 x 9, 6050 x 44, 6051 x 3, 6052 x 12, 6053 x 1, 6054 x 9, 6060 x 17, 6066 x 1, 6068 x 3, 6070 x 3, 6076 x 2, 6080 x 2, 6081 x 2, 6085 x 1, 6087 x 2, 6094 x 1, 6101 x 4, 6105 x 6, 6108 x 1, 6500 x 3, 6501 x 3, 6502 x 2, 6503 x 3, 6505 x 4, 6507 x 1 6508 x 3, 6509 x 13, 6510 x 1, 6511 x 7, 6018 x 3, 6520 x 3, 6521 x 2, 6525 x 9, 6529 x 2, 6532 x 1, 6542 x 1, 6553 x 1, 6554 x 4, 6555 x 1, 6559 x 1, 6563 x 2, 6564 x 2, 6576 x 1, 6577 x 2, 6582 x 1, 6587 x 1, 6592 x 1, 6596 x 12, 6613 x 7, 7000 x 1, SF 4 x 1, Unstratified x 19.

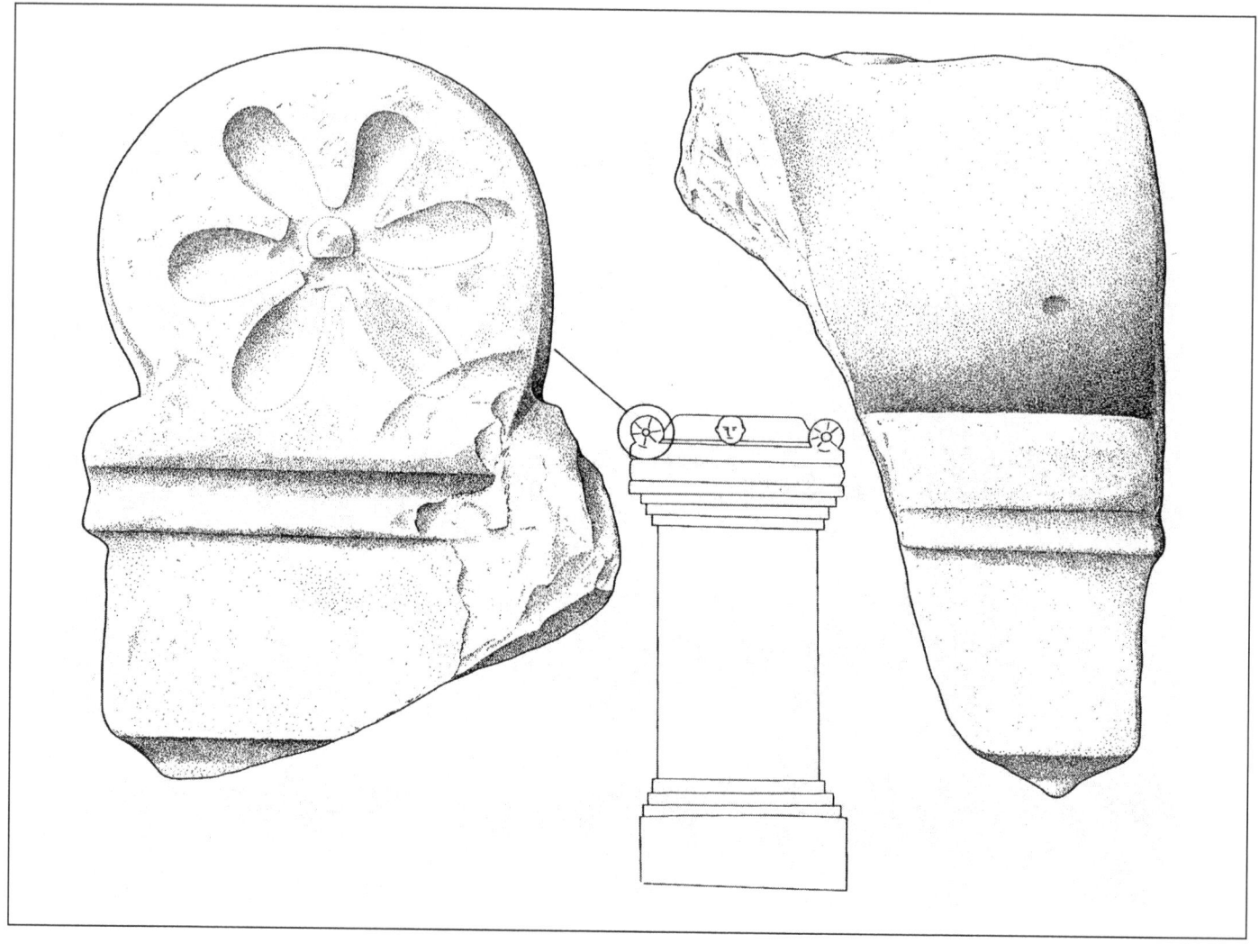

Fig. 30   Altar fragment (Scale 1:2)

Stone Objects
by I.M. Ferris

1.   Fragment from the top of an altar, comprising a portion of one of the two circular bolster mouldings on either side of the top of the altar. The bolster was decorated on its 'show face' with a six-petalled rosette, a common motif in such a context. Context 6511. [Backfill of pit F700]. Fig.30. Plate 14.

2.   Upper stone, rotary quern fragment. Diameter 410mm. Maximum thickness at kerb 100mm. 50% of stone present. Millstone Grit, probably from a Pennine or Peak source. Not illustrated. Context 6001. [Ploughsoil].

The Coin
(identification by A.S. Esmonde Cleary)

1.   Bronze coin; *as*, first–second century, illegible. Context 6519 [Backfill of ditch F715].

Copper-alloy Brooches
by Don Mackreth

Both Brooches 1 and 2 have their springs mounted in the Polden Hill manner: an axis bar through the coils is seated in a pierced plate at the end of each wing, the chord being held by a rearward-facing hook behind the head of the bow.

1.   Each wing has a pair of mouldings at the end. The plain bow has, on each side, a curved plate rising from the wing. The foot-knob has a thin moulding at the top and bottom. The return of the catch-plate has a buried moulding at the top and bottom, and another at a slight angle in the middle. Context 1003. [Backfill of pit F2 (= F604)].

2.   Each wing has a single moulding at its end. The hook behind the head is carried over the top of the bow and runs down the upper part of that to form a skeuomorph of the Colchester's hook. The bow is otherwise plain, tapering to a foot-knob with a think moulding at the top. Context 6511. [Backfill of pit F700].

Both of these belong to a major family spread over the Marches, much of the western side of England mainly south of the Mersey, but occurring in most parts of Roman Britain and even beyond. Brooch 1 is a classic example of the main type of which many are plain, Brooch 2 is also a member even if the plates on the sides of the head of the bow are not really in evidence. The whole family has been discussed before and nothing new has occurred to change the main thrust of the dating: *c.* AD 75 to *c.* 150/175 (Mackreth 1996, 300–1, fig.93,8).

3.   The integral spring has four coils and an internal chord. The section of the spring and the brooch generally shows that it had been forged, not cast. The upper section of the bow is rounded and it tapers to a very fine point. Context 3007. [Backfill of pit F700 (recorded in evaluation as F303)].

The rounded section of the bow shows that this is classifiable as a *Drahtfibel* Derivative, the generally poor form of the brooch, when compared with the more etiolated original, betraying a relatively late date. Close dating is not to be expected in the general group of weak Derivatives both of the *Drahtfibel* or the Nauheim. They run on from the middle of the first century to near the end, no group is demonstrably second century, and there is generally a weak representation towards the end of the first.

THE ANIMAL BONES
by Andy Hammon

Introduction

Due to problems of residuality, identified at assessment stage, it was decided that only the Phase 1 animal bone assemblage would be analysed in detail.

The mammal bones were recorded following a modified version of the method described in Davis (1992) and Albarella & Davis (1994). This system considers a selected suite of anatomical elements as "countable" (diagnostic zones); it does not include every bone fragment that is identifiable. Briefly, the skeletal elements considered are: all teeth (mandibular and maxillary); the skull (zygomaticus); scapula (glenoid articulation/cavity); distal humerus; distal radius; proximal ulna; carpals 2–3; distal metacarpal; pelvis (ischial part of the acetabulum); distal femur, distal tibia, calcaneum (sustentaculum), astragalus (lateral part), naviculo-cuboid/scaphocuboid; distal metatarsal; and proximal phalanges 1–3. At least 50% of the specified area has to be present to be "countable".

The following skeletal elements were always recorded for birds: scapula (articular end); proximal coracoid; distal humerus; proximal ulna; proximal carpometacarpus; distal femur; distal tibiotarsus; and distal tarsometatarsus.

Horn-cores with a complete transverse section were recorded as "non-countable", as were other elements of particular interest, such as deer antler, pathological and neo-natal/very young specimens.

Mandibular fragments were considered to be ageable when there were two or more teeth present with recognisable wear. Mandibular teeth, both *in situ* and loose, were aged using wear patterns. The system recommended by Grant (1982) was used for cattle and pig, whereas the wear of sheep/goat teeth was recorded according to Payne (1973 & 1987).

Measurements are listed in the Appendix Two. Von den Driesch (1995) defines the majority of these. All pig measurements follow the definitions of Payne & Bull (1988). Humerus "HTC" and "BT" and tibia "Bd" measurements were taken for all species as suggested by Payne & Bull (1988). Measurements "BatF", "a", "b", "1" and "4" for cattle and sheep/goat metapodials were taken using the criteria described by Davis (1992).

The differentiation of sheep and goat was attempted on the following elements: deciduous lower premolars (dP_3 and dP_4); humerus; metacarpal; tibia; astragalus; calcaneum; and metatarsal. The criteria defined by Boessneck (1969) were used for all elements except the teeth (Payne 1985) and the tibia (Kratochvil 1969). The distinction between Red deer (*Cervus elaphus*) and Fallow deer (*Dama dama*) was attempted using the criteria of Lister (1996). The chicken/guinea fowl/pheasant (*Gallus/Numida/Phasianus*) distinction was attempted on the following elements: articular end of the scapula, shaft of the carpometacarpus, proximal end of the femur and shaft of the tarsometatarsus.

Provenance and Preservation

Recovery

The majority of the animal bones recovered from the Orton's Pasture excavation were hand recovered. Additionally, 45 samples were taken for flotation and fine sieving. These samples ranged between 3 and 23 litres in volume. Residue from fine sieving was collected on a 1 mm mesh. However, sieving produced very few bone fragments, only a small proportion of which was "countable" using the diagnostic zone system described above.

Residuality and Contamination

Animal bone residuality is notoriously difficult to identify and to quantify. Various methods have been employed in the attempt to identify the volume of residual animal bone within an assemblage. The majority of which have relied on subjective criteria, such as differential surface colour and severity of abrasion. However, all such attempts to quantify animal bone residuality in this way have been problematic (*e.g.* refer to Dobney *et al.* undated). Therefore, pottery residuality is normally used as an indicator of animal bone residuality, although the two may not be directly linked.

The presence of mainly residual pottery in Phase 2 would therefore suggest that much of the animal bone may also be residual. Consequently, the animal bone from Phase 2 was considered not worth full investigation (Albarella & Lawless 1998).

The post-cranial elements recorded from Phase 1 demonstrated quite a low level of canid gnawing, only 8% (11 of 146). This would suggest that the majority of the animal bones was retrieved from their original anthropogenically deposited context, rather than from secondary deposition caused by scavenging dogs. Albarella & Lawless (1998) specifically noted contexts 6030 and 6038 as containing bones with canid gnawing, which were likely to have been the result of scavenging dogs causing secondary deposition.

Preservation

Most of the animal bones from Orton's Pasture were moderately well preserved. However, contexts 6506, 6532, 6548, 6577, 6587 and 6596 were poorly preserved (Albarella & Lawless 1998).

Fragmentation

The level of fragmentation in general was not exceptionally high, although contexts 6010, 6525 and 6526 were extremely fragmented (see below for the explanation). The relatively low number of loose teeth demonstrates the moderate level of fragmentation. It has been calculated that 21% (43 of 208) of the "countable" elements from the hand-retrieved assemblage were loose teeth. This is in direct contrast to highly fragmented assemblages where there are more loose teeth, for example the Iron Age assemblage from Covert Farm, Crick, Northamptonshire. The hand retrieved animal bone assemblage from Covert Farm (Field 2) consisted of 49% of loose teeth (Hammon 1998).

Overview and Discussion

The animal bones from Phase 1 of Orton's Pasture composed a small assemblage, only 211 "countable" fragments (based on the diagnostic zone system described above). Consequently, it has only been possible to make very general observations regarding the nature of the animal utilisation and activity at Orton's Pasture.

It has been possible to make some comparisons of the Orton's Pasture material to that from the nearby New Cemetery site, Rocester (Levitan 1996), located approximately 300m to the west of Orton's Pasture, almost directly in the present village centre (Esmonde Cleary & Ferris 1996). As outlined above, three successive Roman forts and a subsequent "small town" were discovered during the New Cemetery excavation (Esmonde Cleary & Ferris 1996). The archaeology at the two different sites is essentially part of the same Roman complex (Jones & Cuttler 1995).

Phase 1 of the Orton's Pasture excavation is roughly comparable to Phase 1A through to Phase 2B, which covers the period late first century to late second century AD at the New Cemetery (Levitan 1996).

Levitan (1996) divided the seven chronological phases at the New Cemetery into four groups for the purposes of studying the vertebrate assemblage. It is these four phases that have been used for the New Cemetery — Orton's Pasture comparison. They are as follows:

Group 1 – Phase 1A–1B. Late first- to mid-second-century military activity.

Group 2 – Phase 1C–2B. Mid-second- to late second-century military activity.

Group 3 – Phase 2C–3. Late third-century civilian activity.

Group 4 – Phase 3, Structure 6. Late third- to mid-fourth-century civilian activity.

Therefore, Groups 1 and 2 are from the same chronological period as the Orton's Pasture animal bone assemblage, although for the purposes of this analysis Group 1 has been ignored because it is too small to be statistically viable.

Species Composition

The vast majority of the "countable" bones belonged to the major domesticates (Tables 9 and 10). Cattle dominated the Orton's Pasture assemblage, followed by sheep/goat and then pig. Horse (context 6052), dog (contexts 6564 & 7000) and domestic chicken (contexts 6032, 6052, 6108, 6555 & 6564) were also present in low numbers.

A variety of wild animal and bird species was also present in low numbers. These included Red deer (*Cervus elaphus*) (contexts 6097 & 6503), duck (*Anas* sp.) (contexts 6032, 6094, 6101 & 6519), small rodent (context 6094) and small passerine (i.e. the songbirds) (context 6534).

Goose was also recorded in low numbers. The one recorded specimen probably belonged to that of a domestic goose (*Anser anser*), due to its size.

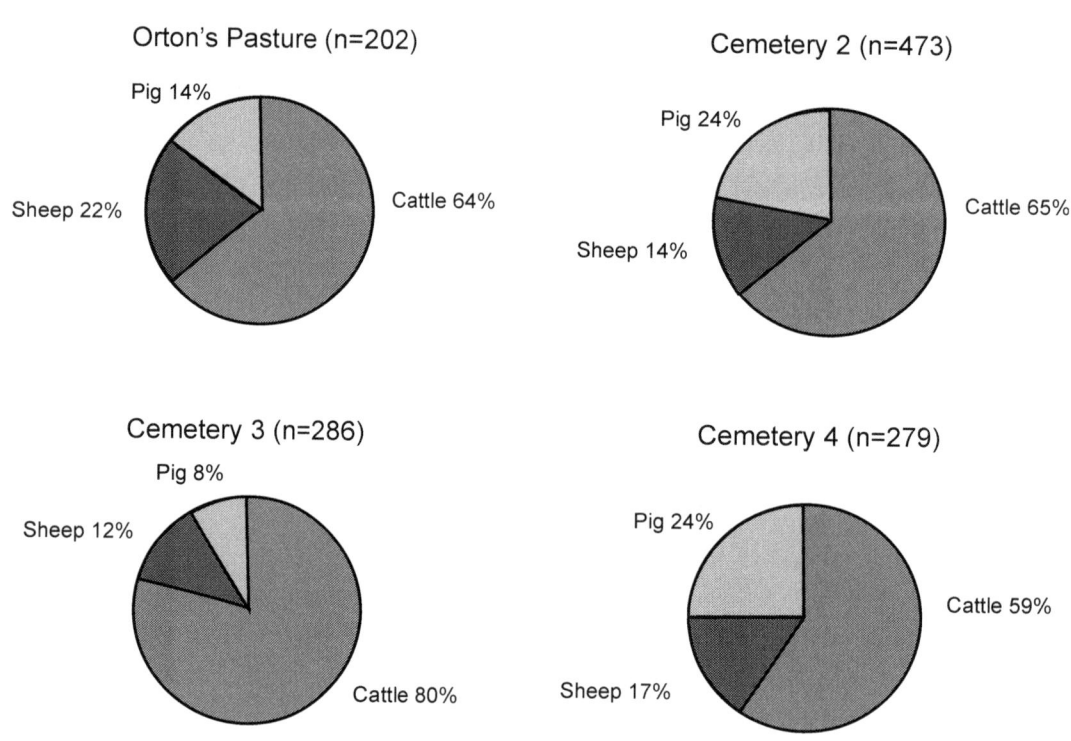

"Sheep" includes both sheep (*Ovis aries*) and sheep/goat (*Ovis/Capra*)

Fig. 31   Animal bone : relative abundance of major species at Orton's Pasture and New Cemetery sites
(New Cemetery data - Levitan 1996)

Each group at the New Cemetery generally mirrors the pattern observed at Orton's Pasture (Fig.31) for the relative abundance of cattle, sheep and pig to one another. Cattle are dominant within each group at the New Cemetery, with only the proportions of sheep and pig varying. Pigs were the second most numerous animals in Groups 2 and 4, whereas sheep were the most numerous in Group 3 (Levitan 1996). The pattern observed at Orton's Pasture is most similar to Group 2 from the New Cemetery. This was to be expected, as both assemblages represent the same chronological period and type of activity/ settlement. Consequently, it would appear as if no significant difference exists between the level of recovery from the two sites.

Due to the small size of this assemblage (see above) it is not possible to comment on the utilisation of sheep and pig. Therefore, as cattle are the most abundant species they will be concentrated upon for the remainder of this report.

It has, though, to be remembered that the importance of cattle may have been over-emphasised by a recovery bias favouring the larger bones from the larger mammals, at the expense of the smaller bones from the larger mammals and bones from the smaller mammals, birds, fishes and amphibians. Taphonomic considerations also cause a bias, with differential post-depositional preservation of different bones (summarised by Nicholson 1996).

Utilisation of Cattle

From the NISP (number of identified specimens) counts mentioned above it is clear that cattle were the most important species at Orton's Pasture (as well as at the New Cemetery). If live weight ratios are considered this becomes even more apparent. Using the mid-point values suggested by Dobney *et al.* (undated) from the Manching data set, the following proportions have been estimated for Orton's Pasture.

Cattle – 90%

Sheep/goat – 4%

Pig – 6%

The Manching data set considers the weight of one cow to be 275 kg, one sheep to be 37.5 kg and one pig 85 kg. Therefore, 7.3 sheep are required to equal one cow or 2.3 sheep to equal one pig (Dobney *et al.* undated).

The heavy reliance on cattle demonstrated by the Orton's Pasture assemblage is quite normal for a Roman military site (King 1984). However, it cannot be conclusively·proven that Orton's Pasture was a military site (Iain Ferris pers. comm.). King (1984) argued that on cultural grounds the species representation and utilisation would vary depending on whether the site was indigenous, Roman, civilian or military in nature. Roman military sites were characterised by this high reliance on cattle; about 42% of Roman military sites in Britain have 70% or more cattle bones within the assemblage (King 1984, 189).

Levitan (1996) concludes that in actual fact there is little difference in the relative abundance of the three major domesticates, cattle, sheep and pig, between any of the New Cemetery groups. The earliest civilian phase at the New Cemetery (Group 3) actually has the highest amount of cattle (Levitan 1996), which is in direct contrast to the hypothesis proposed by King (1984). Levitan suggests that this dichotomy

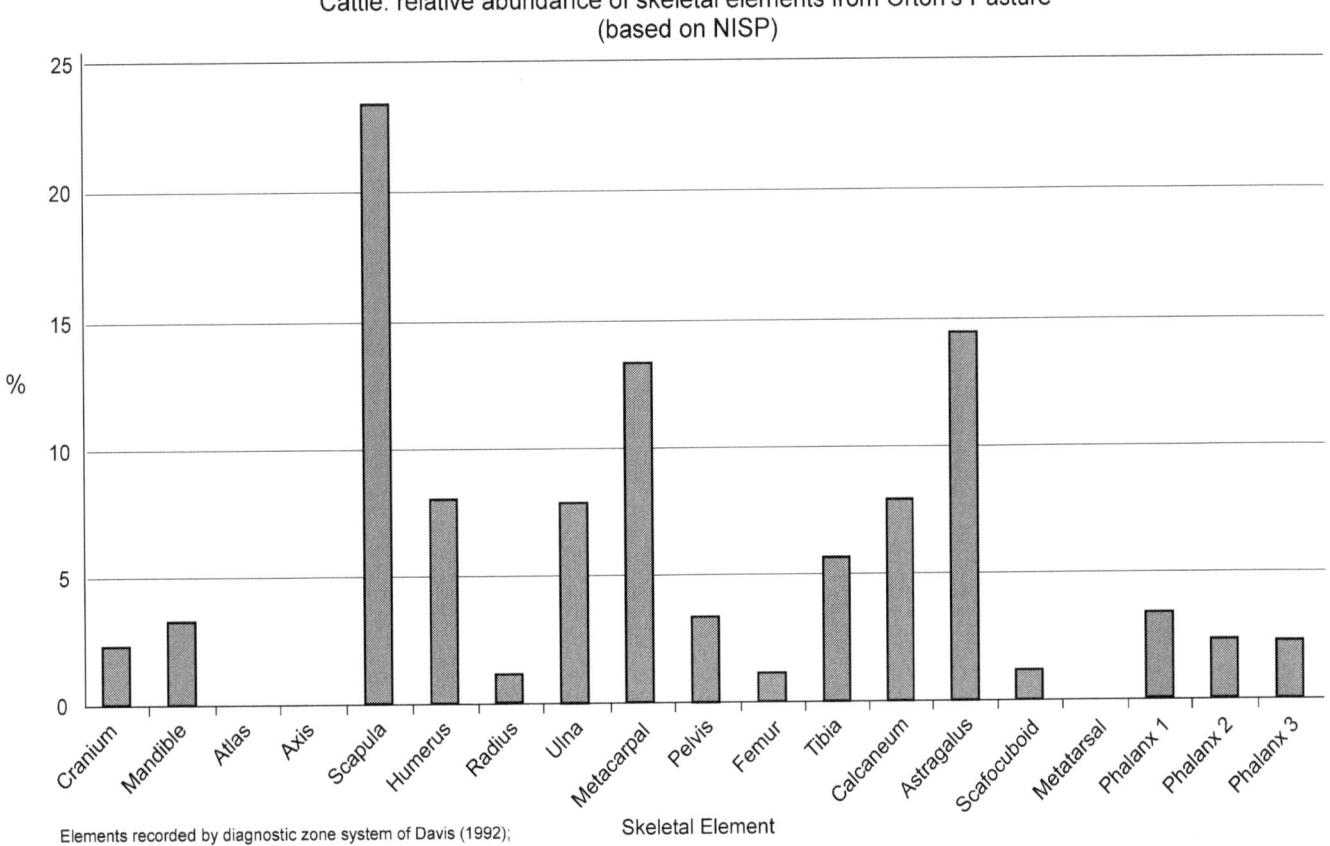

Cattle: relative abundance of skeletal elements from Orton's Pasture (based on NISP)

Elements recorded by diagnostic zone system of Davis (1992); Albarella & Davis (1994)

Skeletal Element

Fig. 32 Cattle : relative abundance of skeletal elements

may be due to the small sample size. As previously mentioned, the Orton's Pasture assemblage generally mirrors the New Cemetery Group 2 assemblage, although it has to be remembered that King's (1984) work is a review and only reflects overall trends, thus site specific characteristics may be obscured (Umberto Albarella pers. comm.)

The relative abundance of cattle skeletal elements (Fig.32) to one another would suggest that cattle were probably being butchered at Orton's Pasture, or in the immediate vicinity, because the assemblage is composed of a selection of most skeletal elements. For example, if cattle had been slaughtered elsewhere skulls and mandibles might have been expected to be absent. Taphonomy and differential preservation to a certain degree dictate the observed pattern (summarised by Brain 1981). For example, craniums and femora generally tend not to survive as well as the more compact, and subsequently more durable, elements such as the calcaneum and astragalus. The high number of scapulae has a different explanation (see below).

There is a slight dichotomy between the numbers of cattle metacarpals and the total absence of metatarsals (Fig.32). Not withstanding recovery biases and taphonomic considerations this may be the result of some particular on-site activity, for example joints of meat (formed by the hind limbs) being consumed elsewhere.

Figure 33 illustrates the relative abundance of cattle skeletal elements from the Orton's Pasture and the New Cemetery assemblages. With the exception of the scapulae from Orton's Pasture there is no discernible pattern that would suggest that cattle utilisation differed between chronological period or site. Levitan (1996, 198) interprets distribution of skeletal elements

as being characteristic of "a fairly mixed set of deposits".

Butchery marks (combined with the degree of fragmentation) are consistent with that deriving from kitchen refuse, the systematic reduction of the carcase into smaller portions. Orton's Pasture demonstrated a higher level of butchery (50%) than did any of the groups from the New Cemetery, which varied between 20% and 30% (Levitan 1996). This variance may have been caused by the different methods used to analyse the animal bone from the two sites. Either level of butchery is by no means unusual for the Roman period.

Several contexts (6010, 6525 and 6526) from Orton's Pasture demonstrate a very high degree of fragmentation and butchery, rendering the majority of bones "non-countable" using the diagnostic zone system described above. Shafts being split longitudinally and epiphyses being chopped across the articular surfaces typified this heavy fragmentation and butchery. This phenomenon has been noted from a number of other Roman assemblages, such as Lincoln (Dobney *et al.* undated).

Most "traditional" interpretations suggest that this phenomenon was representative of a single activity. Once the meat has been removed the bones were smashed into small fragments to be boiled in large cauldrons for the production of bone by-products (Dobney *et al.* undated). Van Mensch (1974) suggested that the similarly butchered assemblage from Zwammerdan (Holland) represents the waste from Roman soup kitchens. However, Dobney *et al.* (undated) refute this hypothesis, suggesting that it may have been linked to the exploitation of marrow and marrow fat. It has also been suggested that this type of butchery may be linked to the production of glue (Umberto Albarella pers. comm.).

Cattle: relative abundance of skeletal element
(New cemetery data from Levitan 1996)

Skeletal element:
1- Orton's Pasture = zygomaticus/Cemetery = frontal,
2 - mandible (tooth row), 3 - scapula (glenoid cavity),
4 - humerus (distal), 5 - radius (distal), 6 - ulna (proximal),
7 - metacarpal (distal), 8 - pelvis (ischium), 9 - femur (distal),
10 - tibia (distal), 11 - metatarsal (distal)

Number of bones/fragments:
Orton's Pasture = 108
New Cemetery 2 = 81
New Cemetery 3 = 31
New Cemetery 4 = 54

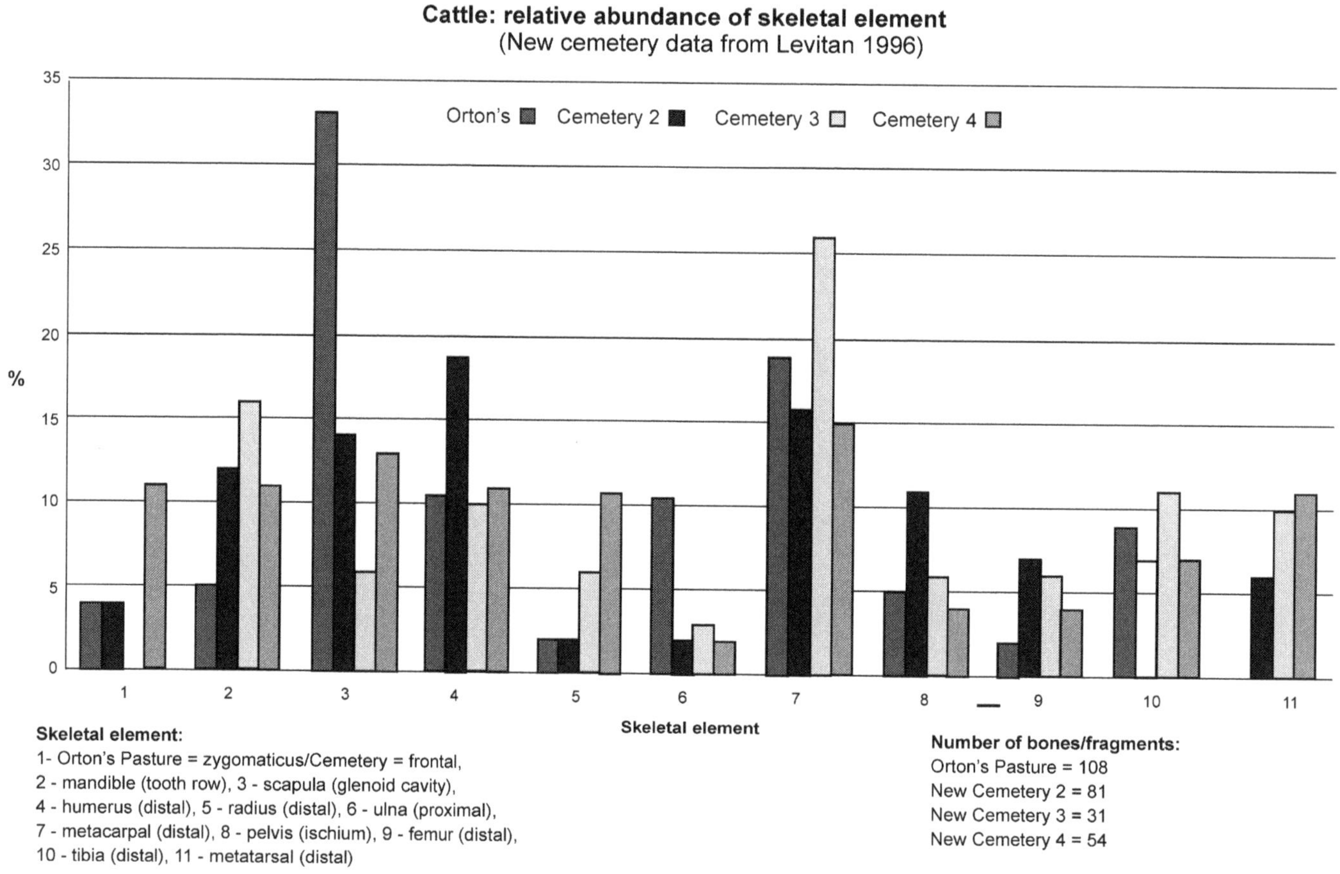

Fig. 33 Cattle : relative abundance of skeletal elements at Orton's Pasture and New Cemetery sites

The eleven scapulae recorded from context 7000 represented another typical Roman butchery pattern. This single context was the major contributor to the relatively high occurrence of this particular skeletal element within the Orton's Pasture assemblage (Fig.32) and probably represented a dump. The butchered scapulae were characterised by what is termed 'hook damage' (a hole through the blade). The butchery on these specimens was also characterised by the pattern described by Dobney *et al.* (undated, 26) in relation to the Lincoln material — "….trimming around the glenoid cavity, removal of the spina (spinous process)….small nicks or shaving marks….on the margo thoracalis". Again, this type of butchery is unique to the Roman period and was also noted from the New Cemetery assemblages by Levitan (1996). The 'hook damage' is thought to correspond to the shoulder being hung up in a "smoker and/ or a brine pit" to be cured (Dobney *et al.* Undated, 26). Thus, the "shaving and nick" marks represent the cured meat being stripped off the bone (Dobney *et al.* undated; Lauwerier 1988, 156).

Unfortunately, due to the lack of ageable cattle mandibles it has not been possible to construct survivorship/mortality curves for the Orton's Pasture assemblage. Therefore, it has not been possible to comment on how cattle were being utilised other than for meat.

Neither Orton's Pasture nor the New Cemetery provided much in the way of biometrical data. Subsequently, it has only been possible to directly compare the distal breadth (Bd) of the metacarpal from the two Rocester sites. The average distal breadth of cattle metacarpals from Orton's Pasture was 54.6 mm, whereas the New Cemetery Group 2 was 53.7 mm and Group 3 was 48.4 mm.

The Orton's Pasture individuals correspond directly to those from Group 2 at the New Cemetery, but are larger than those of Group 3. This is unsurprising, as Orton's Pasture and the New Cemetery Group 2 are from the same chronological phase. This may be significant and could represent deliberate stock improvement by the Romans who were importing cattle from the continent especially for the task (Audoin-Rouzeau 1991).

There are several parallels in Britain, which lends support to this hypothesis. Dobney *et al.* (undated) noted from the Lincoln assemblage particularly large cattle in the third century AD and suggested that they represented recent imports. After the third century the Lincoln cattle decrease in size and this was interpreted as the imported cattle being interbred with the indigenous varieties. Albarella (1997) suggests a similar reason for the existence of a group of large cattle at Great Holts Farm, Essex.

Summary and Conclusion

The Orton's Pasture animal bone assemblage is quite small. This, combined with the moderate fragmentation, meant that it has provided only general information regarding the economic and agricultural utilisation of the various animal species present. Subsequently, all observations are tentative.

The structures discovered at the New Cemetery (Group 2) are contemporaneous with Orton's Pasture. The Orton's Pasture assemblage is very similar to Group 2 from the New Cemetery site (in terms of species composition, size of individual, utilisation *etc.*), all of which correspond to the typical Roman military pattern observed at other sites in Britain and northwestern Europe.

To summarise, cattle by far were the most economically important animals. Sheep and pig were not very economically or culturally important. Cattle were predominately exploited for meat and bone by-products, which is demonstrated by the fragmentation and high level of butchery recorded at Orton's Pasture. Skeletal representation would suggest that animals were being slaughtered at Orton's Pasture, or in the near vicinity.

Large cattle specimens recorded from the animal bone assemblage may have been imported. Imported plant and, possibly, animal species have been noted at other Roman sites. The large cattle at Great Holts Farm, Essex, were interpreted as being continental imports (Albarella 1997), and were found in conjunction with imported plant species, such as Stone Pine (*Pinus pinea*) and olives (*Olea europaea*) (Murphy 1997).

Table 9: Number of "countable" specimens (Davis 1992; Albarella & Davis 1994) from Phase 1 of Orton's Pasture, Rocester, Staffordshire

Species	Total
Cattle (*Bos taurus*)	129
Sheep (*Ovis aries*)	10
Sheep/Goat (*Ovis/Capra* sp.)	35
Pig (*Sus scrofa*)	28
Equid (*Equus* sp.)	1
Dog (*Canis familiaris*)	2
Red Deer (*Cervus elaphus*)	1
Small rodent (R*odentia*)	2*
Chicken/Guinea Fowl/Pheasant (*Gallus/Numida/Phasianus* sp.)	3
Duck (*Anas* sp.)	1
Goose (*Anser* sp.)	1
Passerine (*Passeriformes*)	1*
Total	**211**

* specimens retrieved from sieving, all other specimens from hand collection

Table 10: Number of "countable" specimens (Davis 1992; Albarella & Davis 1994) and proportions of the major domesticates from Phase 1 of Orton's Pasture, Rocester, Staffordshire

Cattle	129	64
Sheep*	45	22
Pig	28	14
Total	**202**	

* combines both sheep *(Ovis aries)* and sheep/goat *(Ovis/Capra)*

Table 11: Bone measurements from Phase 1 of Orton's Pasture, Rocester, Staffordshire

CONTEXT	ELEMENT	TAXA	GL*	Bd	Dd**	BT	HTC	LA***	SD	BaF	A	B
6555	HU	GNP	760	163					76			
6555	TI	OVA		230								
6564	PE	CAF						242				
6564	FE	GNP		131	110							
6565	HU	B					265					
6565	MC	B			249					462	243	240
6031	MC	B		624	298					555	282	298
6032	AS	B	597	370	332							
6032	AS	B			376							
6032	MC	B		459	224					409	218	197
6032	PE	O						224				
6052	AS	B		352	308							
6052	MC	B		503	248					426	239	235
6052	MC	B			285							
6054	AS	B	577	366	315							
6054	MC	B								443		
6054	TI	B		531								
6054	TI	S		302								
6054	TI	S		311								
6010	AS	B	612	382								
6070	MC	B		621	305					558	286	296
6525	AS	B		371								
6080	PE	O						250				
6089	MC	B		522	246					449	248	251
6094	MC	B		540	253					484	256	252
6095	PE	B						710				
6095	RA	O	1370						140			
6095	HU	OVA				272	127					
6108	MC	B		550	258					495	269	259
7000	TI	OVA		224								

Table 12: Mandibular teeth measurements from Phase 1 of Orton's Pasture, Rocester, Staffordshire

CONTEXT	TAXA	dP4L	dP4W	M1WA*	M1WP	M2WA*	M2WP	M3L	M3WA*	M3WC	M12WA	M12WP
6555	O								81			
6565	B							371	151			
6565	O								81			
6031	S					136	144	352		123		
6052	B							339	150			
6052	O					93			90			
6052	OVA		67	71								
6054	OVA		59									
6054	OVA		61									
6054	S										100	102
6054	S	189	81	90	87							
6070	OVA		58	65		73						
6519	B							363	150			
6519	S							362		120		
6085	OVA		60									
6085	S			90	104	125	136					
6095	OVA		61									
6095	S	168	77	95	98							
6097	OVA		58									
6108	S			82								
6503	B							353	148			
6503	O								93			

APPENDIX TWO

Measurements of animal bones and teeth

All measurements are taken in tenths of a millimetre. See text for an explanation of how the measurements were taken. Phase, species and then context order the data (Tables 11 and 12).

ELEMENT CODES
HU = humerus
RA = radius
MC = metacarpal
PE = pelvis
FE = femur
TI = tibia
MT = metatarsal
AS = astragalus

TAXA CODES
B = *Bos taurus* (cattle)

O = *Ovis/Capra* (sheep/goat)
OVA = *Ovis aries* (sheep)
S = *Sus scrofa* (pig)
EQ = *Equus* sp. (equid)
CAF = *Canis familiaris* (dog)
GNP = *Gallus/Numida/Phasianus* (chicken/guinea fowl/pheasant)

MEASUREMENTS
Bone:

* GLl in astragalus and GLC in humerus
** Dl in astragalus and '3' in metapodials
*** LAR in dog

Teeth:

* WA = anterior width in pigs, all other species width of occlusal surface

SHELL
by I.M. Ferris

Small quantities of marine shell (25 fragments) came from 13 contexts, all from the northern enclosure (Enclosure 1) and pits outside the enclosure to its north. All identifiable fragments were of the common European oyster, *Ostrea edulis*.

Contexts containing shell: 6003, 6007, 6025, 6031, 6036, 6038, 6046, 6070, 6076, 6086, 6090, 6509, 7000.

CHARRED PLANT REMAINS
by Angela Monckton

Introduction
During the excavation samples were taken for charred plant remains from the fills of pits and ditches, in order to recover evidence of crops, diet and possibly of activities on the site in the past. An unusual find of charred fruits of dates and stone pine nuts in a pit (F700) in the south enclosure was made during the assessment of the samples which was deemed worthy of fuller investigation.

Methods
A total of 46 samples was taken from features thought to have the potential to produce plant remains. Samples were usually of 10–20 litres in size but included some smaller samples. These were processed by wet sieving, with flotation onto a 0.5mm mesh sieve and the resulting flotation fractions (flots) were air-dried and packed carefully. The flots were then sorted for plant remains using a stereo microscope. Some of the flots were large, so a part of these only was sorted. The residues of two of the samples were found to contain charred material and these were also sorted and the remains added to those from the flots. The type and quantity of remains were then recorded, in order to assess the samples and this information was used to select samples for analysis.

Twelve of the samples were selected for analysis, including the most productive samples from each area and group of features. During analysis, the selected flots were checked for additional plant remains and more of the flot sorted for the sample from F700. However, many of the flots were large and could not be sorted further within the resources available, so further examination may add to the remains found. The remains from the selected samples were identified by comparison with modern reference material in the Department of Archaeology at the University of Leicester. The plant remains were counted and recorded in Table 13, the names and order follow Stace (1991) and are seeds in the broad sense, unless stated. The remains from those samples not selected for analysis were also identified and summarised in Table 14.

Results, the Plant Remains and Contexts Sampled
Cereals
Cereal remains were found in small numbers in most of the samples. The charred cereal remains (Table 13) included both grains and chaff of wheat (*Triticum* sp), grains of cultivated barley (*Hordeum vulgare* sp) and occasional grains of possible

rye (*Secale cereale*). The wheat chaff (glumes) was mainly of spelt (*Triticum spelta*) but a few grains were identified as emmer (*Triticum dicoccum*) because of their characteristic hump-backed shape (Jacomet 1987). Both spelt and emmer are glume wheats where the grains are held firmly in the chaff (glumes) and require several steps of processing to free the grain. This type of grain can be stored or transported with the chaff still present, so that chaff is found on both producer and consumer sites (Hillman 1984). Hulled barley (*Hordeum vulgare*) was found with the occurrence of twisted grains, which indicated the presence of six-row barley, although the presence of other forms could not be excluded.

Stone pine

One of the samples from pit F700 in the the south enclosure contained numerous fragments of stone pine nut shell (*Pinus pinea*) (Plate 15), including 19 whole nuts ranging from 18.5 x 9.5mm to 11.0 x 5.5mm, average 15.5 x 8.5mm, in size. These had not been opened to remove the edible kernel. There were also 65 half nut shells which made a total of 52 nuts. Some charred, shrivelled kernels were also present. In addition, a number of moderate-sized nut shell fragments, possibly amounting to the equivalent of a further 25 nuts, together with a smaller volume of tiny fragments, were found in the same deposit. Therefore a minimum number of 77 nuts was present, with possibly around 90 in all. Cone scales were also found in the sample. A large complete scale measured 32 x 18mm, and there were 44 similar scales and 14 smaller scales making a total of 58 cone scales. Part of a cone apex was also found, with nine smaller scale bases attatched. A complete cone can produce a hundred seeds and the scales can bear either one or two seeds although the upper and lower scales are smaller and often sterile (Kislev 1988). The totals found suggest that the remains recovered were possibly from a single cone. Stone pine is a plant of the Mediterranean region, although it can grow and fruit in this country when introduced, being fully hardy (Brickell 1989). It is an unusual find in Britain.

Dates

In the same deposit from pit F700 came two whole charred date fruits (*Phoenix dactylifera*) and a date stone with the characteristic furrow (Wendy Smith pers. comm.). The dates were almost complete (Plate 16) and measured 37 x 16mm and 39 x 18mm, one of which had part of the stone visible through a break in the flesh. The stone measured 19 x 7mm. Whole charred dates are an unusual find in this country, over 20 were found at Colchester (Murphy 1984) and were then the only recorded find of dates in Roman Britain. The fruits found there compare in condition, although they are rather smaller. Dates grow in the humid-parts of the middle East (Polunin 1976) and in the Mediterranean area, so that these are undoubtedly an import. Date fragments were also found in pit F703.

Other food plants

A single grape pip (*Vitis vinifera*) was found in the sample from F703 in the south enclosure. This plant will grow and fruit in this country and is cultivated here today, and may therefore be from local cultivation in garden or field, or may be an import. A few poorly preserved apple or pear pips (*Malus/Pyrus*) were found, possibly from cultivated plants. Fragments of hazel nutshell (*Corylus avellana*) were found and a possible sloe stone fragment (*Prunus spinosa*), as evidence of probably wild plants used as food.

Wild plants

The seeds of wild plants found were mainly the weeds of arable and disturbed ground, such as cleavers (*Galium aparine*), docks (*Rumex* sp), fat-hen (*Chenopodium album*) and knotweed (*Polygonum* sp). These were either weeds of the cereals or from disturbed ground such as is found near settlements. The most numerous arable weed seeds were those of the large grasses (Poaceae), including brome grass (*Bromus* sp), which are often found with charred cereals. Some of the weeds such as sedges (*Carex* sp) and buttercup (*Ranunculus* sp) grow in damp conditions which may be found in some areas of cultivated fields, field ditches or could possibly have been brought to the site with fodder or plant material used as flooring or animal bedding. Grassland plants possibly from this type of material include knapweed (*Centaurea nigra*) and ribwort plantain (*Plantago lanceolata*), although all these plants could be weeds of the fields or settlement. The perennial plants ribwort plantain and heath grass (*Danthonia decumbens*) are thought to have been weeds of ard cultivation and both were found with abundant cereal grain at a nearby site (Moffett 1993).

The samples

The samples from the pits and ditches of the north enclosure generally had few remains present, consisting of a few cereal grains and weed seeds and occasional fragments of chaff with a few fragments of hazel nutshell (Table 13). This probably represents redeposited material from a general scatter of food preparation waste somewhere in the vicinity. Two of the pits in the south area differed, F700 having a concentration of stone pine nutshell and cone fragments together with the charred dates. This sample from F700 consisted of a lens of charred material (6516) in the pit, a sample from the same pit (6511) contained a few small fragments of pine nut shell, and, although only part of the sample was sorted, remains were not numerous. The pit F703 contained a much smaller quantity of stone pine and date fragments together with a grape pip. There was also a background of the same kind of waste as found in the north enclosure in both these features. The third pit F701 and the south enclosure ditch F705 (Table 13) from a section excavated near to the pits, contained a trace of stone pine nut shell (Table 14), together with similar waste to the north enclosure. Other samples from the south enclosure contained similar remains to the north enclosure, although not all samples could be completely sorted, the remains were also in a generally low concentration.

Discussion

The cereals found consisted mainly of spelt wheat with a little emmer, together with barley which is the situation found on sites of this date in the midlands and the south of England (Greig 1991). Rye was possibly also present, and it was found at the nearby New Cemetery site where it was thought to be a weed of the other cereals (Moffett 1993). In contrast to that site, the cereal remains were few in number, although similar in containing little chaff. The few grains with weed seeds and a trace of chaff may be waste from the final cleaning of cereals for consumption and the small amount found here can only indicate use of cereals in the vicinity.

The sample from pit F700 contained nuts and cone fragments of the stone pine, a date stone and two charred whole dates. Stone pine and dates are both exotic and are rare finds in Roman contexts in this country. Stone pine, also called umbrella pine, is found wild from Portugal to Asia Minor and has been planted in the Mediterranean region for millennia. This tree will grow and fruit in this country if introduced into cultivation. The cones can be harvested and stored until ripe, then opened in the sun to remove the nuts. The nuts are then floated in water to separate the empty seeds and cone scales (Kislev 1988) which may explain the unopened nuts found here. The nuts are opened with the aid of fire (Kislev 1988), so it is possible for accidental burning to occur at this stage. However, the majority of the nut shell found here is in halves or fragments, suggesting that the shell was discarded after consumption, together with the empty nuts and cone fragments. The kernels were a favoured ingredient in Roman food, they were used as a condiment in conjunction with asafoetida as a substitute for the north African plant laserpithum which became extinct due to intensive gathering (Cappers 1995). The seeds are mentioned as an ingredient in many of the recipes of Apicius as a flavouring and accompaniment for meat, fish and game (Edwards 1984).

Of the five other finds of stone pine in England before 1988 (Kislev 1988), two were from temple sites. One of these was the temple of Mithras in London where pottery associated with ritual offerings, chicken bones and other ritual objects were found; the second temple find was at Verulamium. The three other finds, however, were not associated with temples, one was from a waterlogged refuse deposit from London, another from the Royal Exchange site in London and the third from Chew Park, Somerset (Kislev 1988). The cones are pictured in wall paintings and mosaics from Pompeii and Herculaneum and the tree was worshipped in a Phrygian cult which was later celebrated in Rome (Kislev 1988). The find from Rocester is from an area with other ritual associations, the stone pine may provide additional evidence of this. However, the remains may represent food waste. A recent find of stone pine from a late Roman farm at Boreham, Essex, found with other fruits and nuts, was considered to be evidence of the varied diet of the occupants (Murphy 1997).

The only published find of charred dates at present is from Colchester Building 5 and was the only record of the fruit in Roman Britain at the date of publication and was clearly an import (Murphy 1984). The dates found at Colchester had not been pressed into blocks for transportation (Murphy 1984), which appears to be the case with the remains found here at Rocester. At Colchester the fruits were charred in the burning of the building but at Rocester there is no evidence to suggest why the dates were burnt. The find of these fruits shows their importation from the middle East or the Mediterranean region and suggests the relatively high status of the occupants.

Conclusions

Small numbers of cereal remains, mainly grains, were found in most of the features sampled. The cereals consisted of wheat, mainly spelt with a little emmer, and hulled barley including six-row barley. Evidence of probably cultivated plants was found from a grape pip and apple or pear pips. Some evidence for gathered food was found showing that hazel nuts and possibly sloe were consumed. Because of their low concentration, these remains were thought to be part of a general scatter of redeposited waste, probably from food preparation on, or near, the site.

A pit in the south enclosure contained numerous remains of stone pine nuts and cone fragments, which may though represent only one cone, because they can contain around a hundred seeds. The find was from a lens of charred material in a pit, F700, so probably represents a single deposit. These remains were found in one of a group of three pits near to a small stone building in the south enclosure. There were also a few fragments from the other two pits and a nearby ditch section which provide very limited evidence of a scatter from the same or similar material, depending on whether these features were open at the same time. Some of the nuts from F700 were complete and may have been discarded because they were empty. However, the majority of the nutshell was in halves or broken, suggesting the nuts had been consumed and the waste shell and cone fragments burnt for disposal. Stone pine is known to have ritual associations, but is also known from many Roman recipes, so its use here could be from either or both of these uses. The stone pine occurred here with two charred whole dates and remains of both these plants is unusual. The dates would have been imported from the middle East or Mediterranean region and this may be the case for the stone pine, although the tree will fruit in this country. The presence of unusual and imported fruits suggests the relatively high status of the site or the occupants.

Acknowledgements

I am grateful to Ellie Ramsay for the efficient processing and sorting of the samples and for providing information for the assessment of the samples. I am very grateful to Dr James Greig of Birmingham University for help with the identification of the stone pine, for taking the photographs for Plates 15 and 16, and for his helpful comments. I would like to thank Dr Wendy Smith of Leicester University for confirmation of the identification of the date stone, also Lisa Moffett of Birmingham University for reading the report and for her helpful advice and comments. This work was carried out during employment by the University of Leicester Archaeological Services.

Table 13 Charred Plant Macrofossils from Roman contexts of second-century AD date from Orton's Pasture, Rocester, Staffordshire

Area	N	N	N	N	N	N	S	S	S	S	S	S	
Feature No.	602	603	604	719	702	715	700	701	703	704	705	706	
Context	6054	6042	6094	6577	6528	6559	6516	6522	6508	6532	6533	6534	
Context type	Pit 1	Pit 1	Pit 1	Pit 2	D	D	Pit	Pit	Pit	D	D	D	
GRAINS													
Triticum cf *dicoccum*	-	-	-	-	-	-	-	-	-	1	-	-	Emmer
Triticum sp.	5	2	1	1	1	2	4	-	1	4	-	-	Wheat
Hordeum sp. hulled	5	2	2	2	-	-	-	-	1	-	3	3	Barley
Hordeum sp. hulled, twisted	2	1	-	-	-	-	-	-	-	-	1	-	Barley
Hordeum vulgare L.	-	-	-	-	-	1	-	1	-	-	-	-	Barley
Secale cereale L.	-	1cf	-	-	1cf	-	-	-	-	-	1	-	Rye
Cereal indet.	13	10	6	6	7	4	3	2	10	6	9	6	Cereal
Cereal fragments	+	+	-	-	-	-	-	+	+	-	+	-	Cereal fragments
Cereal/Poaceae	3	-	3	-	-	-	1	-	6	-	-	1	Cereal/Grass
Culm node large	1	-	1	-	-	-	1	-	-	-	-	1	Cereal stem
CHAFF													
Triticum spelta L. glume	-	2	-	-	-	-	-	-	-	-	2	1	Spelt
Triticum cf *spelta* glume	-	2	-	-	-	-	-	-	-	-	-	-	Spelt
T. dicoccum/spelta glume	-	11	-	4	1	1	-	-	-	-	2	-	Glume wheat
T. dicoccum/spelta rachis	-	1	-	1	-	-	-	-	-	-	-	-	Glume wheat
FRUIT AND NUTS													
Pinus pinea L. nuts (whole + halves/2)	-	-	-	-	-	-	52	-	2	-	-	-	Stone pine nuts
Pinus pinea nutshell (approx no. of nuts)	-	-	-	-	-	-	25	-	4	-	-	-	Stone pine nuts
cf *Pinus pinea* (immature nuts)	-	-	-	-	-	-	11	-	-	-	-	-	?Stone pine nuts
Pinus pinea nutshell fragments	-	-	-	-	-	-	++	1	+	-	-	-	Stone pine nut shell
Pinus pinea L. cone scale bases	-	-	-	-	-	-	67	-	6	-	-	-	Stone pine cone scales
Corylus avellana L.	3	11	-	1	-	-	3	-	-	1	4	-	Hazel nut shell
cf *Prunus spinosa* L. fragment	-	-	-	-	-	-	-	-	-	-	-	3cf	Sloe
Malus/Pyrus	-	-	-	-	-	1	2	-	-	-	-	-	Apple/Pear
Vitis vinifera L.	-	-	-	-	-	-	-	-	1	-	-	-	Grape vine
Phoenix dactylifera (whole + stone)	-	-	-	-	-	-	2+1	-	-	-	-	-	Dates (whole + stone)
Phoenix dactylifera fragments	-	-	-	-	-	-	4	-	1cf	-	-	-	Dates (fragments)
Nutshell indet fragments	-	-	-	-	-	-	11	-	-	-	-	-	Nutshell
WILD PLANTS													
Ranunculus subgen *Ranunculus*	-	-	-	-	-	-	-	-	-	-	-	1	Buttercup
Ranunculus sp	-	-	-	-	-	-	-	1	-	-	1	-	Buttercup
Chenopodium album type	1	1	2	1	-	-	5	-	-	-	-	-	Fat-hen
Stellaria sp	-	-	-	-	-	-	-	-	-	-	-	2	Chickweed type
Persicaria cf *maculosa*	1	-	-	-	-	-	-	2	-	-	2	-	Persicaria
Polygonum sp.	-	3	-	-	-	-	-	-	-	-	-	-	Knotweed
Polygonum aviculare agg.	-	-	-	-	-	-	-	1	-	-	-	-	Knotgrass
Rumex sp.	-	1	-	1	1	-	-	2	3	-	4	-	Dock
Brassicaceae	-	-	-	-	-	-	-	-	1	-	-	-	Cabbage family
Vicia/Pisum/Lathyrus	-	-	-	3	-	-	-	-	-	-	-	-	Vetch/Peas
Vicia/Lathyrus	-	-	-	1	-	-	-	1	-	1	-	-	Vetch/Vetchling
Medicago/Melilotus/Trifolium	2	4	-	4	-	-	-	1	8	1	-	1	Medick/Melilot/Clover
Plantago lanceolata L.	-	2	-	-	-	-	-	-	-	-	1	-	Ribwort plantain
Galium aparine L.	-	-	-	-	-	-	-	2	2	-	-	-	Cleavers
Sambucus nigra L.	-	-	-	-	-	-	-	-	1	-	-	-	Elder
Centaurea nigra L.	-	-	-	-	-	-	-	-	-	-	1	-	Knapweed
Carex sp	-	1	1	-	-	-	-	-	-	-	11	5	Sedge
Bromus hordeaceus/secalinus	1	-	-	1	1	-	-	1	-	2	6	1	Brome grass
Danthonia decumbens (L.) DC	-	-	-	-	-	-	-	2	-	-	1	-	Heath grass
Poaceae large	4	4	2	5	3	5	-	-	2	2	3	-	Grasses
Poaceae small	-	1	-	-	-	2	-	-	-	-	1	1	Grasses
Indetermined seeds	2	1	2	1	-	1	9	-	4	2	3	1	Seeds
Thorns straight/curved	-	-	-	1s	-	-	1c	-	-	-	-	-	Thorns
Buds woody	-	1	-	-	-	-	5	1	5	-	-	-	Tree/shrub buds
Tuber fragments	-	-	-	-	1	-	-	-	-	-	-	1	Tubers
Culm fragments small	-	-	-	-	-	-	-	-	-	-	2	1	Grass stem
Bark fragments	+	-	+	-	-	-	+	-	+	-	-	+	Bark fragments
Immature cone/catkin	-	-	-	-	-	-	1	-	-	-	-	-	Immature cone/catkin
?Kernels of pine nut	-	-	-	-	-	-	11	-	-	-	-	-	?Kernels
TOTAL	43	62	20	33	16	17	219	18	58	20	58	31	(Items)
Vol sample	21	10	21	15	16	20	21	17	10	21	17	19	(Litres)
Vol flot	400	160	650	180	70	190	600	170	370	140	350	270	(mls)
% Sorted	50	all	25	all	all	all	all	all	50	all	50	50	(%)
Items/litre	4.1	6.2	3.8	2.2	1.1	0.9	10.5	1.1	11.6	1.0	6.8	3.3	(Items/litre)

Key. + = present, ++ = abundant, D = Ditch. Remains are seeds in the broad sense unless described otherwise.

Table 14   Summary of charred plant remains in all Roman samples

Cont	Feat		S.Vol litres	F.Vol. mls.	Sorted %	Grain	Chaff	Seeds	Hazelnut	Pine nut	Other
6054	F602	N/P.1*	21	460	25 +25	28	-	11	3	-	-
6042	F603	N/P.1*	10	160	all	16	-	18	-	-	-
6097	F603	N/P.1	13	130	all	1	-	2	-	-	-
6100	F603	N/P.1	21	190	all	6	3	5	-	-	Fibre
6060	F604	N/P.1	23	560	25	1	-	1	-	-	-
6094	F604	N/P.1*	21	650	25	12	-	7	-	-	-
6095	F604	N/P.1	9	180	all	5	2	11	1	-	-
6108	F617	N/P.1	8	140	all	-	-	-	-	-	-
6096	F727	N/P.2	20	100	all	3	-	5	-	-	-
6577	F719	N/P.2*	15	180	all	9	5	17	1	-	-
6581	F719	N/P.2	10	30	all	-	-	1	-	-	-
6582	F725	N/P.2	13	100	all	3	-	4	1	-	-
6586	F725	N/P.2	20	20	all	1	-	3	-	-	-
6592	F725	N/P.2	10	140	all	3	-	1	-	-	-
6595	F726	N/P.2	11	120	all	-	-	2	2	-	2fs 1ca
6613	F726	N/P.2	20	450	33	3	-	8	2	-	1fs ch
6596	F727	N/P.2	19	460	25	3	-	5	2	-	-
6528	F702	N/D*	16	70	all	9	1	5	-	-	-
6554	F715	N/D	20	400	25	2	-	6	1	-	1 ch
6559	F715	N/D*	20	190	all	7	1	8	-	-	-
6105	F614	N/Pit	18	700	25	3	-	1	-	-	-
6107	F616	N/PH	11	1100	12.5	-	-	-	-	-	-
6109	F613	N/Gu	13	500	25	-	-	1	-	-	-
6038	-	N/Spr	10	1100	12.5	-	-	-	-	-	-
6056	-	N/Spr	22	1600	12.5	-	-	-	-	-	-
6082	F610	N/BS	12	2500	6	-	-	3	-	-	1 ch
6597	F729	N/Sc	8	20	all	3	-	1	-	-	-
6511	F700	S/Pit	20	800	12.5	2	-	7	-	8	-
6516	F700	S/Pit*	21	600	20+80	9	-	14	5	172	5 fruits
6518	F701	S/Pit	21	440	25	1	-	-	-	-	-
6521	F701	S/Pit	22	260	50	1	-	13	-	-	-
6522	F701	S/Pit*	17	170	all	3	-	13	1	1	-
6508	F703	S/Pit*	10	370	45	18	-	21	14	-	-
6532	F704	S/D*	21	140	all	11	-	8	1	-	-
6533	F705	S/D*	17	350	50	14	4	34	4	-	-
6534	F706	S/D*	19	270	50	10	3	12	-	-	3 fs
6541	F709	S/D	20	70	all	1	-	3	-	-	-
6542	F710	S/D	17	100	all	8	-	7	-	-	-
6560	F705	S/D	20	100	all	1	-	-	-	1	-
6562	F714	S/D	22	100	all	-	-	-	3	-	-
6584	F720	S/E.D.	19	60	all	1	-	-	-	-	-
6585	F720	S/E.D.	8	20	all	-	-	1	-	-	-
6605	F730	S/Sc	21	1000	12.5	-	-	-	-	-	-
6616	F735	S/Sc	17	260	50	2	-	1	-	-	-
6509	-	Unph	3	30	all	1	-	1	1	-	-
7000	-	Unph	10	200	50	fr	-	1	-	-	-

Key: fs = fruit stone fragment cf sloe, ca = capsule, ch = charred fragment indet, N/P.1 = North pit group 1, N/P.2 = group 2, S = south, D = ditch, E. = early, Spr = spread, Gu = gully, Sc= scoop, BS = beam slot, PH = post hole,   Unph = unphased. * = sample analysed see Table 1.

Table 15   Numerical Comparison of the Orton's Pasture and New Cemetery Finds Assemblages

	Coarse Pot	Samian	Mortaria	Amphorae	Iron Nails	Iron Objects	Copper Alloy Objects	LeAD Objects	Glass	Coins	Stone Objs. inc. querns	Bone Objects	Total
New Cemetery Count	19,290	2,359	717	1,232	7,684	300	169	19	853	69	47	0	32,739
%	58.92%	7.20%	2.19%	3.76%	23.47%	0.91%	0.51%	0.05%	2.60%	0.21%	0.13%	0%	
Orton's Pasture Count	5,346	740	124	829	434	37	39	3	92	1	2	5	7,652
%	69.90%	9.67%	1.62%	10.84%	5.67%	0.48%	0.51%	0.03%	1.20%	0.01%	0.02%	0.06%	

DISCUSSION

by I.M.Ferris

THE SITE WITHIN ROMAN ROCESTER

The excavated sequence from the site of Orton's Pasture has added considerably to the picture of Roman activity at Rocester that had already been established by the larger-scale excavations at the New Cemetery site that took place in the 1980s (Esmonde Cleary and Ferris 1996), and by subsequent, smaller-scale excavations and evaluations at a number of other locations around the village (Ferris forthcoming). At the New Cemetery there was encountered a sequence that encompassed three successive Roman forts, the first (Phase 1A) being constructed around 100 AD , and soon after abandoned, the second (Phase 1B) dating to the first third of the second century, and the latest and best-understood (Phase 2) being Antonine in date, founded *c.* 140/160, and abandoned *c.* 200 AD

After the abandonment of the final fort, it would appear that in the third and fourth centuries a civilian settlement grew up here, a settlement that at some stage was provided with a clay defensive rampart and possibly a wall, which might suggest its status to have been that of a small town or roadside settlement. The New Cemetery site lay in one corner of this later Roman enclosure.

Other excavations, to the west of the forts, have established the presence here of what has been identified as a *vicus*, contemporary with the third of the forts and quite possibly also with the second. To the east of the forts, further Roman activity was encountered and here too may have been an area that was utilised by the Roman military in the second century, in this case for the grazing or corralling of horses and other livestock.

It is therefore of considerable interest to note that the Roman remains so far encountered around the village extend over a much greater area than was supposed even ten years ago, and indeed that the area of the Scheduled Ancient Monument protects only a relatively small proportion of these zones. While it can now confidently be reported that activity contemporary with the sequence of the three forts at Rocester has been identified outside of the defensive circuits of the forts on three sides — to the east, west and south — as yet there has been no opportunity to assess the presence or absence of further contemporary activity on the fourth, northern side of the forts.

At Orton's Pasture, Phase 0 produced no finds, and may be either later prehistoric or early Roman in date, and will not be discussed further in this report. The dating of the pottery and other finds from the Orton's Pasture Phase 1 features and deposits suggests that this phase is certainly contemporary with parts of both Phase 1A and Phase 1B [New Cemetery phasing] forts lying to the north. The suggested end date of Orton's Pasture Phase 1, *c.* AD 130–150, corresponds to the start date of Phase 2 at the New Cemetery site. The Phase 2 activity at Orton's Pasture would appear to include some material to suggest that it is contemporary with the post-military abandonment and subsequent growth of a 'small town' at Rocester, and therefore that it relates to Phase 3 at the New Cemetery site. This later Roman activity at Orton's Pasture most probably took place outside the defensive or boundary circuit of the civilian settlement, whose main focus, as with that of the earlier forts, again lay to the north. Once more, as there is little

information available to allow the contextualisation of the Orton's Pasture Phase 2 activity beyond that already provided for the later Roman period in the published New Cemetery site report (Esmonde Cleary and Ferris 1996, 225–226) subsequent discussion will focus exclusively on Orton's Pasture Phase 1.

Phase 1

The Functional Characterisation of the Site: Military or Civilian?

The new, enhanced picture of the sequence of Roman activity at Rocester is nevertheless, in places, not altogether clear, and it is difficult to understand how the Orton's Pasture activity is linked to that recorded to the north. The first issue to be addressed relates to the status of the Orton's Pasture site of Phase 1, and in particular, whether it can be classified as a military or civilian site at any period of its occupation. Even though the lines of the southern defences of the three Roman forts are not known, it is assumed that they lie in the field known as Abbey Field, on the north side of Mill Street.

From the Phase 1 horizons at Orton's Pasture very few finds that are military in character were recovered. Only the small copper-alloy military fittings Nos. 15, 16, 17 and 22, and possibly Nos.14 and 18, attest to some activity on the site involving soldiers and other military personnel. There are also no items of weaponry from the site and nothing diagnostically military about the iron knives and tools recovered. All of the copper-alloy military fittings came from contexts and features either within Enclosure 1 or to the north of Enclosure 1. On the other hand, while it is quite feasible to imagine the accidental loss of one or two small items off military uniform, either on this site or through the disposal here of rubbish derived from inside the fort, their discrete distribution perhaps argues against this, as does the fact that the leather strap decorated with repoussé copper-alloy bosses (Nos. 15 and 22) would seem to be too large and bulky an item to represent merely a casual loss.

Conversely, of course, if one looks at the non-ceramic finds assemblage from the site there is nothing here to disallow its assignation to a civilian context either. There are, for instance, no significant numbers of personal items, particularly of jewellery, which might hint at, but not necessarily prove, a civilian presence. Given the generally high level of finds disposal attested at Orton's Pasture, particularly involving the dumping of pottery and animal bone, and to a lesser extent glassware and metalwork, the overall make-up of the integrated finds assemblage (see Table 15, p. 71) when viewed in relation to a similar table prepared using data from the New Cemetery excavations is very interesting and contrasts emerge between the two sites, as will be discussed in detail below. This still though does not resolve the dilemma of characterising the Phase 1 Orton's Pasture activity as exclusively military or exclusively civilian.

The pottery data show that the site has a military-associated supply, with high levels of samian and amphorae. The latter is in particular higher than might be expected on a civil site.

However, *vici* also have military-associated pot supplies, so perhaps ceramic evidence cannot be used to characterise the site in this way.

A total of seven *graffiti* came from the site and are reported on by Roger Tomlin above. Five of the *graffiti* were on samian vessels, one on an amphora and one on a vessel found during the watching brief. It has been suggested (Evans 1987) that *graffiti* on pottery can help to provide an index of levels of basic literacy in Roman Britain, and that distinct patterns can be discerned at different types of sites; that there is a hierarchy of site displaying greater or lesser degrees of literacy in other words.

The rate of occurrence of *graffiti* at Orton's Pasture is 1:1,048, compared to 1:1,242 at the New Cemetery site. Evans noted that such rates of *graffiti* were common on military sites, something which suggests once more that the functional profile of the Orton's Pasture site is more military than civilian rural. At rural sites occurrence rates can be as low as 1:10,585 (Thornwell Farm, Chepstow, Gwent) and 1:12,500 (Catsgore, Somerset) according to Evans (Evans, Forthcoming).

While Anthony King (1984) has argued that there is a distinctive profile to Roman military animal bone assemblages, as has been pointed out by Andrew Hammon in the specialist bone report above, the situation may not be quite as clear-cut as King's statistics, gathered some years ago, show. Nevertheless, according to the criteria laid down by King, the Orton's Pasture animal bone assemblage has a military, rather than a civilian, character. King's military animal bone assemblages would be dominated by cattle, pig and sheep, with cattle being significantly predominant and pig being second in terms of consumption, represented at a greater percentage level than it would be in a civilian context. King has recently revisited this subject (King 1999) but it has not been possible to take on board the results of his new study in this present report due to time constraints.

Again, there are no diagnostically military buildings and structures on the Orton's Pasture site. However, the alignment and orientation of the ditches of the two enclosures at Orton's Pasture is the same as that proposed for the forts which lie to the north, and this could denote a direct relationship between the two complexes, and that the Orton's Pasture enclosures acted as annexes to the forts. The profiles of the ditches of the northern enclosure, Enclosure 1, have the classic V-shape so often associated with military ditches. Those of the southern enclosure, Enclosure 2, are less well-cut and vary a great deal in their profile. On morphological grounds, then, no functional identification of the site can be made.

If the site is militarily related, then the terminology for describing extra-fort, defended areas depends to some extent on the relationship between the fort's defensive circuit and that of the related enclosure. The most in-depth consideration of this topic still remains Wilson's study of 1984, though obviously much new material has been added to the database since that time. The terms annexe, 'defensive outwork', or temporary camp/ labour camp can, according to Wilson, be applied to defended enclosures 'within 500m of a known fort....when the siting makes it clear that it does not form part of the inner defences of the fort itself' (Wilson 1984, 60–61). At Orton's Pasture this relationship is unknown, so the use of the term annexes to describe the enclosures here may not be strictly supportable.

Though it appears that the northernmost boundary of the northern enclosure lies within Orton's Pasture, and therefore that it has been proven that there is no direct connection with the fort's defences, nevertheless the possibilty exists that the turning westwards of the enclosure ditch at this point actually marks the position of an entrance-way into the enclosure here, an entrance-way subsequently blocked or narrowed by pit digging. However, in assessing the Orton's Pasture enclosures against the other types defined by Wilson, they are obviously not temporary camps or labour camps for the construction of the forts themselves, while they also do not appear to be the kind of enclosure, such as at Greensforge in Staffordshire, defined by Wilson as a 'defended outwork'.

The subject of military annexes has received surprisingly little attention from students of the Roman army in Britain, though they were discussed as part of a study of the *vicus* in Roman Britain undertaken by Sebastian Sommer (1984). Sommer makes the point that while the majority of *vici* are quite organic settlements in their planning and growth, a *vicus* can also be laid out and contained within a military annexe, and that the two categories of site are therefore not necessarily exclusive (Sommer 1984, 18–22). However, a *vicus* enclosed within a fort annexe would have been subject to direct military control, both in terms of its planning and layout and in the overseeing of the life and behaviour of its inhabitants. Thus, in such a situation the boundaries between civilian and military would have become somewhat blurred. Excavation inside military annexes has been relatively rare, with the notable exceptions of Newstead and Elginhaugh, both in Scotland, and also rare on an extensive level at *vicus* sites, with a consequence that interpretation of their functions remains somewhat hypothetical (Sommer 1984, 34–40).

A Minimalist Interpretation

There may be said to be a minimalist (processual) and a maximalist (post-processual) interpretation of Phase 1 at Orton's Pasture. The minimalist interpretation can be set out in just a few paragraphs and represents perhaps the furthest that the sensible, grounded archaeologist would stretch interpretation of his or her material.

The minimalist interpretation would recognise that there were three distinct phases of activity on the site: the first (Phase 0), low-level, uncharacterised, and undated by associated artefacts; the second (Phase 1), being either Roman military or civilian in character — which is uncertain — and being dated to the last decade of the first to the mid-second century AD ; and the third (Phase 2), being later Roman, in all probability civilian, activity connected to some kind of industrial activity on the fringes of, or outside of, the main settlement focus.

Ploughing over the years had seriously denuded the archaeological deposits on the site and had truncated features and structures, making interpretation of the remaining, compromised features, structures and deposits difficult and partial. Only in one area of the site did any kind of stratigraphic sequence survive, albeit only partially intact. However, there is still very little that can be said about Phases 0 and 2, due to the limted evidence relating to these phases gathered by the excavation.

The only period for which extensive areas of the site were excavated and recorded in plan was Phase 1. Though large areas of the boundary ditches and interiors of two discrete enclosures were stripped, the interiors of both were proved either to have been largely empty when in use — perhaps being used for the corralling of stock — or that they had contained perhaps ephemeral structures that had been destroyed by heavy ploughing over the years. The only building present, a small stone structure in the southern enclosure, cannot be identified to any particular function, and indeed cannot even be firmly dated by associated finds.

As well as helping to date the phase and assess its longevity, the presence of large quantities of domestic rubbish on the site in Phase 1, disposed of in a number of large rubbish pits, this rubbish principally consisting of pottery, animal bone, glass and plant remains, with some bone and metal items, allows a certain amount to be said about the economic basis of the site, its supply of food and materials, the type of pottery in use here for various purposes and so on. The Orton's Pasture finds assemblage could represent the disposal here of material used and broken off-site. In that case, study of the assemblage will tell us something about the nature of that off-site activity, if it is at all reflected in the make up of the assemblage. Conversely the Orton's Pasture assemblages may represent material consumed, broken and disposed of here on site. If the latter is accepted as being the case, then the various excavated features on the site may throw some light on the nature of that activity or vice versa.

There are more unusual items on the site than might have been expected to be present in a rural location in Roman Britain, and these items — bones of probably imported cattle, exotic plant remains such as dates and Stone Pine — could attest to the high status of some of the inhabitants at the site or in the vicinity, as has been suggested by the environmental specialists writing above. Exotic pottery and metalwork with decoration relating to the god Bacchus could again represent expensive items belonging to high-status individuals, items which may provide some insight into the beliefs of those individuals, or be items which were acquired and treasured more for their aesthetic value than for any other reason. A fragment of a sandstone altar hints tentatively at the religious life of the local inhabitants.

A Maximalist Interpretation

The maximalist interpretation requires the acceptance that in Phase 1 at Orton's Pasture detected repetitive and significant patterns and rhythms within the structural, artefactual and ecofactual assemblages, some contradictory, some complementary and some dissonant, can be interpreted and thus translated into a story in which a coherent set of actions and activities emerges that encompasses both the sacred and the profane, the banal and the extraordinary, much as life in the ancient world may itself have been structured.

A basic description and analysis of the layout of the enclosures and of their internal features has already been given above as part of the exposition of the site's overall structural sequence, while the difficulty of interpreting these features in isolation has formed part of what has been called the 'minimalist interpretation' of the site (above). The key to perhaps understanding, or at least starting to understand, the nature of the Phase 1 activity at Orton's Pasture lies in the analysis of the recovered artefacts and environmental material, and the comparison of this material with the assemblages from the New

Cemetery site, and between the two enclosures at Orton's Pasture. Only then can an interpretation of the structural evidence be offered.

If a very rough comparison is made between the make-up of the overall finds assemblages from the Orton's Pasture and New Cemetery sites at Rocester, some interesting differences emerge in the character of the two assemblages, which may say something about the differing functions of each site.

There are too few small finds from Orton's Pasture to allow the kind of grouping by functional category that Crummy (1983) and Cool *et al.* (1995) in particular have applied successfully to other large Roman small finds assemblages. On both Rocester sites there is activity of the earlier Roman period (first and second centuries) and later Roman period (third into fourth century), so that it was felt unnecessary to try and eliminate this later material from the calculations, even though later activity would appear to have been less intensive at Orton's Pasture. Some recovery biases between the two sites will have doubtless resulted from the very different conditions of excavation of the two sites, Orton's Pasture being a rescue excavation undertaken in poor weather conditions.

In order to allow direct comparison to be made, a numerical count was made of the following Roman finds on each site; samian, amphorae, mortaria, and coarse pottery by sherd count; coins; iron nails; identifiable objects of iron, copper-alloy, lead; bone and stone objects by number of individual items; and glass by sherd count. The total number of counted items making up each assemblage was then produced and the percentage representation of each category of material or object in each assemblage was calculated (Table 15). Percentage-wise there was noticeably a greater amount of all types of pottery at Orton's Pasture, with the exception of mortaria (-0.57%).The amount of amphorae by sherd count increased from 3.76% to 10.84%, though by weight the amphora assemblages were very similar (85.159 kg at the New Cemetery and 89.882 kg at Orton's Pasture). Most of the glass was vessel glass, which at Orton's Pasture was less well-represented than at the New Cemetery (-1.4%). Percentages of copper-alloy and lead objects were remarkably similar, though iron objects at Orton's Pasture were fewer, by 0.43%, as were iron nails, by 17.80%. With only one coin and two stone object at Orton's Pasture, these hardly registered percentage-wise, though both figures were lower than those for the New Cemetery (by 0.2% and 0.12% respectively). There were no bone objects at the New Cemetery, while those at Orton's Pasture made up 0.06% of the overall assemblage.

Thus the functional differences between the assemblages can be seen to be quite marked in certain respects. At Orton's Pasture a greater percentage of vessels of one kind or another was in use (or were disposed of here), though fewer of these were mortaria and glass vessels. Fewer iron objects were in use, and given that objects in this material tended towards utilitarian functions, whether civilian or military in context, this would suggest that certain activities were not carried out at the site. Markedly fewer iron nails perhaps suggests that there may not in fact have been any significant number of timber buildings within the enclosures of Phase 1 at Orton's Pasture, and that though deep ploughing had in certain respects denuded the site over the years, it may not have removed evidence for former timber structures here, as was at one time feared. A generally low number of small finds at Orton's Pasture again probably says something about the nature of activity carried out here, with few personal items being present, only one coin, and only two stone objects, a fragment of an altar and a fragment of a quernstone, though the appearance of bone objects here, totally absent from the New Cemetery, may be of significance. Given that 45 of the 47 stone objects from the New Cemetery site were fragments of quernstones, the virtual absence of such utilitarian objects from Orton's Pasture would again seem to be significant. If an additional element of comparison is introduced, by adding the number of animal bones and bone fragments to the totals for each assemblage and then looking at the bone assemblages as percentages of the whole, again an interesting contrast emerges. At the New Cemetery animal bone represents 11.1% by percentage, and at Orton's Pasture c. 4.5%.

Attention will now be focused on looking at the Orton's Pasture assemblage itself. Certain patterns are immediately discernible amongst the Orton's Pasture artefactual and environmental material, and there is a distinct difference apparent between the finds assemblages from the northern and southern enclosures, which may be a reflection of a difference in their functions (Fig. 34).

The pottery assemblage includes a higher number of whole or almost complete pots than might have been expected on a domestic or settlement site, and certainly were the site to represent a venue at which rubbish from off-site was disposed of and buried, the reconstruction of these vessels would probably not have been possible. The large average size of sherds from the stratified, Phase 1 assemblage, and the unabraded breaks on most of the sherds recovered in contexts in pit fills, again suggests that the majority of this material was both used on site, broken on site, and buried straight after its breaking.

A comparison has already been presented above, in the report by Bevan, between the overall make-up of the Orton's Pasture pottery assemblage and that from the New Cemetery in terms of percentages of different fabrics represented and by weight and sherd count of each fabric. A comparison can also be made between the forms of vessels represented at each site, for which purpose the vessels have been functionally grouped together as; Tablewares — dishes, platters, bowls, beakers and flagons; Storage Vessels — jars and amphorae; Food Preparation Vessels — mortaria; and Miscellaneous Vessels — tazzas, lamps, inkwells, wine strainers/presses, face pots, triple vases etc. In order to allow direct comparison between the sites, a count of identifiable forms has been made for each functional group on each site, and this has been converted into a percentage figure representing the level of their representation within the overall assemblage. At Orton's Pasture Tablewares are c. 43%, Storage Vessels c. 51.5%, Food Preparation Vessels c. 4.8% and Miscellaneous Vessels c. 0.7%. At the New Cemetery site Tablewares are c. 47%, Storage Vessels c. 40%, Food Preparation Vessels c. 13% and Miscellaneous Vessels c. 0.1%. Therefore it can be seen that the Orton's Pasture assemblage has more Storage Vessels proportionally and fewer Tablewares, fewer Food Preparation Vessels and more of the specialised Miscellaneous Vessels, though it is realised that some types of vessels could be assigned to more than one functional category in this exercise.

The assemblage also included more unusual and specialised vessels than might have been expected on an occupation site, whether military or civilian in status, as has been discussed above

by Lynne Bevan. These included four tazzas (Unstratified, 3012 [F705], 1006 and 6563 [F706]), a plain ceramic lamp (3002, F700), an imported ceramic lamp with Bacchic decoration (Ploughsoil), a fourth tazza customised to turn it into what would appear to be a candlestick (Unstratified), parts of two triple vases (1025 [F702] and 6529 [F704]), a face pot (1005, F704), a wine strainer (Ploughsoil), the segmented so-called 'snack tray' (Unstratified) which, it has been suggested could conversely have been inverted to form a ceramic stand or table, and the copper-alloy Bacchic-associated *patera* handle (Ploughsoil). The presence of these more exotic vessels, though in some cases they were recovered from residual or unstratified contexts, nevertheless marks out the assemblage as being in many ways unusual. Ruth Leary, in her published discussion of the pottery assemblage from the New Cemetery site, noted how there appeared to be a larger number of what she termed 'exotics' present in Rocester and that this probably reflected the easy access that the military here had to pottery production centres such as those centred on Little Chester, Derby and perhaps to a supply produced in Rocester itself, or very nearby. Though Leary's use of the term exotic referred more to fabrics with mica dusting and glazes, this is not to claim that unusual, vessel types were completely absent from the New Cemetery pottery assemblage. A plain ceramic lamp, a tazza, a ceramic wine strainer and a copper-alloy Bacchic-motif-decorated jug handle were present in the assemblage. It is generally the case that tazzas, triple vases and perhaps also strainers are more common in North Western assemblages such as those from Wilderspool and Walton-le-Dale (Jeremy Evans pers. comm.).

Tazzas and lamps are relatively common finds on temple sites and in contexts where religious and ritual activity is presumed to have taken place. They are also found, however, in domestic contexts, though this is altogether less common. Indeed an example of each occurred in the Rocester New Cemetery pottery assemblage. One of the best examples of these vessels being unequivocally tied in to religious practice is at the triangular temple site at Verulamium from where, amongst a significant assemblage of religious material, a number of tazzas and what were considered to be tazza lids were recovered, as well as ceramic lamps (Wheeler and Wheeler 1936, 190–193 and 200–202). Much of the other pottery from the site though was strictly utilitarian and would not have been out of place in a domestic context, something that can generally be observed of most temple site pottery assemblages. The characterisation of a ceramic assemblage as being connected to a religious site must then be based on the overall make-up of the assemblage and of its association with other materials, though even then definite assignation is not always possible, as will be discussed below in the case of the temple sites of West Hill, Uley and Henley Wood. The Verulamium triangular temple site also provides a parallel for the appearance of Stone Pine in a ritual context (Wheeler and Wheeler 1936, 118–120).

Some interesting observations have been made on the occurrence and distribution of various types of unusual pottery vessels within York (Monaghan 1997). Tazzas, although interpreted as being 'clear indicators of ritual activity' (Monaghan 1997, 858), their commonly burned interiors suggesting their use as incense burners, have a distribution across the city determined more by the date of activity rather than by functional zoning apparent in the archaeological record. However, the distribution of ceramic lamps and head pots is

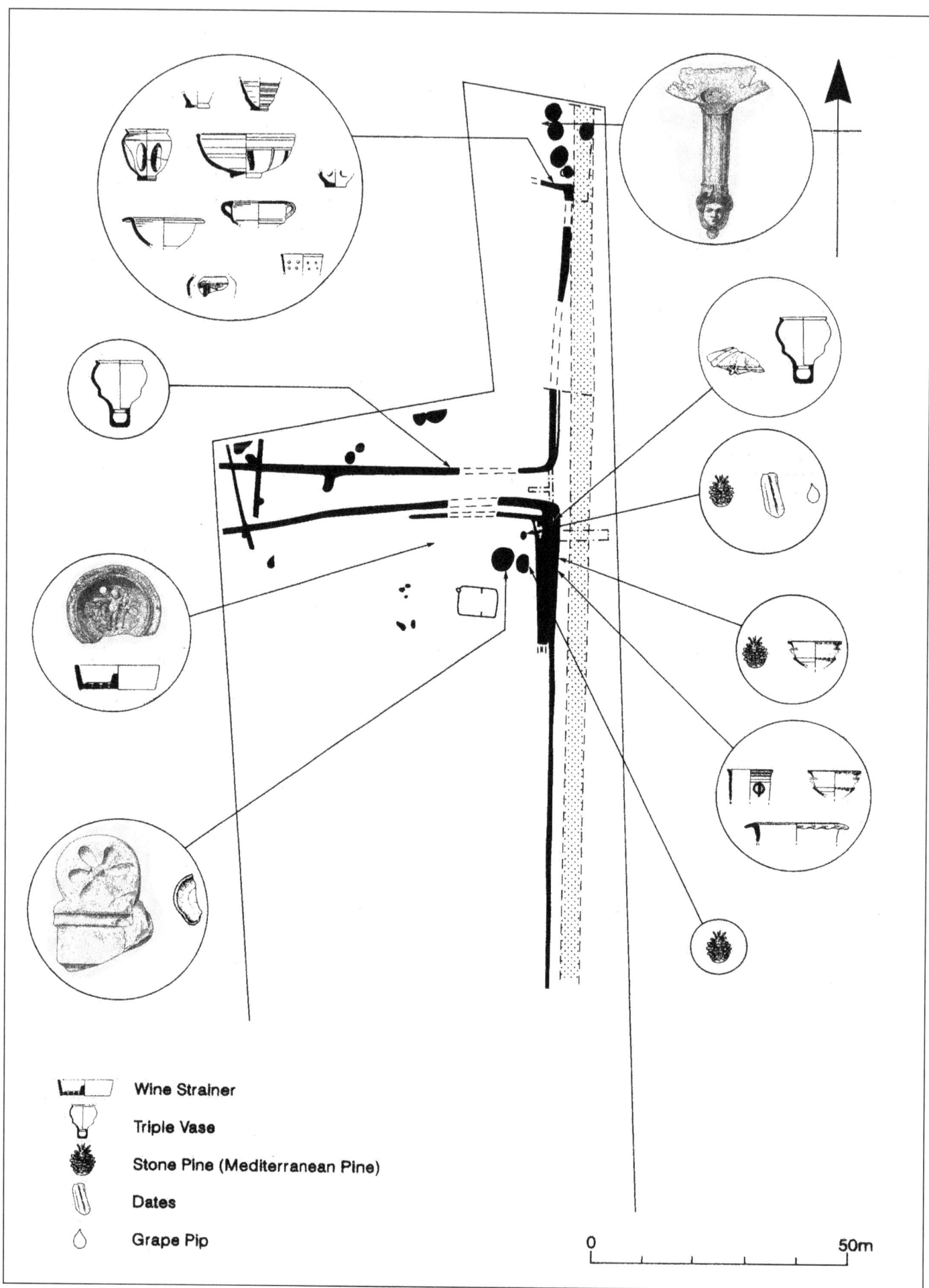

Wine Strainer

Triple Vase

Stone Pine (Mediterranean Pine)

Dates

Grape Pip

0   50m

Fig. 34   Spatial plot of possible ritual/religious artefacts in Enclosures 1 and 2.
(See key for conventionalised items; all others are drawings of actual objects.)

markedly biased towards the extra-mural zones and the Blake Street site 'both of which had high levels of ritual activity' (Monaghan 1997, 859). Ceramic candlesticks would again at York appear to be related to zones of ritual activity. The relative rarity of both face pots and triple vases in the massive York assemblage, while it may reflect a cultural choice not to use such vessels, may more likely serve to highlight the unusual nature of their appearance as part of the Orton's Pasture pottery assemblage.

There are also particularly noteworthy spatial concentrations at Orton's Pasture of either whole vessels that were probably buried in this state, or of particularly distinctive ware types. In the latter instance, the very fact that the majority of the stratified green-glazed pots came from the recut ditch F609 seems to suggest that this is a significant feature, or that burial of selected and chosen material here marks the completion of a significant sequence of acts and actions. This feature also contains the largest single assemblage of samian on the site (70 sherds), including three out of the five examples of samian sherds bearing *graffiti* on the site. Interestingly, at the site of Nettleton Scrubb, Wiltshire — the site of a shrine complex dedicated to Apollo — there was recorded a pattern in the pottery assemblage recovered from the backfill of the pre-Shrine, first-century enclosure ditches and associated features that suggests that colour as well as form/function may have been one of the deciding factors in selection of vessels for use and disposal there at that time. The excavator noted that the 'comparatively rare', imported, green-glazed St Rémy ware, of which eighteen sherds were recovered, representing sixteen vessels, came almost exclusively from this enclosure complex (Wedlake 1982, 244–245).

Other patterns are discernible in the differential distribution of samian across the Orton's Pasture site. From the backfill of the ditches of Enclosure 1 come 132 sherds, from internal pits of Enclosure 1 come 70 sherds, a total of 202 sherds. From the backfill of the ditches of Enclosure 2 come 41 sherds, and from internal pits of Enclosure 2 come 40 sherds, a total of 81 sherds.

Of the more unusual coarseware vessel types, most of which were stratified, there is a notable concentration of these vessels inside, and in the backfilled ditches of, the southern enclosure, Enclosure 2 (Fig.34). The plain ceramic lamp came from pit F700; two tazzas and a whiteware beaker with a painted symbol that may be the top of a *caduceus* came from enclosure ditch F706; a third tazza came from F705; a face pot came from enclosure ditch F704; while unstratified fragments of a wine strainer and the decorated, Bacchic-motif, ceramic lamp came from the cleaning of areas within Enclosure 2.

A similar concentration of environmental 'exotics' is also centred on Enclosure 2. When looking at the charred plant remains from the site, Angela Monckton has noted above that there is a significant difference in the types of material associated with the boundary ditches and internal pits of the northern enclosure, Enclosure 1, and those from the southern enclosure, Enclosure 2. The more exotic material, including the fragments of cone and nuts from the Mediterranean Pine and the dates, is exclusively from the southern enclosure. Mediterranean Pine (nut and/or seeds) comes from pits F700 (contexts 6511 and 6516), F701 (6522) and F703 (6508) and from enclosure ditch F705 (6560). Dates come from pit F700 (6516) and F703 (6508). Grape pips come from F703 (6508), though these need

not necessarily be derived from the fresh fruit, indeed in the circumstances they are much more likely to be from dried raisins (Williams 1977, 329). Also present from the southern enclosure deposits were other 'wild foods' including apple/pear from pit F700 (6516) and ditch F715, hazlenuts from pit F700 (6516), ditches F704 (6532) and F705 (6533), though it should be noted that fragments of hazlenut also came from pits F602 (6054), F603 (6042) and F719 (6577) in the northern enclosure, and sloe from enclosure ditch F706 (6535).

If one though examines the full lists of charred material recovered from pits F700, F701 and F703 some further interesting observations can be made that were neither highlighted nor discussed in the specialist report. In all three pits, tree or shrub buds were recovered (in contexts 6516 [F700], 6522 [F701] and 6508 [F703]), and in addition 'immature cone/catkin' came from F700 (6516). Buds were also present in pit F603 (6042) to the north of the northern enclosure. If all, or even some, of this material remains in its contemporary horizons, and is therefore not residual, then it can be fairly surmised that these deposits were laid down in the spring. It defies the laws of probability that charred buds could have reached all of these features simply by accidental incorporation and it may therefore be useful to look for any parallels to such an occurrence and then to seek to make an interpretation or explanation.

Raphael Isserlin has examined the issue of seasonality and the Roman religious calendar in a now-published paper from one of the Theoretical Roman Archaeology conferences (Isserlin 1994). In it he discussed the issue of whether dedications and/or offerings at Romano-British religious sites could in any instances be tied in to seasonal patterns, and thus reflect the existing literary evidence for a calendar of religious festivals and observances in the wider Roman world. He examined both epigraphic and archaeological evidence from British sites, and from the former deduced provisionally that there was a suggestion that certain times of the year may have been avoided, as inappropriate times for the dedication of religious monuments. The latter, archaeological evidence examined included both artefactual and environmental data from a small sample of sites.

At Jordan Hill, Dorset a repetitive pattern of deposition of artefacts was apparent in a third to fourth-century well or shaft, dug in the courtyard of the temple there, thus probably reflecting cyclical time. At the first-century enclosure at Ashill, Norfolk a number of wells or shafts was encountered, the complex possibly being a focus of ritual activity. In one of the shafts (Shaft 3) a repeated pattern of deposition was again apparent, and again reflected cyclical time. The deposits included a large number of pottery vessels, animal bones, iron objects, copper-alloy brooches, a whetstone, leather shoes, and organic material, including leaves, twigs and nuts, from the hazel tree. Isserlin weighed up the possibility, from the presence and description of the nuts, that either each deposit containing such material was deposited in the autumn over a number of years, with the feature being capped and protected during the interim periods, or that all the deposits were laid down in a single season, between late spring and autumn, in a series of weekly or monthly events. It will be recalled that the excavators of pit F700 at Orton's Pasture recorded a number of interleaved charcoal and clean sand deposits within the pit, which suggested to them the almost deliberate and conscious 'closing-off' of each of the burned horizons towards the base of the pit by the deposition of thin layers of clean sand. Such a sequence could also have been created by the periodic capping or closing-off of the pit.

Isserlin's point was that amongst organic materials in features such as these there might be indicators of seasonal deposition; the presence of nuts and berries might suggest autumnal activity; buds on twigs or branches would hint at spring deposition; animal bones may hint at seasonal slaughtering patterns, as at the site of West Hill, Uley, Gloucestershire discussed in detail below, and at the Harlow temple site in a less pronounced fashion (Dorrington and Legge 1985, 122–134).

As to the animal bone assemblage at Orton's Pasture, it has been characterised as having a profile consistent with its being military, as opposed to reflecting civilian dietary patterns of the time. The interpretation of the material is again very much taken from a socio-economic point of view, and issues relating to other unusual patterns on the site reflected in the ceramic and charred plant remains assemblage have not been discussed. While assemblages of bone from temple sites can be so inherently biased in terms of the assemblage being dominated by one particular species, almost to the exclusion of all other, that its religious context can be established beyond all reasonable doubt, as at West Hill, Uley in Gloucestershire, less clear-cut examples may be difficult or even impossible to detect. The report on the animal bones from Orton's Pasture suggests that there is nothing untoward about the assemblage, beyond its characterisation as being akin to King's military type of bone assemblage.

At Uley, the temple complex excavations, at a site dedicated to Mercury, produced what Bruce Levitan chose to categorise as a votive bone assemblage, comprising exceptionally large numbers, and thus a heavily skewed percentage, of sheep/goat bones and domestic fowl. No such pattern, of course, exists at Orton's Pasture. However, it must be borne in mind that a shrine is not a temple, and certainly not a temple site such as Uley which would have been as much a commercial enterprise in its heyday as it was a religious establishment. The suggested Orton's Pasture shrine was small, possibly dedicated by one individual officer or a group of officers from the nearby fort, and perhaps relatively short-lived.

The annual religious calendar by which the army functioned called for numerous events of sacrifice and/or dedication, and it is likely that many different kinds of animal sacrifice occurred regularly throughout the year. While the so-called *suovetaurilia*, that is the triple sacrifice of a cow, a sheep and a pig, was more associated with imperial piety, similar sacrifices of these beasts in particular, singly, together or in twos and threes, would also have taken place. Following sacrifice of the animals, the carcasses would have been butchered, one assumes in the standard Roman manner, and then the meat would have been cooked and eaten as part of a feast that usually formed an integral part of the overall religious activity.

The specialist observed that 'cattle were probably being slaughtered and dismembered at Orton's Pasture or in the immediate vicinity, because the assemblage is composed of a selection of most skeletal elements' (Hammon above), with a 20–30% higher level of butchery being discernible at Orton's Pasture amongst the cattle bones than at the New Cemetery site. There were also noted some individual contexts where butchery levels were particularly high (6010 [F609], 6525 and

6526 [F702]), all of these contexts being backfills of stretches of the enclosure ditches of the northern enclosure, Enclosure 1. F702 is the southern enclosure ditch, while F609 represents a recut of the northern ditch, a recut which has already been highlighted as containing a distinctive pottery assemblage. The fact that there was also a concentration of cattle scapulae displaying hook damage recovered from the backfill of the eastern ditch of Enclosure 1 (7000 [F612]) further emphasises the spatial patterning here. It is quite possible therefore that the northern enclosure could represent a zone for the corralling, slaughtering and butchering of cattle and perhaps other animals, either under civilian or military supervision, perhaps to supply meat to the fort to the north. It is also possible that animals could have been corralled here prior to their ritual slaughter as part of the military calendar of religious observance which required animal sacrifice as a necessary part of the ritual process.

Both Andy Hammon (the animal bone specialist) and Angela Monckton (the charred plant remains specialist) found parallels for certain elements of their respective assemblages at the Essex site of Great Holts Farm, Boreham. At this site finds were made of both Stone Pine, and another exotic plant, olives, not found at Orton's Pasture, and cattle bones from large, perhaps imported, beasts. These parallels seem at the same time both valid and questionable, in the light of the socio-economic interpretation then placed on the parallels, that they both relate to, and support, the identification of high status activity on the two sites. In the first place, the Phase 1 activity at Orton's Pasture dates to the second century AD while the Great Holts Farm site dates principally to the fourth century. Secondly, Orton's Pasture probably, though not entirely certainly, represents a pair of military annexes, one related to a shrine, while Great Holts Farm is a villa site. Thirdly, the environmental material referred to, in the case of Orton's Pasture was recovered from pits and ditches associated with the shrine enclosure (the Stone Pine and the dates) and more widely across both enclosures (the 'large cattle' bones), and in the case of Great Holts Farm the majority of the material came from the backfill of a well (Mark Germany pers. comm.). While the excavators do not believe that the well deposit at Great Holts Farm constitutes anything other than rubbish disposal, the significance of wells, shafts and pits as occasional venues for structured deposition has already been raised. The importation of cattle in second-century Roman Britain would seem on strictly socio-economic grounds to perhaps represent a very different phenomenon to the importation of cattle in the fourth century, by which time improvements in the country's breeding stock might have been expected to have taken place. The latter phenomenon might in fact be thought to be more extraordinary than the former. Grant (1989, 143) has summarised the differing opinions on the issue of recognising imported as opposed to improved stock.

In order to contextualise further the information from Orton's Pasture, reference will need to be made in particular to the results and interpretation of excavation at the Roman fort site of Newstead in Scotland, both of the campaigns of James Curle (Curle 1911) in the earlier part of this century and of the more recent work carried out by Rick Jones and Simon Clarke of Bradford University (Clarke and Jones 1994; Clarke 1994), and at the Roman fort and *vicus* site of Castleford, West Yorkshire (Cool and Philo 1998).

At both sites there were recorded episodes of pit digging and rubbish disposal which to the excavators appeared to be in some respects unusual and yet at the same time much as one would expect to find on sites where the hygienic disposal of tons of domestic and everyday refuse in a safe and efficient manner would have occupied some considerable and continual effort and expense of time. At Newstead, the campaigns of James Curle exposed large areas within an enclosure, interpreted as an annexe, which lay to the south of the main fort complex. Both within as well as outside the annexe boundary ditches he excavated a number of huge pits which he interpreted in some case as wells that had naturally gone out of use, perhaps with the contamination of the water therein, and which had then been used as ready-made rubbish pits in which material from the forts could be dumped and backfilled.

Within the annexe there were no diagnostically military buildings: indeed, at certain periods the interior of the annexe must have been largely empty, the only archaeologically detectable activity being the digging of pits and the sinking of wells, and the subsequent disposal of rubbish into these features. However, the diversity and range of material dumped in some of these wells/pits was such that questions had to be asked about the definition of rubbish when applied to the contents of the pit backfills.

Not only was there a range of domestic pottery vessels represented but also metal vessels, wooden artefacts, in some cases well-preserved in the waterlogged conditions which existed at the basal levels of some features, and some more extraordinary objects, including the reknowned cavalry parade helmet, which would appear to have gone into the ground in a virtually mint condition. There was also animal bone and other types of environmental material such as wood and leather. In the case of Newstead, the direct physical relationship between the fort and enclosure ditches, and the particularly large quantity of military artefacts and equipment recovered during the excavations, meant that there was no hesitation in the site being characterised as a military annexe. The first extended discussion of the ritual aspects of the Newstead pits, by Ann Ross (1976), suggested that structured deposition was taking place here alongside the more profane aspects of the use of the site.

More examples of such 'Newstead pits', as they have become known, were excavated as part of a rescue excavation campaign carried out by Bradford University in the 1980s and further extended as their Newstead environs research project. While no objects quite as unusual as those uncovered by Curle were recovered in this campaign, nevertheless a significant new data set was added to the pit groups and allowed for a reinterpretation of some of the patterns of waste disposal at the site to be undertaken. In Newstead's south annexe, the pits excavated would seem to have been in use for the disposal of rubbish and deposition of other material around the middle of the second century AD A pattern of the use of these pits was established which suggested that they were not all in use at the same time, with perhaps 15–20 pits being open at any one time. At some period other activity connected with metalworking took place within the annexe at the same time as some of the pits were in use for rubbish disposal.

The analysis by Clarke and Jones showed that while undoubtedly the majority of the material dumped into the pits could be defined as rubbish, nevertheless some items could not, including the aforementioned parade equipment, perfectly serviceable tools

and so on. Certain types of material seemed to appear only in pit contexts, as opposed to the activity areas examined by the later excavators. They concluded that 'some material clearly has a possible ritual significance' (Clarke and Jones 1994, 119) and observed that 'while some items deposited in the Newstead pits were complete, even damaged or fragmentary artefacts may have represented deliberate deposition of significant items' (Clarke and Jones 1994, 119). Certain types of pit tended to be the recipients of certain specific types of material, though not exclusively so. Their re-examination of the Newstead pits phenomenon identified trends in the selection of material for disposal, patterns of structured deposition and, in addition, recognised the existence of 'special deposits' in some pits. The context for these deliberate acts remains uncertain, for specifically religious items were seldom included amongst the dumped material.

At Castleford fort and *vicus*, analysis of the finds from pits suggested that there was a discernible pattern of 'rubbish' disposal within the pits, as at Newstead, and that there was undoubtedly both selection of specific types of material for disposal in this way and in some cases of what must have been complete, or almost complete, pottery and glass vessels (Cool and Philo 1998). Once more, the authors suggested that 'something more than utilitarian rubbish disposal may have been going on in these pits, and that they may reflect some form of ritual or religious activity in this area' (Cool and Philo 1998, 362) and viewed this as being part of the wider phenomenom that includes the common, though obviously not exclusive, use of pits, wells and shafts on Romano-British sites as foci for formalised and structured deposition of material as part of a religious or ritual action.

The recognition of instances of structured deposition in a Romano-British context is not new, and indeed similar deposits were identified by Tony Wilmott in his publication of work in the Middle Walbrook Valley site in London (Wilmott 1991). A very useful summary of votive and ritual deposits in Roman Britain was put together by Merrifield (1987), and includes many examples of structured disposal or placing of pottery and other finds in ditches, pits, shafts and wells (Merrifield 1987, 37–50).

The Newstead, Castleford and Walbrook examples, alongside the tentative observations offered by Raphael Isserlin with regard to the creation of certain well deposits, tend to suggest that the pattern of well and/or pit digging and the disposal of rubbish and other more significantly construed material at Orton's Pasture is part of a more widespread Romano-British phenomenon. In the case of the southern enclosure at Orton's Pasture though it can perhaps be demonstrated to be a phenomenon sometimes also connected with specifically religious acts and observances. At least one, and possibly all three, of the pits in the north-eastern corner of this enclosure should then perhaps more properly be called *favissae*, a *favissa* being a pit dug for the disposal of *ex votos* and other items, sometimes quite ordinary and mundane, used within a temple or its precinct. The controlled disposal of such material inside the precinct would allow for its religious significance to be otherwise retained.

A Simple Shrine

Alongside the repetitive acts of rubbish deposition just discussed above, it could also be said that the recutting and redefinition of parts of the enclosure boundary ditches of both Enclosures 1 and 2 itself represented a significant, repetitive action (see Merrifield 1987, 38–40 on the significance of marking boundaries). In plan, this appears most markedly around the north-east corner of the southern enclosure, Enclosure 2. The very fact that this recutting is around the angle of the enclosure which contains and protects the small stone-footed building that constitutes the only building on the whole site in this phase seems to be rather more than a coincidence when viewed alongside all the other evidence for a distinctive character to the activity here. It does not require a great leap of faith to identify this small stone building as a shrine, and the enclosure as its *temenos*.

If this building is to be interpreted as a shrine, in the absence of direct, *in situ* evidence of its use as such, it is possible to find at least a small number of parallels for similar structures elsewhere in Roman Britain (Drury 1986, 62–64 and fig.3.7). Drury categorises these structures as 'rectangular religious buildings' and notes that they are a relatively rare type in Roman Britain, though more common on the continent (see, for instance, Derks 1998, 150–152). All the known examples (up to 1986) are simple structures, in some cases with an internal sub-division, as occurs at Orton's Pasture, and in one case with a porch or extension. The size of the buildings varies. For example: at Springhead, Kent dimensions are *c.* 4m by *c.* 5m; at Richborough, Kent *c.* 8.5m by *c.* 5m; at Wycomb, Gloucestershire *c.* 11m by *c.* 7m; and at Bowes, County Durham *c.* 3m by *c.* 5m. The Orton's Pasture building, with dimensions of *c.* 8m by *c.* 4m, would fit into the general size range of these shrine buildings.

The shrine at Bowes was of drystone construction, the majority of the others were constructed with bonded masonry walls. Nevertheless, it is likely that all of them had simple, gabled roofs (Drury 1986, 62) and few internal fixtures and fittings, save an altar or altars. A number contained no finds to unequivocally confirm their religious function, and this has been assigned based upon indirect association and context, as is the case at Orton's Pasture. It must be assumed that the worked stone backfilled or dished into the top of pit F701 inside Enclosure 2, perhaps in fact even deliberately spread over the top of the pit at the time of the demolition of the shrine, largely formed part of the superstructure of the building. Other building stone that may have been present in this area was probably subsequently dispersed by the plough.

As has already been detailed in the finds catalogue, amongst this worked but otherwise undiagnostic stonework from F701 was a single fragment from an altar. The exotic ceramic vessels and the exotic and other foodstuffs from pits F700, F701 and F703 and patterns of deposition within the recut enclosure ditches, not to mention the recutting evidence itself, point towards the carrying-out of acts of religious and ritual rites here. Such ceremonies could have taken a number of forms and have been carried out in a number of different ways appropriate to different situations.

A formal procession to the site of the shrine can be envisaged. Entrance into the defined enclosure or religious precinct would have made the crossing of boundary lines a significant act itself, with the individual moving from a world of human experience and endeavour into the world of the gods, where dealings between men, women and their gods could be mediated by prayer, sacrifice and ceremony. Upon arrival at the shrine, offerings of food would have been made on an altar and burned. Prayers may have been offered and gifts dedicated to the gods. Libations of wine may have been poured, herbs and incense may have been burned, candles or lamps may have been lit, particularly as daylight ebbed away towards the end of the ritual feasting, animals may have been slaughtered, and a feast or meal may have been consumed at the site (Henig 1984, 33–34). Afterwards the remains of the meal and the offerings, perhaps also the vessels used in its preparation and consumption, would have been, like the libations, returned to the earth by their burial, perhaps also involving the breaking or 'ritual killing' of the vessels or other dedicated objects as is attested at a number of temple sites, although such material is more-or-less absent from Orton's Pasture.

Containers to bring food to the site need not necessarily have been anything other than ordinary domestic vessels — jars, bowls, dishes, amphorae — and this point has been made quite clearly by Peter Leach, and others, in his analysis of the pottery assemblages from the West Hill, Uley temple complex and the temple site of Henley Wood (Woodward and Leach 1993, 241–249; Watts and Leach 1996, 120–126). At Uley, with the obvious exception of a large number of miniature ceramic vessels — almost like thumb pots — there were no unusual vessels in the pottery assemblage apart from the occasional example of a pot with a drilled or pierced base (perhaps to allow liquid to escape as part of a libation, or to strain something) to suggest that these were other than domestic pots, produced for the ordinary market and only made extraordinary by their final use and destruction here. At Henley Wood the same applied, though analysis of this material by form did allow some intra-site variations to be reported and for comparison to be made between Henley Wood and Uley, where tablewares formed a higher proportion of the assemblage, while storage vessels were less well represented.

It is perhaps in a way remarkable in terms of contrast that at Orton's Pasture, with the exception of the Bacchic-inspired *patera* handle and lamp, and the altar fragment, there were no specifically votive objects present at the site, yet at Uley they were quite common. It was the case that items either dedicated as *ex votos* at temples or shrines, and items otherwise connected to the religious rites there, were not removed from out of the religious precinct, whether that precinct was bounded by a formal *temenos* wall or, as here, defined by a boundary ditch, possibly originally with an associated bank.

Some imagination is required to recreate the setting of the shrine at Orton's Pasture. It is in a physically liminal position, as well as performing a liminal role between the world of men and that of their gods. As has been noted above in the description of the position of this field on the fringes of Rocester village, the evaluation and excavation recorded a number of areas of the site which had been subject to apparently regular seasonal flooding. While the regime of the River Dove will have altered, perhaps drastically, since the Roman period, nevertheless there is evidence that some Roman features, in evaluation Trench 12 for example, were cut into a tail of alluvium, helping to define the zone of the river's encroachment at some stage around about the first or second century. Towards the very bottom of the field, to the south, there was recorded build-up of *c.* 1m of alluvium deposited by the floodwaters of the Dove. This suggests then that at certain times of the year much of the ground to the immediate south of the shrine building would have been under water, giving a spectacular and dramatic context to any activities carried out at the shrine in the period of the late autumn to early spring each year.

It may have been this remarkably evocative scene, with the upper parts of trees sticking out above the water's surface and so on , that first alerted the dedicatee of the shrine to the site. The suitability of the habitat to attract water birds may also have provided an extra fillip in the form of the opportunity to pursue wildfowling here, hunting and religious observance often having a slighty symbiotic relationship in the Roman world. Rural shrines in general were not large or particularly grand, and indeed it has been observed by Henig that there was often a form of inverted cachet associated with the hut-like simplicity of the shrine at its most unpretentious (Henig 1986, 93–95), a classical influence on Roman Britain which he has described as being 'sacro-idyllic'.

Few such shrines have been recognised in Britain and even one of the more remote and inaccessible of these, the shrines of Vinotonus on Scargill Moor, near Bowes, in North Yorkshire, despite their impresively isolated and wild location nevertheless were provided with a suite of impressive inscribed altars by its patrons, military officers from the fort at nearby Bowes who must have come to the moor to indulge their pleasure for hunting and for wild unfettered landscape (Richmond and Wright 1948). Here, Vinotonus is equated with Silvanus, a deity of woodland, groves and hunting, just as a similar dedication of an altar to Silvanus was made by another Roman army officer on Bollihope Common, Weardale, again in northern Britain, though it is uncertain whether this equally remote spot was the location of a formal shrine.

Given the physical setting of the Orton's Pasture shrine, with the potentially dramatic, almost theatrical, effect created by its proximity to a flood-prone area, it is also worth considering the question of the deliberate integration of this feature into the very landscape itself. An important research paper by Tom Blagg, on landscape and religion in Roman Britain, highlighted the commonly shared Roman and British veneration of natural features such as rivers, springs, woodland and so on, and how away from the towns and major road routes this would have been a deciding factor in the location of the smaller religious sites. This would seem to be partially the case at Orton's Pasture, the site being both *in* the landscape and *of* the landscape, quite literally, while at the same time also potentially being linked to the site of the adjacent fort. A study of religious and ritual practices in Roman Gaul by Ton Derks (Derks 1998) also considered the location of temples and other types of religious sites in relation to what Derks termed 'the mythical geography of the landscape' (Derks 1998,134–144). Amongst other favoured natural locations, the significance of sites of springs, rivers and brooks, and of 'particularly the sources, confluences and intersections with land roads' (Derks 1998, 138) could also be demonstrated in the case of Gaul, as in Britain. While scarcely major rivers, it should nevertheless be remembered that the rivers Dove and Churnet meet less than a kilometre to the south of the Orton's Pasture site, while a main crossing over the Dove must also have been immediately close by, in order to take the road route eastwards towards Little Chester near Derby. These locational factors are likely to have been determinants in the choice of such a propitious site for a shrine.

The Identity of the Deity

The question now needs to be briefly addressed as to whether the shrine was dedicated to the worship of any one particular deity, something that is often discernible through the nature of epigraphic evidence or the finds record. Unfortunately, the single altar fragment is not from that part of the altar that would have carried an inscription, if the altar was indeed inscribed at all. There are likewise, perhaps surprisingly in a possibly military context where a higher degree of general literacy amongst the officers and soldiers would be expected, few *graffiti* on pottery vessels or on other objects from the site. Seven *graffiti* in all were recorded. There would appear to have been no, or few, exchanges here between mortals and their gods mediated through written materials, as is found on other types of religious sites in Roman Britain.

There are, however, the two decorated objects from the site, the copper-alloy *patera* handle and the imported ceramic lamp fragment which, it has been suggested, might have been re-utilised after breaking as an *oscillum*. Both these objects bear Bacchic and Bacchic-associated imagery which must be assessed within the framework of analysis established a few years ago by Valerie Hutchinson in her in-depth study of the evidence for the Bacchic cult in Britain. Hutchinson found that knowledge of the cult or use of its imagery, rather than necessarily adherence to the cult, was much more widespread in Roman Britain than had previously been thought. Bacchic-associated artefacts have been found on sites ranging in date from the first to the fourth century, and in both town and countryside, in both civilian and military contexts. They have also, of course, been found in both domestic and religious contexts. Hutchinson noted that *paterae* decorated with Bacchic imagery '**on the basis of form alone** (her emphasis) merit consideration as religious artefacts' (Hutchinson 1986, 23). She also considerd lamps as a general category of object that, decorated or undecorated, were more likely to be used in non-domestic contexts than as objects for everyday lighting (Hutchinson 1986, 26). In her catalogue Hutchinson listed 159 Bacchic-related objects from military sites in Roman Britain, and 28 objects from sites that possibly represent rural shrines. Given that three Bacchic objects now have been found at Rocester, the *patera* handle and the decorated lamp from Orton's Pasture and the jug handle from the New Cemetery site, there would certainly seem to be the suggestion that in the later first or earlier second century there was a small group of cult adherents stationed in the military establishment here or at least associated with the military.

Whether the exotic foodstuffs and plant remains from the southern enclosure can themselves help provide clues to the deity worshipped or invoked at the site also needs considering. It is unfortunate that routine sampling for environmental material post-dates many of the more important Roman temple excavations in Britain. There is, for instance, no environmental data available for presentation in Hutchinson's study of the Bacchic cult. At West Hill, Uley there was little information provided by the analysis of the plant macrofossils, and certainly nothing to enhance the interpretation of the religious function of the site. The presence of mulberry in one deposit may imply the importation of this fruit as a foodstuff or as an appropriate offering. Monckton (above) has noted that Stone Pine has previously been found at two temple sites, the Temple of Mithras in London and the so-called Triangular Temple in Verulamium, as well as on domestic sites. On two of these domestic sites, Chew Park and Great Holts Farm, this material came from well deposits, which may be of some significance itself. Two other finds of Stone Pine, not mentioned by Monckton, can also be seen to be in a potentially ritual rather than domestic context, particularly in the case of the first example. Philpott, in his survey of burial practices in Roman Britain (Philpott 1991, 195), notes the presence of seeds of *Pinus Pinea* 'in a mass of charcoal in a cremation at Mucking, while two complete Stone Pine cones came from excavations at Number 1 Poultry, London (MoLAS 1997,1).

The extremely low level of finds made of metal and bone, and the complete absence of objects of shale or jet, and so on, that is both ordinary domestic objects and those which might have been transformed from the ordinary into the extraordinary by their dedication as *ex votos*, and of specifically manufactured *ex votos*, argues for this being more a private shrine than a public place of worship and sacrifice. Such a distinction needs to be made in the case of religious establishments and their users. It is, though, perhaps significant that two of the three brooches from the site come from pit F700 inside the southern enclosure, and that these objects can certainly be considered therefore as *ex votos* rather than casual losses. Indeed, certain types of brooches are now being recognised as having regular association with ritual sites and deposits (Simpson and Blance 1998) rather than simply being utilitarian objects recontextualised/ transformed by their use in ritual or religious activities. Given that no characterisation can therefore be made of the pattern of *ex voto* deposition at Orton's Pasture, as has been attempted for seven temple sites by Woodward (1992, 74–78), this too would seem to be a dead-end in terms of identifying the cult or cults linked to the Orton's Pasture shrine.

Context and Content

There has been very little work carried out on religious sites of the Romano-British West Midlands, and indeed only one or two temple or shrine sites have been identified. The rescue excavations of the 1970s on the temple site at Coleshill, Warwickshire have not yet been published, though the interim phasing of the site suggested that there had been two successive temple complexes here, ranging from a timber-built structure (Coleshill 1) through to a stone-built temple and a small, simple square shrine enclosed within a D-shaped *temenos* (Coleshill 2 and 3). In the towns, it is only at Wroxeter that temple sites have been located. There has perhaps in the region been an over-concentration on, first, military archaeology, and, more recently, on urbanism and the related concept of the urban hinterland, a conceptual framework for study and interpretation that has found little room for considerations of the region's religious geography.

The identification of the site at Orton's Pasture as the site of a former shrine, probably associated with military personnel from the nearby fort in the second century, therefore makes an important contribution to regional studies, particularly when viewed alongside the other archaeological data that have been recovered more widely around Rocester village in the last several years. There is emerging from the comparative and integrated study of these data, a detailed and fine-grained picture, not only about the sequence of Romano-British activity here and about the transition of the area from a military-dominated and overseen

area to a civilian zone but also most particularly about the military period itself.

In Romano-British military archaeology there is no longer the predominance of studies of fort types and layout, of the identifications of garrisons and of the minutiae of military movements, important though such studies are to the discipline. There is also now a reluctance to try and shoehorn all archaeological evidence into the historical and epigraphic framework for the history of the province, particularly for the first two centuries of Roman rule. Forts are now more often viewed as being settlements, though obviously settlements of a very different character from civilian centres.

Both the internal workings of these military settlements and their external relationships with other settlements and with the landscapes, both real and perceptual, of which they formed a part have become the new themes of research. Artefactual and environmental data allow these issues to be addressed in quite specific ways, thus adding a socio-economic element to the study, in terms of analysing patterns of agricultural organisation, diet and food procurement, and in terms of the manufacture, acquisition and consumption of pottery vessels and other objects — about military supply and demand in other words.

However, in many respects the socio-economic bias of much Romano-British archaeology today has acted in a way to exclude considerations of many other, equally valid, parallel research directions for the discipline, amongst which is the consideration of religious activity and attitudes, both formalised and informal, official and personal. Such issues tend to be seen as the remit of the art historian or the small finds specialist and in many published excavation reports discussion of religious or votive artefacts seems to be ghettoised in specialist reports rather than integrated into the overall site discussion.

It will be evident to the reader of the individual specialist reports in this publication that there are conceptual differences between the approaches to their data taken by each specialist, and that in particular there was a reluctance amongst the environmental specialists to move beyond socio-economic modelling and to move into areas of more speculative interpretation, and certainly into the application of theoretical perspectives. Perhaps the very opposite applies to the coarse pottery and small finds reports, where more open avenues of interpretation have been explored. These differences of approach have been retained within the specialist reports and have not been excised by the editorial red pen. Instead, the opportunity has been taken to highlight the alternative interpretations that can be made of certain phases of the Orton's Pasture site in this extended discussion.

To conclude, the excavations at Orton's Pasture, Rocester in the 1990s have provided evidence of a more complex picture of Roman activity in the area in the later first and early second century AD than had previously been assumed. The study of artefacts and environmental material from the site has provided a tentative insight into the religious life of some of the inhabitants here, possibly of military personnel, and the identification of a shrine and its precinct enclosure makes a very significant contribution to the study of religion in Roman Britain.

Acknowledgements

The excavations of 1996 were directed by Richard Cuttler, assisted by Bob Burrows, Kirsty Nichol, Derek Moscrop, John

Hovey, Ellie Ramsey, Gary Coates, Howell Roberts, Elliot Wragg and Andrew Silver. The work was jointly sponsored by Mrs M.Atkins and Haslam Homes Limited. The 1990 evaluation, sponsored by Philip Atkins, was directed by Iain Ferris and Laurence Jones, assisted by Steve Litherland, Ed Dickinson and Russell Heath, with Alex Jones leading the geophysical survey team of John Dalton, Mike Cooper and Martin Lightfoot. The 1995 evaluation, again commissioned by Philip Atkins, was directed by Richard Cuttler, assisted by Ed Newton, Bob Burrows and Christine Winter. Richard Tabor and Kirsty Nichol undertook the further geophysical survey.

Post-excavation management and liaison with specialists was undertaken by Iain Ferris and Lynne Bevan. Thanks are extended to all the specialists whose analyses form part of the published report. Simon Buteux of BUFAU is thanked for his financial management of the project, as is Ann Humphries for her work in turning the numerous disks into a single consistently formatted text, and to the illustrators Mark Breedon (Bambi) and Nigel Dodds for the plans and finds drawings. Graham Norrie produced the photographic prints with his customary efficiency.

Lynne Bevan would like to thank Richard Cuttler, John Roberts, Katherine Toney, Catrin Jenkins, Elaine Hammond, Adam Holman, Rachel Heaton and Tracey Joyce for their individual contributions towards the cataloguing and quantification of the pottery assemblage, and for their notes and observations on parallels and the significance of individual vessels, in reports which form part of the site archive. Dr Jeremy Evans very kindly confirmed the identification of the face pot and the triple vase, and commented on a draft of the pottery report. Dr Simon Esmonde Cleary of the Department of Ancient History and Archaeology at the University of Birmingham is thanked for his detailed comments on the second draft of the report. A debt is also owed to Ruth Leary whose pottery type and form series for Rocester, compiled following the New Cemetery excavations of 1985–1987, forms the basis for the pottery study.

During the extended period of work at the site the project has been monitored first by Bob Meeson of Staffordshire County Council, and subsequently by his successor Chris Welch. Andy Watson of Haslam Homes Limited helped the work run as smoothly as it could in the atrocious conditions of winter 1996. Thanks go to all of them for their help, advice and on-site observations.

The Cole Charitable Trust provided a grant to allow the further in-depth study of the charred plant remains to be undertaken by Angela Monckton, and we are grateful to Dr John Cole for his continued support in this way for our research into Roman Rocester.

Finally, thanks must go to Jonathon Shepherd of Rocester for his watching brief work as the development proceeded, and for allowing us to borrow and examine the material that he collected and to comment on its significance in this report.

BIBLIOGRAPHY

Albarella, U. and Davis, S.   1994 *The Saxon and Medieval Bones Excavated 1985–1989 from West Cotton, Northamptonshire*. London, Ancient Monuments Laboratory Report 17/97

Albarella, U. and Lawless, F.   1998 *Orton's Pasture, Rocester (Staffordshire): Assessment of the Animal Bones*. BUFAU

Albarella, U.   1997. *The Roman Mammal and Bird Bones Excavated in 1994 from Great Holts Farm, Boreham, Essex*. London, Ancient Monuments Laboratory Report 9/97

Allason-Jones, L.   1989 *Women in Roman Britain*. British Museum Publications

Allason-Jones, L. and Miket, R.   1984   *The Catalogue of Small Finds from South Shields Roman Fort*. The Society of Antiquaries of Newcastle-upon-Tyne Monograph Series 2

Allason-Jones, L. *et al.*   1985 'The Objects of Copper Alloy and other Materials', *in* Bidwell, P.T. 1985, 117–129

Allen, D.   1986a 'The Glass Vessels', *in* Zienkiewicz, J.D. 1986, 98–116

1986b 'The Roman Glass', *in* Buckland, P.C. and Magilton, J.R. 1986, 103–8, 287–293

1988 'Roman Glass from Corbridge', *in* Bishop, M.C and Dore, J.N. 1988

Anderson, A. (with P. Ellis)   1989 'Coarse Wares', *in* Ellis, P. 1989, *103–119*

Anderson, A.C. and Anderson, A.S. (eds)   1981 *Roman Pottery Research in Britain and North-West Europe*. BAR British Series 123. Oxford

Atkinson, D.   1914. 'A Hoard of Samian Ware from Pompeii', *Journal of Roman Studies* 4, 26–64

Audoin-Rouzeau, F.   1991 *La Taille du Boeuf Domestique en Europe de l'Antiquité aux Temps Modernes*. Valbonne, CN

Bailey, D.M.   1980 *A Catalogue of the Lamps in the British Museum 2 Roman Lamps Made in Italy*. British Museum Press

Barfield, L.H. and Kalali, I.   1996 'The Flint', *in* Esmonde Cleary, A.S. and Ferris, I.M. 1996, 182–183

Bell, A.   1986 'Excavations at Rocester, Staffordshire, by Fiona Sturdy 1964 and 1968', *Staffordshire Archaeological Studies*, New Series 3, 20–51

Bevan, L.   1999 'Ecstatic Celebrants: Bacchic Metalwork from the Roman Midlands', *Transactions of the Staffordshire Archaeological and Historical Society* 38, 6–11

Bidwell, P.T.   1985 *The Roman Fort of Vindolanda at Chesterholm, Northumberland*. Historic Buildings and Monuments Commission for England Archaeological Report 1

Bidwell, P. and Speak, S.   1994 *Excavations at South Shields Roman Fort*, Newcastle-upon-Tyne

Bird, J. (ed)   1998   *Form and Fabric. Studies in Rome's Material Past in Honour of B.R. Hartley*, Oxford Monograph 80

Birley, R.   1994   *Vindolanda 1: The Early Wooden Forts*. Vindolanda Research Reports New Series, 1. Roman Army Museum Publications. Hexham

Birss, R.   1985 'Coarse Pottery', *in* Dool, J. (ed) 1985, 90–124

Bishop, M.C. and Dore, J.N.   1988 *Corbridge: Excavations of the Roman Fort and Town, 1947–1980*.   English Heritage Archaeological Report 8. London

Blagg, T.C.   1986 'Roman Religious Sites in the Landscape', *Landscape History* 8, 15–26

Blagg, T.C. and King, A.C. (eds)   1984 *Military and Civilian in Roman Britain: Cultural Relationships in a Frontier Province*. BAR British Series 136. Oxford

Blazquez, J.M. and Remesal, J. (eds)   1983 'Producción y Comercio del Aceite en la Antiguedad', II Congresso. Madrid

Boessneck, J.   1969 'Osteological Differences between Sheep (*Ovis aries Linné*) and Goat (*Capra hircus Linné*)', *in* Brothwell, D.R. and Higgs, E.S. (eds) 1969, 331–358

Boestard Den, M.H.P.   1956 *Description of the Collections in the Rijksmuseum G.M. Kan at Nijmegen, V. The Bronze Vessels*. Published by Order of the Department of Education, Arts and Sciences. Publisher:Drukkerji andThieme, Nijmegen

Boon, G.C.   1967 'Micaceous Sigillata from Lezoux at Silchester, Caerleon and Other Sites', *Antiquaries Journal* 47, 27–42

Brain, C.K.   1981   *The Hunters or the Hunted? Introduction to Taphonomy*. London: University of Chicago Press

Braithwaite, G.   1984 'Romano-British Face Pots and Head Pots', *Britannia* 15, 181–131

Brassington, M. 1971 'A Trajanic Kiln Complex Near Little Chester, Derby, 1968', *Derbyshire Archaeological Journal* 51, 36–69

Brassington, M. 1980 'Derby Racecourse Kiln Excavations 1972–3', *Antiquaries Journal* 60, 8–47

Breeze, D.J.   forthcoming   *The Roman Fort on the Antonine Wall at Bearsden*

Brickell, C.   1989   *The Royal Horticultural Society Gardeners Encyclopedia of Plants and Flowers*. London

Brothwell, D. and Higgs, E.S. (eds)   1969 *Science in Archaeology*. London

Brown, A.E. and Woodfield, C.   1983 'Excavations at Towcester North, the Alcester Road Suburb', *Northamptonshire Archaeology* 18, 43–140

Buckland, P.C. and Magilton, J.R.   1986 *The Archaeoloy of Doncaster: the Roman Civil Settlement*. BAR British Series 148. Oxford

Callender, M.   1965 *Roman Amphorae*, London

Cappers, R.T.J.   1995 'Archaeobotanical Remains', *in* Sidebotham, S.E. and Wendrich, W.Z. 1995, 320–326

Carreras, C. and Funari, P.   1998 *Britannia y el Mediterraneo*. Barcelona

Caruana, I.D.   1992 'Carlisle: Excavation of a Section of the Annexe Ditch of the First Flavian Fort, 1990', *Britannia* 23, 45–109.

Casey, P.J. and Davies, J.L. with Evans, J. *1993 Excavations at Segontium (Caernarfon) Roman Fort, 1975–1979*. CBA Research Report 90

Charlesworth, D.   1959 'Roman Glass in Northern Britain', *Archaeologia Aeliana 37*, 33–58

1960 'The Glass', *in* Petch, D.F. 1960, 66

1972 'The Glass', *in* Frere, S.S. 1972, 196–215

1974 'The Roman Glass', *in* Frere, S.S. and St.Joseph, J.K. 1974, 88–90.

1978 'Roman Glass', *in* Johnson, S.1978, 267–273

1982 'The Glass', *in* Wacher, J. and McWhirr, A. 1982, 106–107

1984 'The Glass', *in* Frere, S.S. 1984, 145–173

Clarke, S.   1994 'A Quantitative Analysis of the Finds from the Roman Fort of Newstead', *in* Cottam, S. *et al.* (eds) 1994, 72–82

Clarke, S. and Jones, R.F.J.   1994 'The Newstead Pits', *Journal of Roman Military Equipment Studies* 5, 109–124

Cleere, H. and Taylor, J.P.   1978 *Roman Shipping and Trade: Britain and the Rhine Provinces*. CBA Research Report 24

Cool, H.E.M *et al.* 1995 *Finds from the Fortress*. The Archaeology of York The Small Finds 17/10

Cool, H.E.M.   1996 'The Roman Vessel Glass', *in* Esmonde Cleary, A.S. and Ferris, I.M. 1996, 106–121.

Cool, H.E.M. and Price, J.   1988 'The Roman Glass', *in* Darling, M.J. and Jones, M.J. 1988, 42–43.

1995 *Roman Vessel Glass from Excavations in Colchester, 1971–85* Colchester, Archaeological Trust.

Cool, H. E.M.   1996 'The Glass and Faience Objects', *in* Esmonde Cleary, A.S. and Ferris, I.M. 1996, 122–127

Cool, H.E.M. and Philo, C. (eds)   1998 *Roman Castleford. Volume 1 The Small Finds.* Yorkshire Archaeology 4.

Cooper, J.   1996 'A Figured Handle', *in* Esmonde Cleary, A.S. and Ferris, I.M. 1996, 134–136

Cottam, S. *et al.* (eds)   1994 TRAC 94. *Proceedings of the Fourth Annual Theoretical Roman Archaeology Conference,* Durham

Cracknell, S.   1996 *Roman Alcester: Defences and Defended Area.* CBA Research Report 106

Crummy, N.   1983 *The Roman Small Finds from Excavations in Colchester 1971–9.* Colchester Archaeological Report 2.   Colchester Archaeological Trust Ltd

Crummy, P.   1984 *Excavations at Lion Walk, Balkerne Lane and Middleborough, Colchester, Essex.* Colchester Archaeological Report 3

Cunliffe, B.W.   1971 *Excavations at Fishbourne 1961–1969. Volume 2. The Finds.* Report of the Research Committee of the Society of Antiquaries of London 27

Cunliffe, B.W.   1975 *Excavations at Porchester Castle. Volume 1. The Roman Period.* Report of the Research Committee of the Society of Antiquaries of London 32

Curle, J.   1911 *A Roman Frontier Post and its People: the Fort at Newstead.* Edinburgh University Press

Dannell, G.B.   1971 'The Samian Pottery', *in* Cunliffe, B.W. 1971, 260–316.

Dannell, G.B.   1992 'The Decorated Samian Ware', *in* Holbrook, N. and Bidwell, P.T. 1992, 40–50

Darling, M.J. and Jones, M.J.   1988 'Early Settlement at Lincoln', *Britannia* 19, 1–57

Davis, S.   1992 *A Rapid Method for Recording Information About Animal Bones from Archaeological Sites.* London, Ancient Monuments Laboratory Report 19/92

de la Bédoyère, G.   1989 *The Finds of Roman Britain.* Batsford, London

Derks, T.   1998 *Gods, Temples and Ritual Practices. The Transformation of Religious Ideas and Values in Roman Gaul.* Amsterdam Archaeological Studies. Amsterdam University Press

Dickinson, B.M.   1992 'Samian Ware', *in* Caruana, I.D. 1992, 51–8

Dickinson, B.M.   1996 'Samian Ware', *in* Esmonde Cleary, A.S. and Ferris, I.M. 1996, 73–95

Dobney, K., Jaques, D. and Irving, B.   Undated. *Of Butchers and Breeds. Report on Vertebrate Remains from Various Sites in the City of Lincoln.* Lincoln: Lincoln Archaeological Studies 5.

Dool, J. (ed.)   1985 Roman Derby: Excavations 1968–83', *Derbyshire Archaeological Journal* 105

Dorrington, E. and Legge, A.   1985 'The Animal Bone', *in* France, N.E. and Gobel, B.M. 1985, 122–134

Driesch, A. Von den.   1995 *A Guide to the Measurement of Animal Bone from Archaeological Sites.* Peabody Museum Bulletin **1**, Cambridge Mass., Harvard University

Drury, P.J.   1986 'Non-Classical Religious Buildings in Iron Age and Roman Britain', *in* Rodwell, W. (ed) 1986, 45–78

Edwards, J.   1984 *The Roman Cookery of Apicius. Translated and Adapted for the Modern Kitchen.* London.

Ellis, P.   1989 Roman Chesterfield, Excavations by T. Courtney 1974–78. *Derbyshire Archaeological Journal 1989 CIX,* 51–130

Esmonde-Cleary, A.S. and Ferris, I. M.   1996 Excavations at the New Cemetery, Rocester, Staffordshire, 1985–1987. *Staffordshire Archaeological and Historical Society Transactions 1993–1994. 35*

Evans, C.J.   Forthcoming. 'Pottery production at The Parks, Godmanchester', *in* Jones, A.E. (ed) forthcoming, *Settlement, Burial and Industry in the Extramural Area of Roman Godmanchester. Excavations at The Parks 1998 and London Road 1997-8.* BAR British Series

Evans, J.   1987 'Graffiti and the Evidence for Literacy in Roman Britain', *Archaeological Journal* 144, 191–204

Evans, J.   1996a 'Roman Pottery', *in* Cracknell, S. 1996, 58–97

Evans, J.   1996b 'The Roman Pottery', *in* Hughes, E.G. 1996, 46–64

Evans, J.   Forthcoming. 'Ceramic Aspects of the Graffiti', *in* Ferris, I.M. and Jones, R.F.J. forthcoming

Ferguson, R.   1996 'The Mortaria', in Esmonde Cleary, A.S. and Ferris, I.M. 1996, 61–63

Ferris, I.M.   1989 'Rocester, Orton's Pasture', *West Midlands Archaeology* 32, 77–8

Ferris, I.M. and Jones R.F.J.   Forthcoming. Excavations at Binchester Roman Fort, County Durham 1976–1981 and 1986–1991

Fox, A.   1940 'The Legionary Fortress at Caerleon, Monmouthshire: Excavations in Myrtle Cottage Orchard 1939', *Archaeologia Cambrensis* 95, 102–52

France, N.E. and Gobel, B.M.   1985 *The Romano-British Temple at Harlow, Essex.* West Essex Archaeological Group Monograph.

Frere, S.S.   1972 *Verulamium Excavations. Volume I.* Research Report of the Society of Antiquaries of London 28

Frere, S.S.   1984 *Verulamium Excavations. Volume III.* Oxford University Committee for Archaeology Monograph 1, Oxford

Frere, S.S.   1987 'Brandon Camp, Herefordshire', *Britannia* 18, 49–92

Frere, S.S. and St. Joseph, J.K.   1974 'The Roman Fortress at Longthorpe', *Britannia* 5, 1–129

Gillam, J.P.   1970 *Types of Roman Coarse Pottery Vessels in Northern Britain,* 3rd edn., Newcastle

Gillam, J.P.   1976 'Coarse Fumed Ware in Northern Britain', *Glasgow Archaeological Journal* 4, 57–80

Grant, A.   1982 'The Use of Tooth Wear as a Guide to the Age of Domestic Ungulates', *in* Wilson, B., Grigson, C. and Payne, S. (eds.) 1982, 91–108

Grant, A.   1989 'Animals in Roman Britain', *in* Todd, M. (ed) 1989, 135–146

Green, M.J.   1976 *A Corpus of Religious Material from the Civilian Areas of Roman Britain.* BAR British Series 24. Oxford

Green, M.J.   1978 *Small Cult Objects from the Military Areas of Roman Britain.* BAR British Series 52. Oxford

Greep, S.   1998 'The Bone, Antler and Ivory Artefacts', *in* Cool, H.E.M. and Philo, C. (eds.) 1998, 267–285

Greig, J.   1991 'The British Isles', *in* van Zeist, W. Wasylikowa, K. and Behre, K. (eds) 1991, 299–334

Hammon, A.   1998 *Covert Farm (DIRFT East), Crick, Northamptonshire: Assessment of the Animal Bones.* BUFAU.

Hanson, W.S., Daniels, C.M., Dore, J.N. and Gillam, J.P. 1979 'The Agricolan Supply Base at Red House, Corbridge', *Archaeologia Aeliana,* 5th Series, 7, 1–98

Harden, D.B.   1975 'The Glass', *in* Cunliffe, B. 1975, 368–374

    1987 *Glass of the Caesars.* Milan, Olivetti

Harden, D.B. and Price, J. 1971   'The Glass', *in* Cunliffe, B. 1971, 317–368

Hartley, B.R.   1985 'The Samian Ware', *in* Pitts, L.F. and St. Joseph, J.K. 1985, 314–22

Hartley, B.R.   1996. 'The Potters' Stamps', *in* Esmonde Cleary, A.S. and Ferris, I.M. 1996, 87–90

Hartley, K. F.   1996 'The Stamps' *in* Esmonde Cleary, A.S. and Ferris, I.M 1996, 64–70

Hawkes, C.F.C. and Hull, M.R.   1947 *Camulodunum,* Report of the Research Committee of the Society of Antiquaries of London 14

Henig, M.   1984 *Religion in Roman Britain,* London, Batsford

Henig, M.   1986 'Art and Cult in the Temples of Roman Britain', *in* Rodwell, W. (ed) 1986, 91–114

Henig, M.   1989 'The Crookham Stand', *in* Soffe, G., Nicholls, J. and Moore, G. 1989, 43–112

Hillman, G.   1984 'Interpretation of Archaeological Plant Remains: The Application of Ethnographic Models from Turkey', *in* van Zeist, W. and Casparie, W.A. (eds) 1984, 1–41

Holbrook, N. and Bidwell, P.T.   1992 'Roman Pottery from Exeter 1980–1990', *Journal of Roman Pottery Studies* 5, 35–80

Hughes, E.G.   1996 *The Excavation of a Late Prehistoric and Romano-British Settlement at Thornwell Farm, Chepstow, Gwent.* BAR British Series 244. Oxford

Hull, M.R.   1963 *The Roman Potters' Kilns of Colchester.* Report of the Research Committee of the Society of Antiquaries of London, XXI. Oxford

Hutchinson, V.J.   1986 *Bacchus in Roman Britain: the Evidence for His Cult.* BAR British Series 151. Oxford

Isings, C.   1957 *Roman Glass from Dated Finds.* Groningen Djarjkarta

Isserlin, R.M.J.   1994 'An Archaeology of Brief Time: Monuments and Seasonality in Roman Britain', *in* Cottam, S. *et al.* (eds) 1994, 45–56

Jacomet, S.   1989 *Prahistorische Getreidefunde.* Botanishes Institut der Universitat Abteilung Pflanzensystematic und Geobotanik. Basel

Jackson, R.P.J. and Potter, T.W.   1996 *Excavations at Stonea, Cambridgeshire, 1980–85*

Johnson, S.   1978 'Excavations at Hayton Roman Fort, 1975', *Britannia* 9, 57–114

Jones, A. and Cuttler, R.   1995 *An Archaeological Evaluation at Orton's Pasture, Mill Street, Rocester, Staffordshire.* BUFAU

Jones, A.   1998 'Excavations at Wall (Staffordshire) by E. Greenfield in 1962 and 1964', *Transactions of the Staffordshire Archaeological and Historical Society* 37, 1–52

Jones, G.B.D.   1974 *Roman Manchester.* Manchester University Press

Kenyon, K.M.   1948 *Excavations at the Jewry Wall Site, Leicester.* Report of the Research Committee of the Society of Antiquaries of London 15

King, A.C.   1984 'Animal Bones and the Dietary Identity of Military and Civilian Groups in Roman Britain, Germany and Gaul', *in* Blagg, T.C. and King, A.C. (eds.) 1984, 187–218

King, A.C.   1999 'Diet in the Roman World: a Regional Inter-site Comparison of the Mammal Bones', *Journal of Roman Archaeology* 12, 168–202

King, A.C. and Millett, M.J. 1993. 'Samian Ware', *in* Casey, P.J. and Davies, J.L, with Evans, J. 1993, 234–49

Kislev, M.E.   1988 *Pinus Pinea* in Agriculture, Culture and Cult, in Kuster, H-J. 1988, 73–79

Kratochvil, Z.   1969 'Species Criteria on the Distal Section of the Tibia in *Ovis ammon F. Aries L.* and *Capra aegrus F. Hircus L.'*, *Acta Veterinaria* 38, 483–490

Kuster, H-J.   1988 *Der Prahistorisch Mensch und Seine Umwelt.* Forschungen und Berichte zur vor und Fruhgeshichte in Baden-Wurttenburg 31

Lambrick, G.   1980 'Excavations in Park Street, Towcester', *Northamptonshire Archaeology* 15, 35–118

Laubenheimer, F.   1985 *La Production des Amphores en Gaule Narbonaise.* Paris

Lauwerier, R.C.G.M.   1988. 'Animals in Roman Times in the Dutch Eastern River Area. Amersfoort', *Nederlandse Oudheden* 12/ *Project Oostelijk Riverengebied* 1

Leary, R. 1996 'Roman Coarse Pottery', *in* Esmonde Cleary, A.S. and Ferris, I.M. 1996, 40–59

Leary, R.   1998 'Roman Pottery', *in* Jones, A. 1998, 26–37

Levitan, B.   1996 'Vertebrate Remains', *in* Esmonde Cleary, A.S. and Ferris, I.M. 1996, 186–205

Lister, A.M.   1996 'The Morphological Distinction between Bones and Teeth of Fallow Deer (*Dama dama*) and Red Deer (*Cervus elaphus*)', *International Journal of Osteoarchaeology* 6, 119–143

Mackreth, D.F.   1996 'Brooches', *in* Jackson, R.P.J. and Potter, T.W. 1996, 296–327

Manning, W.H.   1985 *Catalogue of the Romano-British Iron Tools, Fittings and Weapons in the British Museum.* The Trustees of the British Museum, British Museum Publications Ltd, London

Manning, W.H., Price, J. and Webster, J.   1995 *Usk. The Roman Small Finds.* University of Wales Press, Cardiff

Marsh, G.   1981 'London's Samian Supply and its Relationship to the Development of the Gallic Samian Industry', *in* Anderson, A.C. and Anderson A.S. (eds) 1981, 173–238

Martin-Kilcher, S.   1983 'Les Amphores Romaines à Huile de Bétique (Dressel 20 et 23) d'Augst (Colonia Augusta Rauricorum) et Kaiseraugst (Castrum Rauracense). Un Rapport Preliminaire', *in* Blázquez, J.M. and Remesal, J. (eds.) 1983, 337–347

Martin-Kilcher, S.   1987 *Die Romischen Amphores aus Augst und Kaiseraugst,* Bern

Megaw, J.V.S. (ed)   1976 *To Illustrate the Monuments.* London

Merrifield, R.   1987 *The Archaeology of Ritual and Magic.* London

Millett, M.   1987 'Boudicca, the First Colchester Potters' Shop and the Dating of Neronian Samian', *Britannia* 18, 93–124

Moffett, L.   1993 'Charred Plant Remains' *in* Esmonde Cleary, A.S. and Ferris, I.M. 1996, 206–218

MoLAS   1997 *Annual Review for 1996.* Museum of London Archaeology Service

Monaghan, J.   1997 *Roman Pottery from York.* The Archaeology of York. The Pottery 16/8

Monckton, A.   1998. *Charred Plant Remains from Orton's Pasture, Rocester, Staffordshire.* University of Leicester Archaeological Services Report

Murphy, P.   1984 'Carbonised Fruits from Building 5', *in* Crummy, P., 1984, 40

Murphy, P.   1997. *Plant Macrofossils From a Late Roman Farm, Great Holts Farm, Boreham, Essex.* London, Ancient Monuments Laboratory Report 7/97

Neal, D.S.   1974. *The Excavation of the Villa at Gadebridge Park Hemel Hempstead 1963-8.* Report of the Research Committee of the Society of Antiquaries of London 31. London

Nicholson, R A.   1996 'Bone Degradation, Burial Medium and Species Representation: Debunking the Myths, an Experimental Based Approach', *Journal of Archaeological Science* 23, 513–533

Oswald, F.   1936–7 *Index of Figure-Types on Terra Sigillata ('Samian Ware').* University Press of Liverpool

Page, W. 1898 'Notes on a Romano-British Pottery Lately Found at Radlett, Herts.', *Proceedings of the Society of Antiquaries of London* 2nd Series 17, 261–271

Payne, S.   1973 'Kill-off Patterns in Sheep and Goats', *Anatolian Studies: Journal of the British Institute of Archaeology at Ankara* 23, 281–303

Payne, S.   1985 'Morphological Distinctions Between the Mandibular Teeth of Young Sheep, *Ovis*, and Goats, *Capra*', *Journal of Archaeological Science* 12, 139–147

Payne, S.   1987 'Reference Codes for the Wear States in the Mandibular Cheek Teeth of Sheep and Goats', *Journal of Archaeological Science* 14, 609–614

Payne, S. and Bull, G. 1988 'Components of Variation in Measurements of Pig Bones and Teeth, and the Use of Measurements to Distinguish Wild from Domestic Pig Remains', *Archaeozoologia* 2, 27–65

Peacock, D.P.S. and Williams, D.F. 1986 *Amphorae and the Roman Economy* London

Petch, D.F. 1960 'Excavations at Lincoln', *Archaeological Journal* 117, 40–70

Pirling, R. 1997 *Das Römisch-Fränkische Graberfeld von Krefeld-Gellep 1975–1982*. GDV Series B17, Stuttgart

Philpott, R. 1991 *Roman Burial Practices in Britain: a Survey of Grave Treatment and Furnishing*. BAR British Series 219, Oxford

Pitts, L.F. and St. Joseph, J.K. 1985 *Inchtuthil: the Roman Legionary Fortress, Excavations 1952–1965*. Britannia Monograph 6

Polunin, O. 1976 *Trees and Bushes of Europe*. Oxford University Press

Price, J. 1974 'The Glass', *in* Jones, G.D.B. 1974, 131–134

1976 'Glass', *in* Strong, D. and Brown, D. 1976, 111–126

1978 'Trade in Glass', *in* Cleere, H. and Taylor, J-P. 1978, 70–78

1980 'The Roman Glass', *in* Lamrick, G. 1980, 63–68

1987a 'The Roman Glass', in Frere, S.S. 1987, 71–76

1987b 'Glass from Felmongers, Harlow in Essex, a Dated Deposit of Vessel Glass Found in an Antonine Pit', *Annales du 10e Congrès de l'Association Internationale pour l'Histoire du Verre*, Amsterdam, 185–206

1995 'The Glass Vessels', *in* Manning, W.H., Price, J. and Webster, J. 1995, 139–191

Price, J. and Cool, H.E.M. 1983 'Glass from the Excavations of 1974–76' *in* Brown, A.E. and Woodfield, C. 1983, 115–124

Richmond, I.A. and Wright, R.P. 1948 'Two Roman Shrines to Vinotonus on Scargill Moor, near Bowes', *Yorkshire Archaeological Journal*, 37, 107–116

Rodwell, W. (ed) 1980 *Temples, Churches and Religion: Recent Research in Roman Britain*. BAR British Series 77. Oxford

Ross, A. and Feachem, R. 1976 'Ritual Rubbish? The Newstead Pits', *in* Megaw, J.V.S. (ed) 1976, 230–237

Seager Smith, R. and Davies, S.M. 1993 *Black Burnished Ware Type Series. The Roman Pottery from Excavations at Greyhound Yard, Dorchester, Dorset*. Wessex Archaeology

Sidebotham, S.E. and Wendrich, W.Z. 1995 *Preliminary Report on the 1995 Excavation at Berenike, Egyptian Red Sea Coast*. School of Asian, African and Amerindian Studies, Leiden

Silver, I.A. 1969 'The Ageing of Domestic Animals', *in* Brothwell, D.R. and Higgs, E.S. (eds.). 1969, 283–302

Simpson, G. and Blance, B. 1998 'Do Brooches Have Ritual Associations?', *in* Bird, J. (ed) 1998, 267–279

Soffe, G., Nicholls, J. and Moore, G. 1989 'The Roman Tilery and Aisled Building at Crookham, Hants. Excavations 1974–75', *Proceedings of the Hampshire Field Club* 45, 43–112

Sommer, C.S. 1984 *The Military Vici in Roman Britain*. BAR British Series 129. Oxford

Southwark and Lambeth Archaeological Excavation Committee 1978. *Southwark Excavations 1972–1974*. London and Middlesex Archaeological Society and Surrey Archaeological Society Joint Publication 1, London

Stace, O. 1991 *A New Flora of the British Isles*. Cambridge University Press

Stanfield, J.A. and Simpson, G. 1958 *Central Gaulish Potters*. Oxford University Press, London

Strong, D. and Brown, D. 1976 *Roman Crafts*

Todd, M. (ed) 1989 *Research on Roman Britain 1960–1989*. Britannia Monograph Series 11

Toynbee, J.M.C. 1964 *Art in Britain under the Romans*. Clarendon Press, Oxford

Tyers, P. 1996 *Pottery in Roman Britain*. Batsford, London

Ulbert, G. 1971 'Romische Bronzeknopte mit Reliefverzierung', *Fundberichte aus Schwaben, n. s.* 19, 278–292

Van Mensch, P.J.A. 1974 'A Roman Soup Kitchen at Zwammerdam?', *Berichten van de Rijksdienst voor het Oudheidkundig Bodemonderzoek* 24, 159–165

Wacher, J. and McWhirr, A. 1982 *Early Roman Occupation at Cirencester*. Cirencester Excavations I

Watts, L. and Leach, P.J. 1996 *Henley Wood, Temples and Cemetery Excavations 1962–1969 by the Late Ernest Greenfield*. CBA Research Report 99

Webster, G. 1958 'The Roman Military Advance under Ostorius Scapula', *Archaeological Journal* 115, 49–98

Webster, G. 1962 'Excavations on the Roman Site at Rocester, Staffordshire, 1962', *North Staffordshire Journal of Field Studies* II, 37–52

Webster, G. 1996 'Objects of Copper Alloy — Roman Military Objects', *in* Esmonde Cleary, A.S. and Ferris, I.M. 1996, 136–142

Wedlake, W.J. 1982 *The Excavation of the Shrine of Apollo at Nettleton, Wiltshire 1956–1971*. Report of the Research Committee of the Society of Antiquaries of London 15

Wheeler, R.E.M. and Wheeler, T.V. 1936 *Verulamium. A Belgic and Two Roman Cities*. Report of the Research Committee of the Society of Antiquaries of London 11

Williams, D. 1977 'A Consideration of the Sub-Fossil Remains of Vitis Vinifera L. as Evidence for Viticulture in Roman Britain', *Britannia* 8, 327–334

Williams, D.F. and Peacock, D.P.S. 1983 'The Importation of Olive-Oil into Roman Britain', *in* Blázquez, J.M. and Remesal, J. (eds.) 1983, 263–280

Williams, D.F. 1996 'The Amphorae', *in* Esmonde Cleary, A.S. and Ferris, I.M. 1996, 70–72

Willis, S.H. 1997 *The English Heritage Samian Project. Report on the Results of Phase 1*. University of Durham Press. Durham

Willis, S.H. In Press Samian Pottery in Britain: Exploring Its Distribution and Archaeological Potential. *Archaeological Journal* 155.

Wilmott, A. 1991 *Excavations in the Middle Walbrook Valley, City of London, 1927–1960*. London and Middlesex Archaeological Society Special Papers 13

Wilson, B., Grigson, C. and Payne, S. (eds) 1982 *Ageing and Sexing Animal Bones from Archaeological Sites*. BAR British Series 109. Oxford

Wilson, D.R. 1984 'Defensive Outworks of Roman Forts in Britain', *Britannia* 15, 51–62

Woodward, A. 1992 *Shrines and Sacrifice*. London, English Heritage/ Batsford

Woodward, A. and Leach, P.J. 1993 *The Uley Shrines. Excavations of a Ritual Complex on West Hill, Uley, Gloucestershire, 1977–9*. English Heritage Archaeological Reports 17

Young, C.J. 1977 *The Roman Pottery Industry of the Oxford Region*. BAR British Series 43. Oxford

Zeist van, W. and Casparie, W.A. (eds) 1984 *Plants and Ancient Man*. Rotterdam

Zeist van, W., Wasylikowa, K. and Behre, K. (eds) *1991 Progress in Old World Palaeoethnobotany*. Rotterdam

Zienkiewicz, J.D. 1986 *The Legionary Fortress Baths at Caerleon Vol.2. The Finds*. CAD W Cardiff

Plate 1   General view, looking eastwards, along line of southern ditch of Enclosure 1 and northern ditch of Enclosure 2   (R. Cuttler)

Plate 2
Section of ditch F702, Enclosure 1 (R. Cuttler)

Plate 3   Excavation in progress of pits F602–F604, north of Enclosure 1, looking south   (R. Cuttler)

Plate 4   Section of pit F603   (R. Cuttler)

Plate 5   North-east corner of Enclosure 2, looking west   (R. Cuttler)

Plate 6   Pits F700 and F701   (R. Cuttler)

Plate 7   Section of pit F701   (R. Cuttler)

Plate 8   Section of pit F701   (R. Cuttler)

Plate 9   Section of pit F700   (R. Cuttler)

Plate 10   Structure 1, Enclosure 2, looking westwards   (R. Cuttler)

Plate 11   Section of foundation trench F728, Structure 1   (R. Cuttler)

Plate 12   Ceramic lamp decorated with Bacchic scene   (G. Norrie)

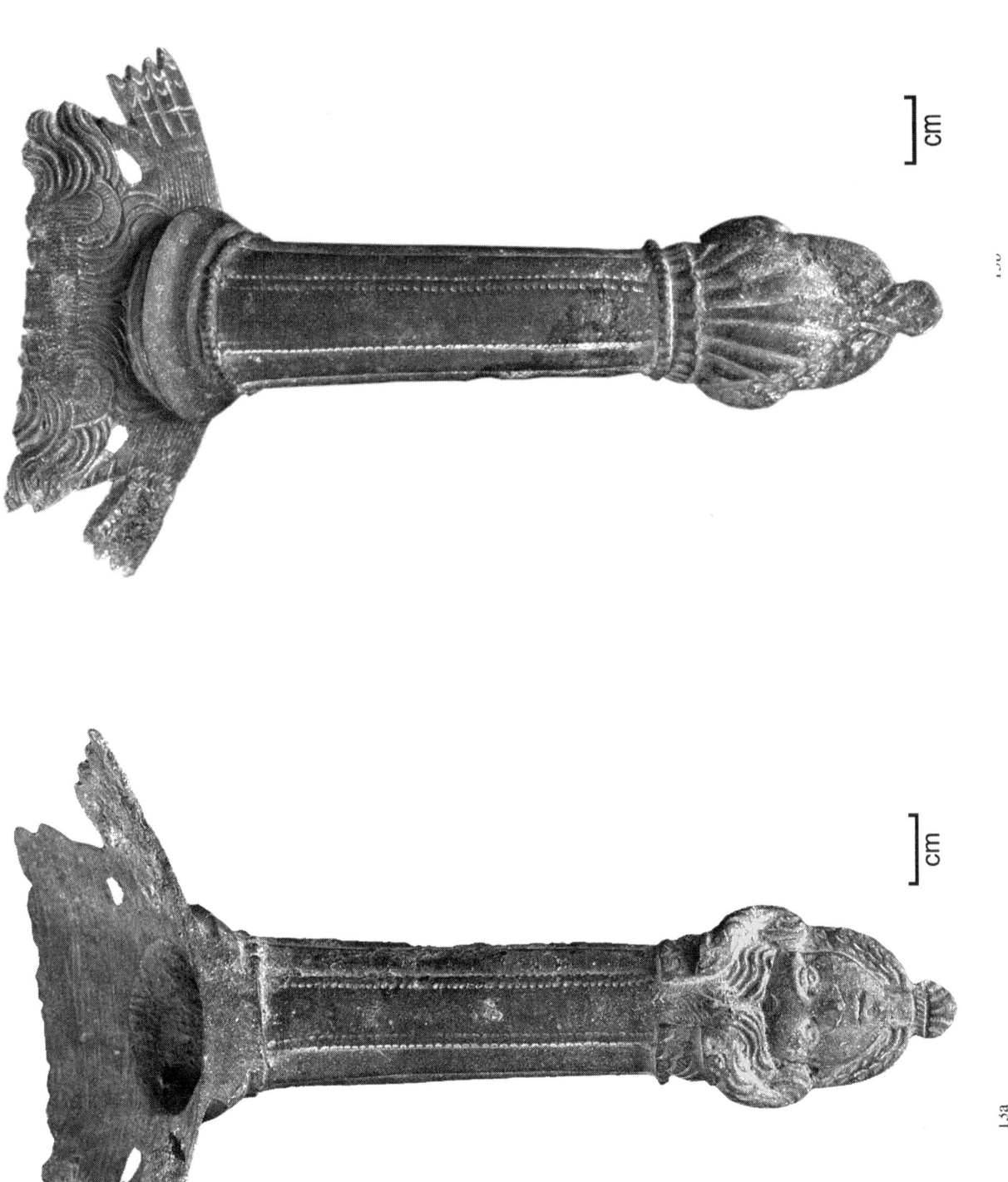

Plate 13   Copper alloy patera handle with Bacchic motifs   (G. Norrie)

Plate 14   The altar fragment

Plate 15   *Pinus pinea* remains from Enclosure 2 (J. Greig)

Plate 16   Date remains from Enclosure 2 (J. Greig)